Athena PERSECUTING

PERSECUTING
ATHENA

The True Story of a Young Rape Victim
and Her Fight for Justice

MARION
SCHULER

PERSECUTING ATHENA
THE TRUE STORY OF A YOUNG RAPE VICTIM
AND HER FIGHT FOR JUSTICE

iUniverse books may be ordered through booksellers or by contacting:

iUniverse
1663 Liberty Drive
Bloomington, IN 47403
www.iuniverse.com
1-800-Authors (1-800-288-4677)

ISBN: 978-1-4917-7065-8 (sc)
ISBN: 978-1-4917-7066-5 (e)

Library of Congress Control Number: 2015910614

Print information available on the last page.

iUniverse rev. date: 7/16/2015

This book is dedicated to the
thousands of young Canadian women
who have been raped and forsaken.

Acknowledgments

I am so very indebted to all who supported us in our time of such desperate need. Thank you for the beautiful and heartfelt letters of support for Athena, for listening when we needed to talk and for coming to court to provide emotional encouragement.

To the dedicated workers at "Hope House", we needed you, and you were there for us. Thank you for your support at Athena's trial and for the many hours of much needed counselling.

I would especially like to thank my friend and cousin Lynda, not just for being there, but for all her dedicated hours editing this book.

And to my brother, Roger: Thank you. Your assistance and support helped us more than you could ever know.

CONTENTS

PREFACE

> "This case begins with the astonishing proposition that if a 15 year old girl reports a sexual assault, police will interview the alleged perpetrator. They will decide who they think is telling the truth. And the loser of that beauty pageant will be charged with a criminal offence."
> - Mr. Cupito, criminal defense lawyer for Athena

This is the true story of a sexual assault victim. Not just any victim, my daughter. This story is told from my perspective as the mother of a beautiful, caring and honest child who becomes irreparably damaged: first as the result of being raped by a boy she thought was a friend, and then repeatedly by the police and the legal system my family once believed in.

I have written this book for several reasons. There is a silent epidemic in North America, it is the rape of teen-age girls by boys they know, and very often trust. It is not the dark alley and strangers that you need to fear most for your child. According to familytimeccc.org /sexual-assaults, *eighty two percent of sexual assault victims know their assailant.* By the time your daughter is *eighteen years old, she will have a one in four chance of having been sexually assaulted* (Copyright 2012 Rape Victim's Support Network @ www.assaultcare.ca). *Eleven percent of those victims are under the age of eleven at the time they are assaulted* (©Canadian Women's Foundation @ www. canadianwomen.org/facts-about-violence).

A report from the Canadian Centre for Justice Statistics Profile Series on Sexual Assault in Canada 2004 and 2007 (Catalogue no. 85F0033M-No.19

ISSN 1496-4562, ISBN 978-1-100-11163-6) states that "about" one in ten sexual assaults are reported to police.

Following my daughter's rape, I learned that there were three other *reported* rapes at her school in the same year. This school is in a rural town with a population of less than six thousand. The student population at the school was under one thousand.

If statistics are correct–and according to all other research, a ten percent reporting rate for sexual assault is very high–there were *at least forty young women in one year at this small high school who were sexually assaulted*. And sadly, this is not an unusual school; similar rates of sexual assault occur all over North America.

My other motivation for the writing of this book is this: The treatment my child and my family suffered at the hands of police and the legal system was unfathomable. Prior to experiencing profound disrespect, intentional humiliation, and complete disregard for the wellbeing of a child, I would not have believed this would both happen, and be condoned in Canada. This lack of ethics, professionalism, and integrity began with the police, and remained constant throughout the entire legal system up to and including the Justice Department.

While this book is from my perspective alone, I have tried to be as honest and open about the events as I possibly can. The legal system not only failed my daughter, but actively tried to destroy her for seeking justice.

The effects of sexual assault are more profound than I could ever have imagined. Rape does not just steal the victim's body; it destroys the victim's soul. When atrocities provided by police and the legal system are added, the very survival of the victim is at risk. For several years I did not know if my daughter would survive this ordeal, and it was treatment by police and the legal system that pushed her close to suicide. While rape is horrendous, being raped repeatedly by the people you believed in and believed were there to save you is beyond what many of us can emotionally deal with. If those who are there to save us actually persecute us instead, our faith in God, and all people is irreparably destroyed. I hope this book will make people angry, and willing to speak out about the shambles our legal system is in. Change will only happen if we make it happen.

Finally, I write this book in an attempt to change societal attitudes. Sexual assault is one of the last taboos of our culture. Topics that were once never mentioned in polite society are now openly discussed and accepted, for example; colon and prostate cancer, sexual orientation, and mental health issues. But mention that you have been raped, and one of two things will happen. Either the room will clear, or the victim will be scoffed at and bullied. The victim soon learns that speaking of the assault is socially unacceptable, which leads to feelings of isolation and shame for something they had absolutely no control over. We have cultural traditions that teach us what to do when there is illness or death in a family. We have no guidelines to tell us how to provide comfort in the case of a rape. Yet because the incidence of rape is so out of control, we are in contact every day with women and girls who are victims of this crime, and we are unlikely to even know it.

I hope this book will outrage you. I hope it will spark the conversations and debates that are needed to end the appalling treatment of young women in our culture. It is time to demand that society and government take the lives of our daughters seriously. The one very sad truth I have learned is that in Canada we are only minimally better than the countries we see on the news who place no value on the lives of women. We give an incredible amount of lip service, but it ends there. The number of young women in North America who are raped daily is horrifying. To quote Mother Theresa: "Love begins by taking care of the closest ones-the ones at home." And it is time we took care of these young women.

Because *Every minute of every day, a woman or child in Canada is being sexually assaulted....* " And according to www.womensnetwork.net, over half of these assaults will involve victims younger than eighteen.

INTRODUCTION

I began keeping notes after my daughter was interviewed by police for the second time following her rape. I intended, and did, use those notes to file a complaint against the police officer who interviewed her.

As contact with police increased, I became more and more disturbed by the lack of respect, integrity and professionalism, and my notes became a journal. The journal entries are shown with the day and date as they were written. As this nightmare went on for far longer than anyone imagined possible, it became appropriate when writing this book to sometimes condense several days or even weeks of entries. This is made evident in the book by showing the range of time in which the events occur.

At times I have added personal reflections as I look back, and these reflections are made in italics.

I have given you the story as I learned it, and many times while we were living this nightmare I had questions I wanted answered, just as you will. Be patient, just as I eventually got answers, so will you. This, I believe is the only way to prevent the incredible amount of information from overwhelming the reader.

In Canada, we own the letters we write, and so I have included copies of the letters I wrote. The flip side of this is that letters written to us remain the property of the writer. The recipient of a letter has no legal ownership to that letter. This means that I cannot legally include letters written in response to my queries or complaints, and must instead re-phrase the contents of those letters. I have done this as accurately as possible.

All of the names, dates, and locations in this book have been changed.

The story is true. In this book I consistently refer to the boy who raped my daughter without adding the fact that I can only allege he committed this crime. Given that he was never convicted or even charged with this offence, I ask the reader to understand that the word "alleged" should always be assumed to exist before any such statement. This book is my interpretation of the events that took place. I have absolutely no doubt that others, particularly those in the legal system, would prefer to see the events differently. I have, however, tried to be as accurate, honest and open as I am able.

CHAPTER 1

Ground Zero

For many months I thought of ground zero as the day my daughter was raped. Looking back, I see it differently; an event that once seemed removed from the Kafkaesque night-mare in which we now live, was actually the beginning of it all.

In the fall of 2010, Athena was in grade ten. Fifteen years old, she was extremely intelligent and had a wonderful sense of humour. She was outgoing, self-confident, and very attractive. She was, to quote from a letter written much later by her boyfriend, 'probably the nicest person I know.' I have described her as a much better person than me and I mean that sincerely and with pride. That I could raise such a beautiful person makes me feel quite humble, and incredibly proud. She was completely accepting of people regardless of age, sex, sexual orientation, appearances or social status. She had always been troubled by catty girls, and friends who were fair-weather. They were beyond her comprehension. As a friend, she was fiercely loyal, and completely accepting. She expected her friends to be there for her, just as she was there for them. She was at the same time remarkably mature, and extremely naive.

She grew up in the country, an hour drive to the closest city, and lived in the same farm house on the same farm all her life. Although we consciously made trips to the city to expand her horizons, she knew precious little of life off the farm. She was raised with two television channels, yet only watched one, a public broadcast station. She watched warm and fuzzy educational shows for children when she was young, and graduated to British humour as she got older. She loved old Disney movies, communicated well with adults, and had never shown even a hint of a negative attitude. Many teachers over the years commented on how polite, genuine, and caring she was. Countless parents over the years had told me they hoped their children would grow up to be like Athena.

GROUND ZERO:

It was early fall. Athena was attending the same rural high school she had attended the previous year. She loved to be physically active, and was enrolled in a Physical Education class. On this particular day, the class was practicing soccer skills outside. Running after the soccer ball, Athena and another girl collided. Athena lost consciousness and was taken to the hospital. She was diagnosed with a concussion, a broken nose, and a sprained jaw. She was told to ice her nose, and sent home.

After two weeks of massive headaches, Athena returned to school to find her entire world changed. She had gotten behind during the time she was away, and was expected to compete with other students for the limited academic help. She had never been assertive, let alone aggressive, and was rarely successful in this competition. She suddenly found herself unable to concentrate, and could not remember even the simplest steps. Literally overnight she went from being a top student to struggling. Her final math mark at the end of the term was forty-six percent, a fail.

Her father and I met with the math teacher, the special education teacher and the principal. They were completely unwilling to compromise, and were not willing to factor in consideration for the injury she suffered. She was told she would have to repeat the math course. Although her grades in other courses also showed marked decreases, she managed to pass them, but with far less than her previous honour student marks.

With the same suddenness, Athena began to have social issues, and seemed unable to accurately read, or deal with social situations. Immediately following the injury, she became unable to comprehend innuendos, and the subtleties of words and comments. She lost the ability to assess the world around her in a way that made her seem even more naive. Almost immediately she became the focus of a group of nasty, mainly female, bullies but she refused to say who was bullying her. She was diagnosed with depression.

By Christmas Athena was in counselling and on antidepressants. She managed to maintain a few friendships, but was no longer comfortable and confident around the big group she once had been a part of. She felt isolated and very alone.

At this time, information about acquired brain injuries was not common knowledge, and no one, not her father or me, or her doctor, or the school made the connection between her depression, mental confusion, or inability to concentrate, with her head injury. Within months of her accident, the media began to showcase the dangers, symptoms, and treatments for concussions. Unfortunately at this time, there was no treatment, no recommendations to improve healing, and no support.

As parents, we struggled to determine what was at the root of her sudden academic and social problems. Was being bullied the cause of her depression and plummeting marks? Was it possible she had undiagnosed Attention Deficit Disorder that had suddenly caught up to her after years of easy marks because of her intelligence level? Why couldn't she remember even simple details and steps? And was it possible that her head injury had something to do with all this?

Athena had been diagnosed as an intellectually gifted student in grade seven, with scores in the 98th and 99th percentile. These tests would serve as a baseline to compare the results of new tests against her original test scores. I made an appointment to have her retested by the psychiatrist who had initially identified her. The testing took two days, with one day of testing completed just after Christmas, and the final at the end of January, 2011. The results took some months to be analyzed.

Between being bullied and not getting the support she needed to achieve, Athena began to dread school. She began to talk about transferring to a different high school, in a town called Rivertown. Initially, her father and I were against this move, but when the situation continued to deteriorate I visited the Rivertown high school with the intention of just 'checking it out'. I learned that Rivertown high offered a program that would enable Athena to recover the areas of math she failed, without re-taking the entire course. The staff seemed very accommodating, and she would be away from the bullies. I decided on the spot. We would bite the bullet, and enroll her at Rivertown starting the next semester, the beginning of February, 2011.

The decision was not without logistical problems: The school was twenty-eight kilometers from our home, and we were outside the school bus catchment area. In order for her to attend this school, her father and I would have to drive her to, and pick her up from, the closest bus stop, about five kilometers from our home. Athena would be a "border crossing" student, crossing not just school, but county boundaries.

Athena was elated; happier than she had been in months. The new school was bigger and offered more choice of courses. It had a much better reputation. Athena had a couple of acquaintances at the new school. One of which, within the first two weeks, would change her life forever.

CHAPTER 2

February 15th 2011

EXACTLY TWO WEEKS FROM ATHENA'S FIRST
DAY AT RIVERTOWN HIGH SCHOOL.

The phone call came shortly after noon. The principal of the school where I was teaching came into the classroom and told me my husband had phoned. There was an emergency, he said, and I was to phone home immediately. My husband, Sandy, had taken the day off work, and was at home, but for him to call me at work meant a serious problem. I left the principal with the class, went to the office, and called home. My very distraught husband told me the high school had phoned. Our daughter, Athena, had been sexually assaulted. She was in the principal's office. That was all they would tell him.

I felt like I had been punched in the gut, which was immediately followed by overwhelming numbness. I remember going through the motions of what I needed to do without being fully present; thick fog with snippets of absolute clarity. I went to the principal and quietly told him, "I have to leave. My daughter has been raped."

With no further comment, I picked up my belongings, and I walked out, leaving him responsible for the class. Several weeks later one of the students remembered that I had left suddenly, and asked me why I had been crying when I left. This surprised me. I didn't know I had been crying, although I did remember feeling like my facial muscles were very tight and pulled out of shape.

The twenty minute drive to Rivertown high-school seemed an eternity, and yet the only memory I have was when I noticed a muddy, overflowing ditch in a farm field, and realized I had no idea where the rape had taken place. In my confused state I wondered if Athena had been found in a ditch or in a field. Had I been thinking rationally I would have known she would be in hospital had that been the case.

I drove as fast as I felt I safely could, while my mind started to reel. Was this somehow connected to the bullying at her last school? How badly was she hurt? Was she at school when it happened? Rumors among students at her last school told of sex in the school washrooms and stairwells-was it the same in this new school? I had the image of a dark stairwell, my daughter.... One assailant? My God, what if there was more than one. When I was part–way, I called the school on my cell phone. I asked the person who answered to tell Athena I would be there in ten minutes.

Having only been in this school once before, I parked by the doors I thought were closest to the office. As soon as I was in the hall I realized I had gone to the wrong door, and I did not know how to get to the office. I felt barely controlled panic at this realization: I needed to find the office and I needed to find Athena. I didn't think I could speak coherently enough to ask for help, and anyway, the halls were empty. I started walking quickly down a long corridor, hoping I was heading in the right direction. Suddenly the office was right in front of me.

The office staff, perhaps from the look on my face, seemed to know why I was there. Before I even had time to speak, I was shown to an office where Athena was sitting in a chair.

She was extremely pale. She appeared to be dazed and in shock. I had not known what to expect: Knowing Athena, I did not expect she would be raving and screaming, but I had no idea how she would react. Still, I was surprised that she was so unresponsive. She stood up when I went to hug her, but she seemed completely deflated; like the life had gone out of her. I was completely focused on Athena, and it wasn't until I had hugged her that I noticed she was not alone. The woman with her identified herself as the school principal.

I pulled an empty chair as close to Athena as I could, and held her limp hand. I didn't want to bombard her with questions, so I waited a few minutes while we all just sat there; Athena staring silently into space, wiping an occasional tear. I didn't see obvious signs of physical injury, and I felt thankful for that. Finally I asked her what had happened. I don't remember her exact words, I only remember learning that Conn had invited her to have lunch at his house, and while they were in his home, he raped her.

⚖

Connor Mann was a boy who had gone way out of his way to befriend Athena. At the time she was assaulted, she had known him about two years. They met through a mutual friend, and started communicating on Facebook and later through texting. Their 'friendship' was really just a social media one, but at this new school, where Athena knew almost no one, he was at least someone familiar. She and Connor; he usually went by 'Conn,' had run into each other a couple of times at hockey games, and Athena had once, many months ago spent a few hours visiting with Conn and his parents. Conn had been invited to our home once, but at the last minute he had cancelled. I had seen him twice, but only at a distance. I felt uneasy both times, wondering if he deliberately avoided having to meet me.

Although I never learned why, Athena ended all contact with Conn at one point. At that time she said only that she did not approve of his behavior.

We raised Athena to see the good in everyone, to believe that boys and girls could be just good friends, and to believe that people could learn and grow and change. I remember her telling me that he had changed for the better, and she let him back into her life a little. That was just after her brain injury, during the time she began to have problems socializing, and he convinced her that he too was having trouble making friends and being accepted.

The final catch came over Christmas. I remember Athena yelling down the stairs to me from the computer room, "Mom! Mom, I knew it! Conn is gay!" His Facebook status had been changed to reflect this. My accepting and supportive daughter was now convinced. He was in need of a friend, and she would be there for him. He was gay, so in her mind not interested in being more than a friend. Hence, he was 'safe.' He knew that Athena was dating someone else and had been for the past nine months. A very short time after this, we made our decision to move Athena to the same school he attended. Conn being there was definitely not a selling feature for Athena's dad and me, but it was for Athena. Texting increased between them, and he started phoning her. We were uneasy about this kid, but with no concrete reason. We certainly never imagined this would happen...

⚖

Athena began to tell me that she went to Conn's house for lunch. When they arrived, he went upstairs. She didn't know what else to do, so she followed him. She became side-tracked by something, and he disappeared. She wandered into what she thought was his room, noticed his DVD collection and started to look at them. Suddenly she realized he was beside her, naked. The principal interrupted her at this point, and suggested that since the police were coming, it would be easier on her if she waited, so she would only have to tell her story once.

I felt a surge of shock at hearing he came into the room naked. My mind struggled with this. It seemed such an aggressive act; like he never doubted he would be successful in his seduction. What young man would take such a chance at rejection? To walk into a room naked is to invite complete ridicule, rejection, anger, or even disgust.

And then I realized. He wasn't afraid of her reaction because it didn't matter to him what her reaction was. His intent was to have sex with her, and her willingness did not enter into it. Being naked gave him a huge advantage over Athena, not just with the shock factor, but with the fact that he did not need to get his clothes off, only hers. This was not about romance and a planned seduction gone wrong; this smacked of the intent to be exactly what it ended up being: rape. I remember wondering if taking his clothes off first had been his own idea, or if he had looked up 'how to sexually assault someone' on the internet. Or perhaps he had learned from previous experience.

Until the principal mentioned the police, I had not even thought about them. I hadn't wondered why we were sitting in this little room, nor questioned what we were waiting for. I felt a sudden, but brief, flash of concern at that point. We have all heard horror stories about police mistreatment of rape victims, but I believed that would not be the case in Canada in the year 2011.

Maybe Athena asked for the police, or perhaps the school simply went ahead and made the call. It didn't matter; I had no issue with the police, and I believed this decision was Athena's to make. I knew Athena would want to do the right thing.

As we waited, Athena said nothing. A few tears escaped from her eyes. Beyond that, it seemed that she had gone to some inner place, where I could not reach her. And indeed she had.

I didn't realize it at the time, but my daughter was already gone from me. She would never again be the same person. I lost my child that day. She has almost been destroyed by this boy, and by the police she believed would help her.

The police officer assigned to the school came into the room. Officer Firth seemed a very fatherly man; likeable and open. I remember only that Athena said Conn's name, and he confirmed he knew who Conn was. He checked that he was indeed "the short guy," and seemed a bit surprised by this, but he also remained very concerned looking and was the first to start the lie we would hear many times that day: "I believe you."

Looking back, there is so much I can't remember. We were at the school for quite some time. It could have been an hour, it could have been two. For some reason I didn't question, Officer Firth directed me to move my truck to the parking lot closest to the school office, and sometime after that, I drove Athena and myself to the local hospital. Officer Firth told me what to do, and on auto pilot, I complied. I vaguely remember leaving the high school; I certainly don't remember driving, but Athena and I arrived at the hospital and parked, as instructed, in the emergency parking lot. I don't remember showing Athena's health card, or filling in any forms. Perhaps the school had taken care of these details, but it is equally possible that in shock, I have simply forgotten.

The very next thing I remember is being in a room in the emergency department of the Rivertown hospital. I remember waiting. I remember thinking that time had lost all shape and meaning, yawning and stretching like some drug-induced nightmare. I had no idea what we were waiting for, and it didn't matter. Nothing mattered but the empty shell that had been my daughter. I watched Athena, and was profoundly worried to see her so remote and despondent. She simply stared into space. At one point a nurse wanted to take her blood pressure, which required Athena to take her sweater off. She did so without any indication that she knew what she was doing. Only once did she say anything to the nurse, and that was to ask her about sexually transmitted diseases. Once she heard the answer, she resumed staring into space.

The room was very cool, but Athena was completely oblivious, her sweater left lying on the bed where it had been removed. I asked if she was cold. She didn't answer, but accepted my help to put the sweater back on. She only spoke once to me, and that was to ask if she could die from being raped when she was having her period.

People came and went, and several times I was asked to leave the room. No one explained why I needed to go, but I assumed they were taking care of her medical needs. I later found out that taking her blood pressure was the extent of that hospital's medical involvement.

Officer Firth spoke to Athena again at the hospital in my presence, and she told him Conn had ejaculated on her leg. I felt I was interrupting, but consoling Athena came before my concern for protocol. I told Athena that ejaculating on her leg meant less chance of both pregnancy and disease. I was hoping this might ease her fears a bit, but I realized she didn't understand, and so I explained that it is the semen that carries many of the diseases, and not having it inside her meant much less chance of illness as well as pregnancy. Firth asked some other question, and Athena told the officer the semen was wiped off on the bed sheets, but she also went into the bathroom and scrubbed the area that he had ejaculated on before she dressed and ran out of the house. She did not see Conn at his house after he raped her. He left the room, and she escaped. She could not remember anything between leaving the bathroom, and arriving at the school. She ended up in class, and didn't realize she was crying until another student pointed out to the teacher how distraught she was.

For some reason, and I think it may have been that we left the school without Athena's coat or boots in spite of it being winter, Officer Firth offered to return to the school and pick up the items from Athena's locker. Athena told him her locker and combination number, and off he went. He later returned with not just her coat and boots, but her backpack as well. At the time I thought it was very kind of him.

Later, once my dealings with police ended the trust I preciously had, it occurred to me that this offer, and our acceptance, had allowed Firth to search Athena's locker, and I wondered if this 'kind' offer was actually motivated by an attempt to find incriminating evidence to use against her.

Someone from a service that supports victims of crime introduced himself and gave me a business card. I forget every word he said to me. Other people came and went. I remember remarkably little. Is this what shock does? At the time I was simply thankful that there were trained professionals to help us, and I trusted them to take care of us at this time of incredible need and vulnerability.

Somehow, perhaps from Officer Firth, we learned that we were waiting for a female police officer from another location to arrive. It seems day one is intended to be warm and fuzzy for victims, and the belief is that a woman makes a female sexual assault victim feel more comfortable. We waited for several hours, Athena completely oblivious to everything and everyone.

The nurse who had taken Athena's blood pressure returned and asked Athena if she would like to see our family doctor. Dr. Grace, bless her heart, left her busy practice to provide emotional support to Athena. She held Athena's hand and spoke quietly to her. I don't believe Athena said anything at the time, but this kindness is one of the few things she remembers of that day. It meant a great deal to both of us. Dr. Grace scheduled an appointment to see Athena the following week, and handed me a note addressed to the school informing them Athena would be absent until further notice.

Finally the officer we had been waiting for arrived. In spite of chattering almost constantly, Officer Lana Chompsky seemed like a straight shooter. She spoke to Athena, and I was asked to leave during this time. Chompsky later questioned me, out in the room where ambulances unload the injured. I have a vague feeling that someone else was with Athena at that time.

I told Chompsky of Athena's obsession with cleanliness and her extreme fear of germs. I explained that she would be the only girl in the washroom scrubbing her hands before eating. I told her Athena would not consent to sex with anyone who had had other partners because of her extreme phobias, and with the increased risk of sexually transmitted disease, she would certainly never have consented to sex with someone she believed to be actively gay. She would never agree to sex without a condom. In short, I explained that Athena had quite pronounced obsessive-compulsive tendencies; cleanliness due to germ phobia being one of them.

I told her Athena's dream and goal was to have only one sexual partner in her entire life. It ripped my heart out to realize that someone had forcefully destroyed this dream, and turned something beautiful into an ugly act of violence. I told the officer that Athena asked if she could die as a result of being raped when she was menstruating. I answered as openly and as honestly as I could. I was an idiot.

The waiting went on. Athena had been assaulted around 11:00 a.m. It was now late afternoon. Once again I had no idea why we were waiting. I don't think anyone told me, and I don't remember wondering. We were just going through the motions of being alive. It really didn't matter if we were one place or another; the fact of my daughter's rape remained the same. Eventually we were told it was time to leave for the forensic sexual assault centre in a city about an hour drive away.

Officer Chompsky asked if I wanted to drive myself, or if I wanted to drive with her to the hospital. I knew I was not fit to drive, so I accepted her offer. The three of us got into a plain, dark, car that showed no outward sign of belonging to the police. Chompsky told Athena to sit in the front seat, and I sat behind Chompsky in the back.

Soon after leaving town, Athena received a text message from a boy at school asking if she and Conn had 'fucked' at lunch time. When she read it, Athena made a small distressed noise, and she told Chompsky what the text said. Chompsky told her to just reply "no." Incredibly, this text, and Athena's response would later be questioned in court.

When we arrived, Officer Chompsky parked directly in front of the hospital in a spot reserved for police. Not only was the car unmarked, but Chompsky was in plain clothes. A man immediately stopped her and pointed out that the spot was for police only. She flashed her badge and he retreated.

I had never been in a city hospital emergency department. It was wall to wall people crushed into a small space, running noses, bleeding cuts, pale faces mingled with children crying and parents trying to console them. Chompsky led us directly to the front of the line, flashed her badge again, and the slow process began. Forms were completed, and then we were shown to a very small private sitting room. I wondered if it were reserved for traumatized and grieving people, and realized that we now were both. Another wait: This time for the sexual assault team to gather at the hospital from other work locations and even from other nearby cities.

While we waited, Officer Chompsky chattered on, but I remember only two things. One was her offer to mediate between Athena and Conn, if Athena ever decided she wanted to ask Conn why he raped her. I could see from the look on Athena's face that this idea appalled her. She later told me how shocked she was that Chompsky would even suggest such a thing. She said she never wanted to set eyes on Conn again, and could not imagine ever wanting to talk to him. I realized then that Chompsky failed to understand the extent of Athena's trauma.

The other thing I remember was Chompsky assuring us that Conn would have legal restrictions placed on him to prevent him contacting Athena. Legal restrictions would also be in place to prevent him from being around, and potentially harming, children younger than himself.

Finally we were informed that the sexual assault team arrived. A hospital worker led us to a suite reserved for victims of sexual assault. Safe and comforting, like a rabbit warren, this suit of rooms was buried deep in the belly of the hospital. With the door closed to the outside world, it felt safe from the world that suddenly had become so terrifying.

The door opened into the side and end of a tiny sitting area, like a cozy little nook. Straight ahead was the examining room; larger and with several areas including a shower and a washroom. Off the sitting room was a small galley type kitchen, and from the couch I could see a couple of chest type freezers. The freezers, I was told, were there to preserve forensic evidence collected from sexual assault victims who were not sure they wanted to report their rape to the police. I remember being amazed by this: Why wouldn't a victim go to the police? Look at all the support we were getting! Athena was repeatedly told she was believed and respected for her decision to come forward; told that she had done *the right thing.*

I was not allowed to be with Athena when she was examined for evidence. Several workers told me the team would go over every inch of her body with "a fine tooth comb" looking for forensic evidence. Unfortunately, this proved not to be the case. Blood was taken for testing, and Athena was given a teddy bear—which she clung to—and a new set of green hospital scrubs to replace her clothing which allegedly was sent for forensic testing.

Officer Chompsky kept busy, writing in her notebook, and she left the room at least once, but perhaps more, to talk on the phone. These events were so unimportant to me at the time, I took very little notice. I think

Chompsky may have gone into the examining room at some point, but I am not even certain about that.

One of the team members commented that victims very rarely bring anyone, let alone a parent with them to the assault centre. This made me incredibly sad. I could not imagine anyone having to go through this alone.

When Athena returned from the examining room, I gave her a hug, although I don't think she realized. She held the ubiquitous teddy bear like it was her life line. She complained again that her head really hurt. She was offered a Tylenol by one of the nurses.

A social worker talked to Athena then, and asked her if she had any specific concerns. Sexually transmitted diseases were Athena's biggest fear, and after that, she was concerned about her boyfriend. How could she tell him she had been raped? The worker asked what he was like, and Athena shared a little about him. The worker reassured Athena by saying that based on what she heard; he would likely be there for her.

Athena was offered a feast of drugs. Drugs to counter as many sexually transmitted diseases as are available. And Athena, who was terrified of all drugs, and had only once in her life taken antibiotics, went for the entire feast, including some extra because Conn is gay. In spite of this cornucopia of drugs, she would still be tested several times during the next six months for sexually transmitted diseases.

When we left the hospital, it was night. Officer Chompsky took a wrong turn and got lost somewhere in a new shopping development. She phoned a friend of hers to get directions, and eventually we got back on the right road again. Athena stayed curled in a fetal position on the front seat. She mentioned again how tired she was, and how badly her head hurt.

Only then were we told that Athena still needed to make a formal statement, and that this had to be done at a police station. Conn was still being held at the police station in Rivertown, and so we would go to the police station in the town of Zend, about a twenty minute drive from Rivertown. She told us that we would stop in Rivertown first to get something to eat. It was now past ten o'clock p.m. and I realized Athena had not eaten since breakfast, some sixteen hours ago. She had been raped, gone back to school and in shock had gone to class. A student in her English class noticed she was in obvious distress, and had suggested to the teacher that she be allowed to go to the guidance department. Athena could not remember being in class at all. When she got to the guidance department she apparently told the counselor she had been raped. Next, she had been sent to two hospitals, invasively searched for forensic evidence, and now, many long hours after the most horrific experience in her life, she would have to tell the story while being video-taped.

Athena and I went in to the Subway restaurant; I ordered for us, hoping food would somehow help. Officer Chompsky stayed outside. I thought she was on the phone the entire time, but months later I learned she went to the Rivertown police station, which in the state I was in I failed to realize was just across the street.

It was raining when we arrived at the Zend police station, and we parked in a dark lot near a rear door. The door was locked, and Chompsky unlocked it for us to enter. As we walked through the dark room, I noticed two police officers viewing a computer screen. Given that there were no lights on, and no vehicles in the parking lot, I was surprised to see them. They were already gone when we left.

Once again we waited. It took a very long time before Officer Chompsky was ready, and Athena and I waited in a small room just off the public entrance. I called Sandy again as I had several times to keep him informed about what was going on. He had already started to shut himself off from the world.

When Sandy and I finished talking, I called Athena's boyfriend. Their usual routine was for him and Athena to text message in the evening. He attended a school well over an hour drive in the opposite direction from the school Athena now attended. After having received several text messages from him, Athena felt she couldn't put off answering him any longer. He would already sense something was wrong, and would be worried. Her text back to him said only that something had happened and she would tell him more when she could. I worried about him. I knew he would be extremely upset, who wouldn't be? I suggested to Athena that I phone and tell him. I knew it would be incredibly painful for her to explain, and I wanted to spare her more suffering, both in the telling, and possibly in his reaction. This would be a huge shock to him. He too would need emotional support to get through this, and he may need some time to collect his emotions before talking to her.

Athena then sent a text to say she would be calling, but in fact I made the call.

He listened silently when I told him Athena had been sexually assaulted, but he immediately wanted to talk to her. I could hear him telling her he loved her, while Athena silently wept.

And then it was time for Athena's interview. Once the interview finally started it seemed to take forever. My best guess was the interview started at around eleven o'clock, but I really don't know for certain. There were clocks, and I wore a watch, but my brain just couldn't register the reality of the time: time simply stopped having any meaning. I was exhausted. I could not imagine how Athena felt. How could she be expected to think, let alone communicate a coherent thought?

Eventually Chompsky and Athena reappeared. Officer Chompsky was telling Athena she had tried in the interview to prompt her to say how phobic she is about germs. By that point, I don't think Athena cared much about anything, including her statement to the police.

Finally we were done. On the drive back to Rivertown hospital– where decades ago I had left my truck–Chompsky chatted on. She talked about a sex offender registry, accessible to only a few individuals in the entire country. We were led to believe that Conn would now be in this book, regardless of a conviction. It had, she said, been established in response to other horrific acts against women, and to bridge communication between police forces and detachments. The goal of the registry, she said, was to have one location where all reported sexual assaults are recorded and can be tracked.

She also informed us that, as of the next day, she would be off work for two weeks of training. As a result, her partner, Officer Derk Delwood, would be taking over the investigation. Officer Delwood had interviewed Conn, and so was already fully involved. Chompsky said Athena would likely be interviewed again to clear up a few details, and that the interview would be conducted by a woman officer.

Chompsky left us at Rivertown hospital, and somehow I drove home. By then it was well after midnight.

Athena felt 'dirty' and wanted to scrub herself clean of the assault. She showered and scrubbed, and then had a bath. She said her nipple was really sore where Conn had sucked or bit it. She also said he had tried to force his penis in her mouth. She complained that she was very sore 'inside', and she still had a pounding headache. She did not go into details of the assault, and I did not think it would help to ask her to tell this story again.

Months later I learned Athena called her best friend later that night. She also called her older brother and sister. Athena asked her sister if she knew if it was possible to have a normal life after being raped.

At some point in the night the phone rang, and it was Officer Chompsky, calling to tell us something about Conn's phone, and him not being able to contact us now. Nothing made much sense, but once again, we just trusted that the professionals were taking care of us, and we were thankful.

It was a long, sleepless night for Sandy and me. Athena fell asleep, and it wasn't until the next day that I realized this was more than a way to shut out the world. It was likely the result of another concussion.

CHAPTER 3

Living in Fog

THE FIRST TWO WEEKS FOLLOWING ATHENA'S ASSAULT

We stumbled through life in a deep fog. It was impossible to think or talk about anything but the assault and its' devastating effect on Athena. In one day our lives had become unrecognizable, and our child a complete stranger.

Sandy and I were both consumed by feelings of complete helpless, but especially for Sandy, the belief that he had failed to protect our daughter cut him to the core. We had no idea how to cope, what to do, how to help our child who was in such obvious emotional pain. While Athena had been diagnosed with depression following her brain injury, she had responded extremely well to treatment. But being raped sent her into a depressed state so deep we were afraid for her. She was suddenly terrified to be around people, but also terrified to be alone. She was remote and withdrawn, completely changed from the person she had been. At times she became incredibly angry and would verbally lash out; responses we never imagined her capable of. Other times she was terrified that Conn would find a way to hurt her again. We had no idea how to reach out to the child we used to know. We thought that other than death or extreme illness, this was the worst thing that could happen in our family.

FEBRUARY 16, 2011   •

The day after Athena was sexually assaulted. A date I expect has been burned in our minds forever. Sandy and I stayed home, exhausted. Athena stayed in her new found shell. Completely withdrawn, most of her day was spent on the couch, curled in the fetal position. We needed Athena to respond to us in some way. We needed to know that this was temporary; that she would come back to us. Athena was gone, and whether she would ever come back to us, we had no way of knowing. In my ignorance I tried to get her to talk about the assault. I thought talking about it would help, and that needing to talk about it was normal. It was the only thing she showed some passion about. She was adamant; she did not want to talk about it. She did not want to think about it. She wanted to forget it had ever happened. It was always in her head, she said. It would not go away.

It seemed the phone didn't stop ringing that first day, although I forget most of the calls. I know someone from the sexual assault unit at the hospital phoned early in the day, as did someone from Services for Victims. One call was from a telemarketer, which shocked me. How could the world go on as if nothing had happened? The police did not call, and that surprised me.

A very dear friend took the day off work, just to be available if we needed her. We did. We contacted a few of the people close to us, and understood when they didn't know what to say or do. Society gives us detailed rituals to deal with many things; death, illness, accidents. There are none to deal with sexual assault. Just knowing that friends cared, just hearing their concern, helped a lot. One friend brought Athena flowers, and Athena, for a very short time, seemed almost herself. Another friend baked us a cake.

We told everyone we spoke to how well we had been treated; by the school, the police, and the sexual assault centre. I specifically praised the police, and was not prepared for the surprise expressed by those I spoke to. Most did not expect the police to treat a rape victim well. An overwhelming majority said they would not have reported the assault. I was disturbed by the attitudes I encountered: I believed it was important that rape be reported in order that those responsible be punished. How else would we stop rapists?

That afternoon, Athena discovered a welt on her head. It was about two and a half centimeters wide and five or more centimeters long; it was not hard, as I would have expected, but felt more like an over-filled water balloon. It ran horizontally on the right side of her head. She said it didn't hurt, and instead had me feel a spot on the back of her head, just up from where her neck and head met; that she said was extremely tender. I was completely confounded. I asked if Conn had hit her. She was adamant that he had not; and the depth of her conviction surprised me. She had no idea how the injury had occurred. I asked her what the nurses at the sexual assault centre had said about it. She told me they hadn't checked her head. I knew this couldn't be right, and believed instead she had just been too emotionally distraught at the time to notice and remember. After all, the entire reason we went to the sexual assault centre was to find evidence of violence. Several times I was told the assault centre workers would 'go over every inch of her body with a fine tooth comb.' And while I naively believed this had been done, I was most unhappy I had not been told about another head injury.

As Athena took my hand and guided my fingers to the welt on her head, I noticed some extremely thin scratches on her arm. Once I started looking, I noticed quite a number these scabbed-scratches. Each was about two centimeters in length, and thinner even than a cat scratch; about the width of a very fine pen line. Almost all were single, and were scattered on both arms, but there were also a couple on her torso, and on the back side of one hip. Each one was perfectly identical, and perfectly executed; no ragged edges, no varying width, perfectly straight. They seem too shallow to have bled, yet each had an identical scab. They weren't serious, just very, very odd. I asked Athena how she got these scratches, but she had no idea.

Sandy and I discussed the welt, and vaguely wondered if we should 'do something' about it, but we couldn't decide what that something was. The very last thing I felt like doing was returning to the hospital emergency department, and really, there seemed no point. As a head injury, it was past the time to worry about concussion, and as a part of the assault, well, sexual assault is an act of violence. Sandy felt these injuries were just part and parcel of the whole violent act, and to him it paled in comparison to the sexual part of assault. I was just too exhausted to know what to do. I reasoned that the sexual assault centre must have noticed, and had some legal or privacy reason, for not telling me. Or perhaps they simply forgot. Either way I was not impressed.

⚖

Some days later, when I was thinking more clearly, and was a bit more emotionally stable, I tried to contact the sexual assault centre. I left a number of messages, none of which were returned until it just didn't matter anymore.

Several times in the following weeks Athena would blurt out a detail about something that had happened the day she was raped. She would state something, and it was done. No further discussion. I wondered if she even knew she had spoken these words out loud.

In the days after the assault Athena complained that she really hurt 'inside', but the rest of her comments were made only once. When Conn appeared naked in the room, she remembered saying, "What the fuck?" This was the first time I had ever heard Athena say the 'F' word. Another time she said she couldn't move her hands when Conn was raping her, and not knowing what prevented her from doing so upset her greatly. She made random comments about Conn's sexual organs. Each time the description was very odd: Conn's penis was small; he appeared to have only one testicle. Another time she described this testicle as black and ugly. She told me the sexual assault centre found blood in her bra. Weeks later she made the connection between Conn biting or sucking on her breast really hard with the blood in her bra, but at that time thoughts seemed to pop into her mind, she would verbally express that thought, and it would be gone. We quickly learned not to press her for more details; if we did, she became very distressed. It seemed she could share these 'pop up' thoughts without becoming emotionally involved, but to deliberately remember or think about the assault caused her more emotional distress than she could bear.

The night following the rape, Athena's best friend Jessie came to stay with her. Many months later Jessie told us that night, Athena, still asleep, began fighting and punching; as if she were fighting off an attacker. More and more agitated, she kept repeating Conn's name. Jessie was afraid she would be inadvertently hurt by Athena's flying fists, but was afraid to try and wake her. During their years of friendship, nothing like this had ever happened before; nor did it happen again. In concern, Jessie left the bed. Athena also got out of bed. Jessie went out and shut the bedroom door behind her. Still asleep, Athena banged on the door, saying Conn's name over and over. Athena eventually stopped, and went quietly back to bed. After awhile, Jessie followed.

⚖

For years Athena had dreamed of becoming a swimming instructor and a life guard. Her training had been postponed once because of her concussion. Now she was facing an even bigger obstacle.

Athena had completed the classroom component of the swimming instructor course, now she needed the practical experience of assisting a qualified swimming instructor. Planned long before the assault, Athena's first day was to be the Saturday just days after she was raped.

That we even attempted to have Athena go to the pool that morning shows how incredibly little we knew about the emotional repercussions of rape.

FEBRUARY 19

When we got to the pool, Athena was too terrified to go into the change room alone, so I went with her. Then the thought of having to undress and put on a bathing suit completely flipped her out. She could not even remove her sweater, let alone put on and wear a bathing suit. She felt exposed and vulnerable. There was no way she could go in the pool, and certainly could not help teach lessons.

With Athena's approval, I told the head lifeguard briefly what had happened. The guard was wonderfully considerate, and let Athena observe for the day. The room the pool was in was very humid and hot, and unlike anyone else on the pool deck, Athena was wearing jeans, a shirt and a sweater. She was visibly sweating, but she could not force herself to take off her sweater. She couldn't even pull the zipper down. Finally she rolled her pant legs up, just a bit. At one point she was asked to go into a room with one of the male instructors to get some lifejackets. Later she told me she almost couldn't do it, even though she knew the instructor, and had previously trusted him.

In the past I would have dropped her off at the pool and returned to pick her up at the end. Now she was terrified to be alone. I stayed and sat on the pool deck where she could see me at all times, and she constantly glanced over to reassure herself I was still there, and that she was not in danger.

⚖

Athena had completely lost her independence. She was in many ways like a very young child, terrified of people and completely dependent. She was unable to go into a store or a public washroom alone. If someone she didn't know came within a meter and a half of her she would grab and cling to me. She trusted few people, male or female.

I don't think there was a conscious plan to get Athena out in public, but it seemed like the right thing to do. For the next two weeks I tried to get Athena out every day. We went to stores, or restaurants; anywhere that forced her to be around people. She was constantly withdrawn and morose. Occasionally she would become very angry. She used to love shopping and eating out, she had been outgoing, gregarious and self-confident. All of that was gone. She wasn't interested in what we were doing, she just went along. I tried to make it interesting, tried to get her to look at clothes, but on the one occasion she showed some minor interest in an outfit, she panicked at the thought of going into the change-room to try it on.

After a number of outings, perhaps a week or so after the assault, Athena and I went to a department store. When we got there, she wanted to try going beyond where she could see me. We agreed that I would stay in one spot, and she would go one aisle over, and then return. She was back within seconds, breathing heavily with anxiety. But she had done it. I almost cried. Where had Athena gone? How could she have been so independent, so confident, and have it all disappear in one terrible hour? Before she was raped, Athena had absolutely no fear of speaking in front of any number of people; she was outgoing and remarkably self confident. Now she was terrified to speak to a sales person in a store.

At some point in the week after the assault, I called Derk Delwood, the police officer I was told was now in charge of the investigation. At this point I had not even spoken to Officer Delwood, and I found this very odd. Chompsky had told us we would be kept fully informed, but then she left, and Delwood had taken over. I don't recollect much of the call, only that I felt chastised by him. I was left feeling I had no right to ask what was happening in the case of my daughter's rape, and in fact I was told only that it was too soon for any results, and that he was looking into some text messages.

Sandy commented that this did not bode well. I preferred to believe it would all be fine.

School presented a huge problem. Since her head injury, school had become such a challenge for Athena, and missing classes would only compound the problem.

Thank heaven for good friends. Sandy talked to one of his closest friends and told him about the assault. Almost immediately after hanging up, his friend's wife, Nancy, called; Nancy explained to us that she was a sexual assault survivor —something we had not previously known— and asked if she could take Athena for a drive to talk to her.

Athena went willingly; thankful to find someone who really understood what she had gone through. When they arrived back at our home, Nancy told us her story, and used it to help us understand what Athena was feeling and fearing. She explained that Athena was not ready to return to school. We started to realize that healing was going to take a very long time. We started to realize that the life we had was gone, and that the new reality was looking very grim.

And so we stopped pushing Athena to return to school. I arranged to have school-work set aside for her which either Sandy or I picked up and returned to the school once completed. The Vice Principal I spoke with came across as very accommodating and willing to help in any way he could. We discussed options to facilitate a safe and less stressful return to school. Even though we believed Conn had a restraining order legally preventing him from any contact with Athena, she was terrified to be in the same building as him. We devised a plan to have designated students walk Athena to and from her classes, and the bus. Athena would never leave the safety of the school. Her locker had been close to Conn's, and it was moved. We decided that she would start by going to just one class, exactly one week after she was raped.

FEBRUARY 24

All night Athena worried about the possibility of seeing Conn at school, and by this morning was so exhausted she seemed about to shatter. Instead, we went out in public again, and practiced being strong. But something suddenly flipped again, and just before dinner Athena became terrified that Conn would come to our home and hurt her again. The fact that he lives twenty-four kilometers away, and cannot legally drive, did not alleviate her fear one bit. She feels completely vulnerable in her own home, and it hurts that she doesn't believe her dad and I can protect her. It feels like we are failing her again by not providing a home she feels safe in.

FEBRUARY 25

This morning out of the blue, Athena decided she would go to school and meet Angela for lunch.

I called the school to give them a heads up, and off we went. We had a plan: I would walk her into the school where Angela would be waiting for her. I would then wait in the truck. After having lunch together, Angela would walk Athena to where I was waiting.

Athena was back in less than ten minutes, out of breath, but with a small feeling of accomplishment. I told myself it is all about small steps.

FEBRUARY 28

Athena had an appointment at the medical clinic in Rivertown, once again to test for sexually transmitted diseases, a fear that constantly plagues her. Delwood, the police officer now in charge, finally phoned today, but not to give us any information; to talk about text messages. Apparently, when Conn was interviewed, he claimed Athena agreed to have sex with him, *in a text message*, although Conn had not been able to produce the message to prove his claim.

Consent via a text message? I have never heard anything so ridiculous. Even I know that consent to have sex can't be made in advance. In Canada, consent must be made at the time, and must be ongoing. This means that regardless if consent is given, it can be rescinded by either person, at any time during the act, and all sexual activity must stop immediately, or it becomes the criminal act of sexual assault.

In spite of this, Delwood asked to speak to Athena, saying he wanted to obtain copies of her text messages for the three days prior to the date Conn claimed to have been granted this consent. Athena readily agreed. I wondered, but did not ask, why they didn't obtain Conn's messages.

When Athena and I discussed this unusual request, she said she didn't think there had been any texts between her and Conn the entire week prior to the assault. She told me she had almost completely ended contact with Conn, which reminded me: Athena had made a comment sometime in the week previous to the assault about Conn's behavior at school. Since attending the same school, she had been rethinking how close a friend she wanted to be with Conn. He regularly skipped classes, was constantly in detention, and had a reputation for fighting. She said she didn't want to make an enemy at this school where she knew so few people, but she didn't approve of these behaviors, and did not want teachers and other students to think she was like that. How unfortunate she didn't completely stop all contact.

After Athena spoke to Delwood, she started to worry. Like most teens, Athena indiscriminately lets other kids play with her phone. Being new at the school made her even more vulnerable; her phone was new, and she didn't want to seem unfriendly by refusing to let other kids check it out. Her biggest concern was the possibility that someone else may have sent a message that set her up. I asked her who she had permitted to use her phone. She could name a few; but she didn't know the names of most of the students. They were friends of people she had just met in her new classes. She hadn't thought it was a big deal to let other students play with her phone. Suddenly she was rethinking that wisdom. She also told me that she and Conn had shared a sexual joke when texting.

Athena obsessively worries about anything and everything, and always has. I suggested that rather than worry, she simply call Delwood back, tell him about the joke, and tell him that other kids played with her phone. She asked me if I would do that for her, so I did.

First I spoke to Delwood, and then Athena spoke to him again. She told him about the joke. I certainly don't condone Athena joking about sex, but since her concussion there are times she doesn't realize what is, and is not, appropriate. Until her head injury, this was not the case, but since, she seems to have lost some of her verbal filters. Regardless, I don't get the importance. No one has the right to rape. I assume this texting thing must just be a hurdle to be cleared in order that the charge against Conn will successfully end in a conviction.

FEBRUARY 29

Athena decided she would go to school for one period, but before she even left home she was visibly shaking and felt like she was going to vomit. When I picked her up after the one class, she was sullen and angry. This is not like Athena, and I really don't know how to react to her now.

We had a date with Services for Victims to register Athena for counselling. It was like being with a stranger who looked like my daughter. I don't know the angry person she has become. She was short tempered and terse both with me and with the intake worker, something I have never seen before. I cried when my turn came to talk to the worker. I feel like I am grieving. I feel like I have lost my daughter, and I am terrified I might never have her back. I don't know how to cope with this incredible loss.

We learned that Athena does not qualify for sexual assault counselling because she is only fifteen, and the service is limited to those sixteen years or older. How ludicrous. One look at this child and her need for help is blatantly obvious. Instead we were referred to a counselor from a woman's support group and shelter, called Hope House.

MARCH 2

Athena went to school on the school bus and stayed for the first two periods. It did not go well. Before school had even begun, Conn walked by her locker twice, stopping to stare at her each time. She was terrified. In her Civics class the topic for the day was sexual assault. Why in hell would the teacher teach this lesson when she knew Athena had just been raped?

Later we had an appointment with Terry, the counsellor from Hope House, and once again Athena was visibly angry and extremely uncooperative. She offered no information, and barely answered the questions asked of her. Terry didn't seem to take it personally or even really notice. I wondered if this was something Terry dealt with often; perhaps she is used to clients displaying such raw anger. It is entirely new to me. It makes me so sad to see Athena so full of hurt and anger, and I am filled with hate for the monster who did this to her.

I was really surprised when Athena agreed to meet with Terry again. Shockingly, there are enough victims of sexual violence at the high-school that Terry counsels there on a regular basis. Athena could see Terry at the school, but this would mean missing classes. When I expressed my concern, Terry offered to have a counselling session with Athena after school at her office downtown. This poses yet another problem: I really have to get back to work, and so can't be there to drive her, and Athena is terrified to walk alone. Terry offered to pick Athena up at the school, and keep her safe until I could come for her after work. Thank god for such wonderful people.

Athena and I then went to find Firth, the school police officer to inform him that Conn had been watching Athena. Firth was not at the school, and we found him at the police station. He said he would have a word with Conn.

For some reason, perhaps just remembering that shopping used be a happy experience, Athena wanted to go to a store. I was completely burned out, and told her I would wait in the truck, while she went on her own. She tried. She was back within minutes, an emotional wreck. She was terrified when people came near her. She said she felt like they were all staring at her. She was afraid they would touch her. She cried. I cried too. The extent of her emotional trauma hit me really hard. I don't know how to help, how to react; how to fix this. I know about grief, and I thought she would go through the stages of grieving, but what I see goes way beyond grieving.

I looked up sexual assault on the computer when we got home, but I found very little. The only information I found was about Post Traumatic Stress Disorder, which I learned sexual assault victims often have; but it comes several months after an assault. Some of her symptoms seem to fit PTSD, but there is so much that doesn't. Her total loss of self-esteem, even her loss of self is so profound. She is terrified to the point she can't function or think rationally, and she is so incredibly angry. I feel utterly helpless. It's my job as a mother to be there for my daughter, but how do I fix a broken child?

CHAPTER 4

Kafkaesque Nightmare

Athena finally went to sleep with me beside her, but her sleep was fitful and restless. She said she couldn't face school, and I didn't push her; we were both totally exhausted. I have been sleeping with her because she is terrified to be alone.

Officer Delwood phoned a day, maybe two days ago; the days are all running together. He wanted to set a date to talk to Athena again. We agreed on today. It is exactly two weeks ago that Athena was sexually assaulted. Today she will have to recall all the details of the assault she has tried so hard to forget.

Our visit to the police station started innocuously enough. We waited in the dingy, long, narrow hall while a number of people came and went. There were a few chairs lined up against the wall, and we sat there, uncomfortably conscious of people having to pass close in front of us just to walk through the hall. We waited for well over half an hour and it appeared the receptionist had closed up and gone home for the night.

Finally, a man came out into the hall, closed the door behind him, and spoke to us. *This was Officer Delwood, and it would become his signature to come out into the waiting room hall, close the door behind him, and 'talk'.* Whatever he said at that time has all but been forgotten. I remember when he saw I had a Sudoku book with me, he claimed to also enjoy this past-time. Then he re-opened the door to the hidden world of the police, and took Athena away with him. I stayed behind. I trusted him. I believed that he represented justice and integrity. I believed that he would be caring and respectful to a young girl who had been through what would likely be the most horrific experience of her life. I was wrong.

It was more than an hour before Delwood brought Athena back into the hall. Her appearance was shocking. She looked as horrified as she had on the day of the assault. I assumed this was the result of being forced to recall the disturbing details of being raped, but she and I had no chance to talk. Delwood invited me to come in and discuss the investigation.

I wasn't really comfortable leaving Athena alone in the hall, but there wasn't an option. I reasoned to myself that this should be the safest place in town.

Delwood, who had shut the door behind him when he brought Athena back into the hall, re-opened the door, and led me into a large open room, filled to capacity with male police officers. I was shocked to see so many police in this town of fifty-five hundred people, and wondered if we were interrupting a county–wide staff meeting. There were far more police than I could believe worked in this small town, and every one of them turned and watched as I came in. I remember thinking how intimidating it must have been for Athena. Obviously no consideration had been given for her emotional needs.

The room had three television screens mounted on one wall, and another behind one of the sectioned off desks. One screen showed an empty chair; the rest were blank, and I wondered if this was to monitor the waiting area, though I didn't see Athena.

Delwood directed me to one of the sectioned off areas and only then did I see a woman–the only one in the sea of men– seated there. Delwood introduced her as Officer Bonnie Shepard. Shepard was sitting in front of a single monitoring screen, shielded from the main part by a desk and an 'L' shaped wall. Delwood explained that Shepard had replaced Lana Chompsky as his partner on this case. At Delwood's direction, the three of us went through the crowded room and into a hall at the back of the station. A sharp turn right, and a tiny interview room was visible through a glass window. I was shown inside, and invited to sit in one of the two chairs. Delwood and Shepard discussed which of them would get the chair. In the end, Delwood stood and leaned against the wall; Shepard sat.

The atmosphere was non-threatening, and at the time I thought it was simply an information exchange. Chompsky said I would be kept informed, and I believed that this meeting was intended to finally bring me up to date.

It is trying to recall details like this that makes me wonder how victims can be expected to have any sort of coherent recall. I know that I was under huge stress and some degree of trauma, but nothing compared to Athena, and yet even for me, so many details are simply gone.

I remember Delwood said this was the toughest case he had ever worked on. He said he went a little bit tougher in his interview with Athena. "No tougher than she would be put through in court though. But the interview only muddied the waters further," he said.

After being told that Athena's story varied, and she had trouble remembering details, I told them again about her head injury, and her inability to recall even simple steps and events. I suggested they call Dr. Rose, who had conducted testing to determine the extent of brain damage Athena had sustained when she had her head injury. I had concerns that Athena's injuries would affect her ability to recall this horrific event. I knew from speaking to Dr. Rose that Athena's short-term working and verbal memory had been seriously impaired, as well as her ability to sustain mental focus. We had not been given a formal report yet, but I believed Dr. Rose would assist them in any way she could. Due to both the seriousness of her brain injury, and the seriousness of this situation, I believed the police would be concerned enough to make this phone call. I was wrong again.

We talked informally —or so I believed; remember I am in a room that is literally wired—and then one of them casually asked if I had been formally interviewed 'yet'. They both exhibited some surprise when I said I had not, and asked if I would be willing to do an interview at that time.

I was willing to do whatever was necessary to move the investigation along, and so I agreed to the interview. They made it sound as if formal interviews of the family members of victims was the norm, but looking back, I realize they knew I had not been interviewed, and this was just a little act put on for some reason.

Once I had agreed to a formal interview, the next decision was who would conduct it, and who would be in charge of the recording device outside the room. The decision seemed to have been settled randomly, and Delwood left Shepard and I in the room.

I told Shepard anything I thought could possibly help with the investigation;

I told her what Athena had been like before the assault, and what she had been reduced to as a result.

Shepard asked why Athena would follow Conn to his bedroom. I answered that Athena wouldn't see this as dangerous; even prior to her brain injury she had an innocence and a trust level such that she wouldn't comprehend that this action could be misunderstood. Since the injury, she had been seriously unable understand social innuendos. We raised her to believe that boys and girls could be 'just' friends. She would follow a female friend to her room; she would not see any difference with a male friend. Athena knew they were just friends, he did too. Besides, he was gay.

Shepard asked me if I had noticed any physical injuries on Athena following the assault and I explained some of what I had observed. The conversation kept changing, and I wished I had known ahead of time I would be interviewed so I could have been prepared.

"Did Athena say anything about Conn's physical appearance?"

I told her about the weird things she had said about his sex organs. I did not say anything about the scars on his chest; Athena saw these the day they met, which was at the swimming pool, and I assumed Shepard was asking about the day of the event. Much later a friend asked me if Shepard might have been fishing to see if Athena had ever said she found Conn attractive. This had never occurred to me; physical appearance had no place in Athena's choice of friends, or even boyfriends. Athena always saw beyond physical characteristics to the person inside. It was one of the traits that made her such a good and caring person.

Shepard told me two things; one, they were considering use of a special resources team to gain insight into the problems Athena has. I strongly encouraged this, particularly in conjunction with contacting Dr. Rose, and two; they asked Athena if she would be willing to take a lie detector test. Before answering, Athena asked how the test works, and how reliable it is. This was explained to her, and she readily agreed to take it. In spite of this, they interpreted her caution as fear of taking the test.

I thought Athena's concerns reasonable, and exactly what I would expect from her. She would not agree to something she didn't know about. If everyone else jumped off the bridge, Athena would still be standing there. She would decide for herself after determining the facts. I said as much.

I should explain that unlike many teenagers, Athena has had no exposure to TV Police/Crime/Court programs where lie detectors and other court processes are shown. She knew absolutely nothing of the ways of criminality.

At some point Shepard shut off the recording device, but we kept on talking, and she kept on asking questions. At the time I wondered vaguely why she had done that, but I trusted both her and Delwood, and at the time I had no reason to question her actions. I certainly would now.

When the interview was over, Shepard gave me her card and told me if I had any other thoughts that may help, to be sure to call. I called her a few days later, after thinking about her questions and concerns. Like Athena, my mind works better if I have a chance to think and mull things over. I pushed again for police to contact Dr. Rose.

Athena is essentially an only child; we never yell at her and she really doesn't know how to respond to people who come on aggressively, as Delwood had implied he had. I thought this may be the reason they did not get the results they were looking for. Athena had been raped only two weeks prior for God's sake. She was so fragile she seemed ready to break at any moment. The absolute last thing she needed was to be intimidated by the police.

Delwood had mentioned that while he went 'a bit tougher' on Athena, he could not go very hard on Conn. The reason for this, he claimed, was that Conn's mother was with him as is mandated under the Youth Criminal Justice Act. This irked me. Athena is the victim, but he went harder on her than the boy who raped her? This convoluted logic disturbed me greatly, and I suggested they use a different technique, like just talking with her, and letting her go through the story in chronological order.

When I left the interview room, it was Delwood who led me through the still packed office of openly staring cops, and I met with Athena in the hall. He closed the door behind him, and said to us, "Conn is a good kid."

This outrageous statement hit me like a bucket of ice water. I was horrified, confused, livid and speechless, all in the same instant. Praising the boy that raped my daughter was not only ruthless, it was appallingly unprofessional. I looked quickly at Athena to see how she responded to this brutal verbal abuse. Her eyes were wild and wide, and she paled even further. She said nothing. This is when I wish I had been raised to be rude. I wish I could report that I told him exactly what I thought about his comment, but I did not. I was literally speechless with shock.

Before we had even left the building, Athena made three statements: "He believes Conn. He doesn't believe me. Now I know why people don't go to the police when this happens."

She curled up in a fetal position on the front seat of the truck, and wept all the way home. I was beyond furious. As a victim she should have been treated with even more respect and sensitivity than a person off the street. I asked her if Bonnie Shepard had been decent to her in the interview, and was shocked again to learn Athena did not even know who Shepard was. In fact, until I told her, Athena was not even aware there had been a woman present, and she certainly had not been given the option of being interviewed by her. How utterly intimidating for a young female rape victim to have to wade through a sea of men, and then be interviewed and interrogated by a man who is obviously devoid of compassion. It was at that moment I decided I would be filing a formal complaint against Officer Dirk Delwood, and I began recording every interaction we had with the police.

MARCH 5

For the first time since being raped, Athena went to school all day, but she came home an emotional wreck. The VP at the school said he would arrange for other students to walk Athena to and from classes, but no one showed up to walk her. She got to the washroom at lunch time and was too afraid to come out. She stayed there crying until lunch ended. Conn and two of his friends stood and pointedly stared at her when she did walk down the hall.

I have been sharing with my friends both the outrageous statement Delwood made about Conn, as well as the appalling way Athena was treated. Keeping such a thing quiet simply allows it to continue. I am really surprised by people's response. While they are outraged, I find far more people than I ever imagined expect this sort of behavior from the police, and infinitely more than I would expect have themselves had bad experiences with the police. This is a real eye opener, the people I know socially are respectable, law abiding citizens, and almost all are educated professionals. How is it Sandy and I had no idea?

I find this incredibly disturbing. I have trusted the police all my life. Aren't all young children taught that police are their friends and they can always go to the police for help? Until now I have always been the one standing up for police, proclaiming them heroes, ready to give their lives for us, and I always assumed those who did not like police were not law abiding people. Now I see that police are not all good or even decent people.

I don't understand why Delwood would treat a victim, especially a child this way, and I do not see where he gets off saying that a rapist is a 'good kid' to the victim of this creep. I can find no reason in the world that would excuse this comment. Doesn't it matter that this boy continues to stalk and harass Athena? In Delwood's mind do 'good kids' engage in criminal harassment and sexual assault? Delwood appears to be a rogue cop, out of control, with his own agenda that I believe higher-ups must be unaware of. I do not believe his actions would be anything but condemned.

I now document all contact with Delwood, and I am trying to find out how to make a formal complaint against him. I know that timing is everything, so I am not going to do it immediately, but it will be done. I am starting to fear the power this man has, and would like to see some justice achieved before I start to rattle chains. I am afraid if I complain now, Delwood will not even bother to pursue a sexual assault charge. While he certainly seems to be biased toward Conn, I still don't believe it could be considered ethical or professional to treat a rape victim the way he has treated Athena.

There is such silence surrounding sexual assault. As a society we talk openly about almost everything these days, believing it is healthier that way. The once taboo topics like colon cancer, breast cancer, menopause, sex, being gay are now discussed openly. We talk freely about assault, but when it becomes sexual assault, this is not the case. To openly admit that one has been sexually assaulted makes people extremely uncomfortable, and is still a complete social taboo topic. It is impossible to even determine the frequency of rape because the vast majority of rapes go unreported. Most crisis centres claim that one in three or possibly four women will be sexually assaulted at some point in their life, and the silence only serves to make victims feel more alone and isolated. It also prevents the public from realizing how disturbingly common sexual assault is.

MARCH 6

Yeah! Athena managed to go into the pool with a big tee shirt covering her bathing suit. She took it off at the edge of the water with some hesitation, but she managed. Small steps. Jessie is staying over for the night, and I can sleep in my own bed. Athena has only been able to sleep if someone is with her.

This afternoon, Athena went on a bit of a telling spree about her interview with Delwood: He compared her (very negatively) to his own daughters. Athena said he openly showed disgust when she told him she had a boyfriend and hoped to spend her life with him. He said his daughters would never even think of such a thing at her age. He asked her what her boyfriend 'wanted to do' to Conn. She was afraid to tell Delwood the truth; that Evan said he had better not ever run into Conn, or he may not be able to control himself. She was afraid Delwood would go after Evan too, so she kept that to herself. This seems to be the reason she started talking about the interview: she is upset because she with-held this information, and is afraid it will get her in more trouble. I reassured her she was not a terrible person for not telling Delwood. I told her Evan's reaction is probably completely normal, and I understand her not trusting Delwood. I know I will never trust him again.

Delwood told her he liked Conn; but does not like her. She said he got mad and he yelled at her. She claims she yelled back–I have difficulty imagining this–I expect Athena's version of Athena yelling is more likely that she actually spoke back to him. She told him over and over that there were parts of the assault she could not remember. She said he wouldn't let it go and kept telling her that wasn't true. He said she was lying; that she had consented to have sex with Conn. Athena told him (again) about her head injury, and her memory issues, but he wouldn't accept this. Any time she tried to think before she answered, he got in her face about it. He fixated on how Conn managed to get her shirt and bra off. Athena doesn't know how this happened; her memory of this part of the attack is entirely gone, but Delwood would not accept this.

Athena just wanted this interrogation to stop, *so she finally tried to fill in the missing pieces with what made sense, just so he would leave her alone, and let her go home.*

To say this made me furious would be an *extreme* understatement. Never will I let her be alone with the police again, at any time, for any reason. This is beyond cruel and unusual punishment; this is beyond anything I would have believed could happen in Canada. I want this man to pay, and I intend to make that happen. He has taken the exceptional power he holds as a police officer, and used it to bully and re-victimize a fifteen year old rape victim. This is the reason Canada has a Youth Criminal Justice Act; where does this pig get off ignoring it?

MARCH 7

Not a good day. Athena is extremely overwhelmed by the amount of homework she needs to catch up on.

In researching how to make a formal complaint against a police officer, I have found a website for a formal organization that does just this. Most, if not every police force in Canada has an organization whose mandate is to oversee the integrity of a particular police force. This organization claims to be independent, and hence completely objective. The director is not a part of the police force, and is (theoretically) unbiased as a result. (Note: I have been advised not to point fingers and leave myself open to a charge of liable, and so I will refer to this organization as The Police Watchdog.) I have become very serious about keeping notes now, detailing any interactions with police, and keeping the many emails to the school complaining about Conn constantly stalking Athena.

MARCH 8

A good day! Athena went to school and did not see Conn once. Good is a relative term now, and means only that when she is at home she is not curled in a fetal position crying. I realize she never laughs any more, and I can't remember the last time I saw her smile.

MARCH 9

The school day started badly with Conn passing Athena's locker first thing in the morning. At lunch, Athena was talking to her English teacher about the work she has missed, and Conn came with three friends and stood just outside the door, close enough to hear their conversation. At one point Athena had to push through him and his buddies to go to her locker to get her English books. When she returned, the boys were in exactly the same place, six inches from the door. She was forced to walk right in front of Conn to get back into the class. Ten minutes later, Conn and his buddies were still there, but Conn had moved so he could stare in the door at her. The other boys moved out of sight, but Conn kept walking by the door and looking in at Athena. Athena moved so she could not be seen, and told the teacher how terrified she was.

The teacher knew Athena had been sexually assaulted, but not by whom, and she made a comment about one of the other boys at the door, letting slip that he had previously been accused of sexual assault by another girl, and hence she had assumed it was this same boy who had raped Athena. The teacher attempted a quick cover up when told it had been Conn who had raped her, and not the boy she assumed.

When I heard this, my first thought was to wonder if Conn and his friends shared rape tips, and I wondered if *this* might explain where Conn got the idea of showing up naked.

MARCH 10

Athena was awake all night crying. She says she can't get the attack out of her mind; it keeps running over and over it in her head. She says she feels like she is getting an ulcer. Her stomach always hurts, and she is so upset when she sees Conn, she feels like she is going to vomit. She stayed home, and I emailed the vice principal yet again to tell him that Conn continues to stalk her.

MARCH 11

Athena didn't sleep at all last night. Good thing it's a snow day. In her head she keeps going over and over what happened at school, and says she is really worried that Conn or one of his friends will 'do something' to her. She took a Gravol and went back to bed until noon. This child that I used to know so well is a stranger to me. My god I miss my daughter.

MARCH 12

Another snow day. Athena seems completely unable to focus when she tries to concentrate on school work–or anything else for that matter. She is like the walking dead she is so tired. She says she hates to sleep; all it brings are horrific dreams.

MARCH 13

Today is the last day of in-class instruction for Red Cross Assistant Water Safety Instructor. We were so afraid Athena would not pass it. She constantly has to fight to control panic attacks when she has to get close to people. It helped immensely that there were no males in the class, but she still can't bear to physically touch or be touched.

Oh my god, she made it! She successfully completed the course. We celebrated with ice cream.

MARCH 14

Evan is here and Athena is very clingy. I am afraid she is having a nervous breakdown. She says she is terrified that Conn will find her. He knows where she lives, and may come here to get her. We tried to discuss this rationally, to get her to see how unlikely this is, but we failed. She wants to go to her godparent's house for the night. She says Conn doesn't know where they live, so he would never find her there, and she would be safe. How can we say no?

MARCH 15

I contacted Corry from Services for Victims to ask for advice on how to stop Conn from stalking Athena. Corry said she would look into it, and called me back soon after. She contacted the school police officer, and a new plan has been put in place. Athena is to phone the police office if she is feeling threatened. The police receptionist then would contact the officer at the school, who would come to Athena' assistance. Athena doesn't think this will help much, for one thing she always feels threatened, and Conn doesn't usually stick around, he just keeps walking by; repeatedly. Athena doesn't believe the police want to help her, and she commented that by the time the police arrive, Conn will be long gone.

Corry also suggested we meet with the school to ensure whatever can be done is being done.

MARCH 16

I took Athena to the dentist today to get a mouth guard. Her jaw aches from constantly clenching her teeth. I am hoping this might also help prevent the constant headaches she is having. While I was waiting at the dentist, I picked up a Readers Digest, to read the diction section. A word jumped out: Kafkaesque. Interestingly, when I have been telling people what my life is like now I have said I feel "like I am living in a Kafka novel" and now here it is, our lives in a word: Kafkaesque.

Athena had a complete melt down this afternoon. I've never seen such anger in her. The anger stayed until she crashed and fell asleep after supper. When she woke again at nine-thirty she told us she dreamt Conn viciously attacked her in our bedroom.

MARCH 20

Athena and I were awake most of the night. Sleeping with Athena has become the norm now, although I don't think either of us gets more than an hour or so of restless sleep at a time. Athena is constantly moving and crying in her sleep. The fear from last night hasn't subsided at all. Athena is terrified to be in our home. She talks about wanting to get away from here, and asks if she could live with my brother, several thousand miles away, or in another province with my friend Robin, or with her sister in a far off city; anywhere but here. Sandy is really stressed out, and though I try to convince him to get counselling, he says he won't until this is over. He says he could not discuss how he feels and stay whole. His emotions are so raw and so close to the surface I am afraid he will self destruct.

MARCH 22

Sandy and I met with the vice principal, and explained our concerns for Athena's safety. The teacher who was with Athena when Conn was outside the classroom door did not know Conn by sight. We agreed the school will forward a photo of Conn to Athena's teachers. If Conn is hanging around Athena's class again, the classroom teacher or Athena will be told to buzz the office and ask for the VP to go to the classroom.

I have no idea whether the school has discussed the ongoing harassment and stalking with Conn's parents, so I suggested they need to be informed. I also suggested that if Conn were to go home for lunch daily, it would at least prevent him from harassing Athena during lunch hour. I hope Conn's parents are sufficiently concerned about his actions to actually consider this. Wouldn't normal, caring parents?

The VP informed us that one of the guidance counselors has talked to Conn several times about harassing Athena. I remarked that it obviously has had no effect on Conn's behavior. The VP claims they are doing all they can. I wondered, but didn't ask why the police aren't talking to Conn, and why the school wasn't told by the school officer about the plan to have Athena call the police for help. There seems to be incredible disconnect and a serious lack of follow through. I suggested the school treat Conn's stalking as a bullying issue, since the school board has made such a big deal about the wondrous new anti-bullying legislation. The VP thought this was a good idea.

I left the meeting feeling far less confident about the school's response. Does the VP even know what is in the bullying legislation? Why didn't he think of this solution?

Athena is to either go directly to the VP, or tell me and I will email him outlining any and all issues with Conn. This will enable the school to document the ongoing harassment. This also tells me that he has *not* been documenting the ongoing issues to date. Mr. VP also said *he will formalize the plan that was originally set in place to have friends walk Athena from class to class!* No wonder it wasn't working well, it wasn't even put in place! What the hell.

I am really pissed. The VP has not carried through with *anything* he said he was going to do to protect Athena. The plans to have students walk Athena from class to class was to supposed to have been put in place in February. Why wasn't it done? Why is this man not concerned about my child's safety?

MARCH 23

Conn and his group appeared to be AWOL from school today, but instead of this making Athena feel better, she is now beside herself with fear, convinced they may be on their way to our home to find her.

Athena is really distrustful of the police now thanks to Delwood. She did, however, finally get up the nerve to tell the school officer about a girl at the school, who, without knowing that Athena was assaulted, claimed she had been cornered by Conn, and he tried to get her clothes off. Athena decided she should tell the school officer. This shows that the attack on Athena was not an isolated event, and she feels she can't justify keeping quiet when it seems there is a pattern of sexual assaults. Since she was attacked, Athena has been haunted by the fear that Conn will rape again. After hearing he has already tried, she feels obligated to tell the officer. Once again the school officer says he will 'take care of it.'

As of this day, Athena has been to school for only four full days since the assault. There have been several days when school has been cancelled because of bad weather, but most often she is either emotionally unable to go, or she manages only part of a day. I have hardly worked since the assault. My first priority is to be there for Athena, but finances are becoming a serious issue.

MARCH 24

Delwood phoned this afternoon to say he received Athena's text messages from Telus. He says there are things he wants to clarify in the texts, and wants to get together with Athena to go over the messages. We agreed on Monday after school to look at them.

MARCH 25

Another day at home in the fetal position. Athena wants to quit school and get a job so she doesn't have to see Conn and his gang any more. She wants to complete her National Lifesaving Society training so she can work as a lifeguard and swim instructor. She promises to go to school tomorrow, but she feels she just can't face Conn today.

MARCH 30

Athena went to school as promised, and had a 'pretty good' day. I picked her up from school and then we went and waited and waited for Delwood at the police station. During this time Athena seemed lighter and more relaxed than she has been since the assault. Thanks to the police, this small step toward healing is now completely ended.

CHAPTER 5
Living a Nightmare

We were kept waiting a very long time at the police station. I started to wonder if Officer Delwood had been called out to attend some other crisis. Finally the door to the station opened, Delwood came out into the hall, and closed the door behind him.

The only words I remember him saying are: "I'm arresting Athena for Public Mischief."

My brain could not register what I was hearing. I felt a ringing sensation in my head, and I felt like I might vomit. I looked at Athena. She was ghostly white and in very obvious shock.

I had no idea what Public Mischief was, and I didn't know what being arrested really meant. My first terrifying thought was that Athena may be put in jail; my child, who since being raped could not even sleep alone, and was paralyzed with fear of both being alone, and being with strangers. She was so stressed she seemed ready to snap. I was terrified at what being in a jail cell would do to her.

I was afraid this would kill my daughter, and if it did not, I feared that she would never be emotionally whole and healthy again. I was afraid she would never recover. I see what being raped has done to her, and I know being thought guilty of a crime would multiply that emotional damage many, many times. This was so far beyond anything I could ever imagine or comprehend. My child was raped, and she had gone to the police for help. How could the people who were supposed to help her do this to her?

I was not invited to go into the interview with Athena, but there was not a chance in hell I was letting Delwood be alone with her again. I followed Athena and Delwood into the inner sanctum. No one tried to stop me.

Again the room was completely filled with male police officers. Again they all stood staring at us. Did these cops have nothing better to do? They parted to let us through, and there, at her same post, was Shepard, again sitting at the desk with the television monitor. I was furious. I wanted to ask her how she could live with herself treating a young rape victim like a criminal. I wondered how she lost her humanity. I stared straight at her as we went past. God how I wished that looks could kill.

Athena and I followed Delwood into the tiny interview room. My emotions were out of control; I was livid, terrified, horrified, and in severe shock. Athena was deathly white. Several times through this ordeal I was afraid she would pass out. Delwood found another chair so we could both sit down.

Contrary to proper protocol, the Canadian Youth Criminal Justice Act, and Canadian human rights, from his lack of preparation, it appeared Delwood had not planned to invite me to this party.

Delwood read a document out loud, and I think Athena signed something. The ringing in my head was so loud it interfered with being able to think, and I could not shake away the shock enough to focus. I felt like I was looking at these events from the outside; like I was looking through thick glass, and was not really there at all. It was surreal; a nightmare that made absolutely no sense. Delwood said Athena could have something called 'duty counsel' or she could call a lawyer. Stupidly, I believed that this was some terrible mistake, and since we were law-abiding, responsible people, we could work this out. I believed we could discuss this unfathomable mistake, and make it go away. Athena did not request duty counsel or a lawyer.

Delwood informed Athena I could be present in the interview if she desired. She did. He said she could speak to me alone if she wished. She said she wanted to speak to me alone, but Delwood just kept talking and we were never allowed us that opportunity. *I later learned this was another breach of the Youth Criminal Justice Act.*

I was raised in a family that respected and adhered to the law. We are all upstanding, law abiding citizens who have absolutely no experience with the legal system; no experience with police interviews, being arrested, or needing lawyers. We have always prided ourselves on our good citizenship. Prior to these events, we held the police in high esteem. When other people maligned the police, we would adamantly defend them. We actually believed they were heroes.

At one time Athena wanted to be a police officer, believing policing was a helping profession. She had never had any dealings with the police; had never been in any form of trouble. I had the ridiculous idea that this would matter; that it would count for something, perhaps a shred of respect. I had no idea that Athena could ask to speak to a lawyer by phone from the police station; I had no idea what duty council was, and Delwood certainly did not explain. None of this would have really made a difference anyway; Delwood actively prevented me from providing any guidance to Athena, so my ignorance did not come into play.

What I wanted was to take what was left of my daughter and go home. I didn't fully believe this was happening. I may have been in shock, I may have been in serious denial, I simply could not believe that my daughter, who had just suffered a horrendous and devastating sexual assault, was being put through this hell by the very people who are paid to help her. This was not some third-world, or middle-eastern country where women are persecuted and prosecuted for being raped, this is Canada.

At that time, I did not believe that such audacities could happen in Canada. I know differently now.

On the small table in front of us was a thick stack of papers; the thickness of a very large textbook. Someone had highlighted some of the lines on the top page. We could see printing, and highlighting, but could not make out any words. Delwood claimed they were Athena's text messages.

I registered then that this had something to do with the text messages Delwood said he had obtained, but that couldn't be right. Delwood said he was getting three days of text messages sent between Conn and Athena. There was no way *anyone* could send and receive this many messages in three days. I wanted to look at them. Delwood would not allow either Athena or me to touch or look at them. He kept bullying her, trying to get her to say they were her text messages. Athena adamantly denied that it was even remotely possible that they were hers, and for a ridiculously long time he kept refusing to let us look at them. Around and around this argument went, with Delwood trying to get Athena to say they were her texts, and Athena saying they certainly were not.

Finally he picked up the stack, and held one page open so that both Athena and I could see. The page showed a grouping of five messages that were highlighted. Of the five, three of them were to, or from, Conn's phone number; one was a phone number Athena did not recognize, and one was from Athena's boyfriend. None of the texts were even remotely sexual. This left us even more confused, but Delwood would not explain, nor would he show us other texts. He tried again to make Athena say these were her messages. She would not.

I was so confused: Why were there texts from other people? Why were some, apparently randomly, highlighted? They were neither sexual nor singularly from Conn. I tried to ask questions. Delwood would not answer my questions, and kept hissing at me to be quiet. I wanted to look at the texts, but was not allowed. I believed there had been a huge mistake, and I wanted to know how the messages had been obtained. I wanted to know who had physically taken the messages from whatever big message machine spit them out, and verified them.

I questioned the reliability of Telus, the company who had provided the texts, and Delwood severely chastised me for questioning the Telus god.

Every time I tried to speak, Delwood told me to be quiet. I eventually quit trying. Athena said later that he told me to shut up, and this upset her greatly. I don't remember. I know that every time I tried to speak he shushed me. His manner was rude, condescending, and more chauvinistic than I had been subjected to in decades. Much later I realized he never once called me by my name, but in fact, called me 'Mom' even when speaking directly to me. This is in retrospect. At the time I was completely focused on Athena. She was on the verge of hysteria.

Athena was getting more and more agitated every minute, her eyes had a feverish, watery glow, and she was shaking. At one point when Delwood left the room I was afraid she was going into serious shock. I shook her shoulder and called her name repeatedly. She didn't respond. I kept on shaking and trying to make her talk. Finally she answered, but she was anything but alright. Not one of the two or more dozen cops watching 'The Delwood Show' on the monitors outside bothered to see if this could be a medical emergency.

Delwood said, "Think how hard this has been on Conn's mom; just think how she feels. She calls every day to ask what is going on."

I was dumbfounded. This woman's bastard raped my daughter, the very victim he was saying this to. We have all heard disturbing stories about how police treat rape victims, but until this come out of his Delwood's mouth, I would never have believed it. I lost my last iota of respect for the police at that moment.

Call me an absolute idiot. I still didn't get it. I still thought we were talking about text messages. I still thought he was investigating the sexual assault. How could he not? This was the year 2011, in the civilized country called Canada, not the 1940's where the woman is blamed. I had no idea what the real problem was with the text messages; why he thought they were so important, why there were so many pages. I failed to see any connection between text messages and the rape of my daughter.

Athena kept refusing to give in to Delwood. She did not believe this stack of papers were hers, therefore, she would not say they were hers.

Delwood kept blathering on. "You liked talking to Conn; you enjoyed texting with him. You liked the attention he paid you."

Athena responded, "Yes, I did like having him as a friend."

Delwood kept pushing and pushing. He got nowhere. Athena would half agree where applicable, and she would deny outrageous accusations. She held her conviction, but she was obviously exhausted, and this was starting to show in her weary sounding voice and repetitious responses.

Eventually, Delwood signaled me to go out into the hall with him. I left Athena in the small room, half afraid she would freak out at being alone, and half wondering if she even knew I had left. The door had a window in, so she could see me simply by looking up, but she had shut down. She sat hunched in her chair, as close to curling into the fetal position as was possible. I felt like there was a tight band around my torso, and I could not get enough air. I felt like I was suffocating.

In the hall, with both the door to the main part of the station and the interview room closed, Delwood said, "She has to say she did it, or I will charge her."

I told him, "She doesn't believe she did anything, so she will never say she did."

Again he said, "She has to say she did it or I am going to charge her."

"She will never admit to something she does not believe she did," I responded.

We went around and around this same topic again and again. I was becoming more and more upset, and said, "How can you expect her to admit they are hers when you're not even willing to show them to us?"

Finally he flipped through the enormous stack of papers which he had picked up and brought with him until he found a text that was somewhat sexual. It looked like stupid teenage joking around to me, although I didn't say as much; what did it matter? I could not tell who had sent or received this text, or even Athena's phone had been involved. He would not show me more, and once again I was not allowed to touch the papers.

We went around and around the circle. Delwood would say, "She has to say she did it, or I will charge her."

And I would respond, "She's never going to say she did it, she doesn't believe those are her text messages." I was getting more and more upset. I felt like I was being crushed between the preverbal rock and a very hard place, and I just wanted it all to go away so we could get back to the real issue; the rape of my daughter.

I remember looking at my one hand, and envisioning that hand as Athena being charged with a crime, and knowing that being charged and possibly going to jail would permanently, and irreparably, destroy her. I looked at my other hand and I knew Athena would never admit to something she had not done, and she did not believe that stack text messages were hers. The two were completely irreconcilable.

I broke down and cried, and I remember asking him "How do we get out of this nightmare?"

He simply repeated himself once again, but slowly this time, with each word clearly enunciated, "She-has-to-say-she-did-it."

Suddenly I heard what Delwood was *not* saying. *Not once* had he said she has to tell the truth. I realized this was because he knew she was telling the truth. And then I realized: Delwood was telling me the only way out of this mess was for Athena to lie. It was irrelevant that the texts were not hers; Delwood was telling me that the only way Athena would not be charged was by lying and claiming the texts were hers.

My mind was suddenly very clear. My brain started to fly through the scenarios. I didn't trust Delwood, but I felt like I had no choice. I wanted to believe he was honestly there to help us, and that this was what had to be done to save Athena. There was no time to mull this over; I had only a few seconds in which to decide, but I needed to make certain that what I heard was what he meant. I restated what he had been telling me all along.

I said "All she has to do is say she did it, and you won't charge her?"

And he replied, "Yes, all she has to do is say she did it."

A million thoughts were charging through my brain. The thought flashed that if Delwood was lying to me and actually did charge her, I would come forward with what had transpired in the hall. If it came to it, I would accept any repercussions as a result, but I also knew without question that if he screwed Athena around, I would take him down with me. I made a choice, although choice is not the correct term: choice means there was an option. Not telling Athena to lie and say "she did it" would result in her being charged with a criminal offence. I did not know if she could survive being charged as a criminal. I believed this would destroy my already broken and victimized child. What parent would ever consider that a choice?

"All right," I said to him.

But as I turned to open the door into the interview room, he added, *"And it has to be convincing."*

Had I not already been convinced that Delwood was counselling me to tell Athena to lie, those words absolutely sealed it. Whether or not Athena really 'did it' did not matter in the least to Delwood.

Delwood did not follow me back into the interview room.

In the three seconds between hearing this, and being back in the interview room with Athena again, I had more decisions to make. I couldn't tell Athena to tell the truth; she already was. I could only tell her to lie, but I certainly couldn't do that out loud. *Although in retrospect, I should have, I should have walked in and said: "Delwood told me that if you lie and say the texts are yours, he won't charge you. That would have had an interesting reaction, I'm sure.*

You see, I had finally realized that all those male cops in the room outside were watching and listening to every word said in the interview room. But because I had no other option, I clung to the hope that Delwood was actually trying to help us out of this nightmare.

I went into the room, and made a move to hug Athena. She stood up, and into her very thick hair I whispered, "You have to lie, and it has to be convincing."

She tried to whisper something back, but I hushed her, afraid of being heard. We sat back down in silence for a few minutes, and then she told me to go get Delwood. I stood up and opened the door, but Delwood had obviously been watching and listening from outside, and was already coming in.

Delwood asked Athena, "Are the text messages yours?"

Athena responded, "I guess they are mine."

He asked, "What is in the texts?"

"What you said before, I guess," was her answer.

Delwood pushed and pushed and Athena started breaking. He suddenly changed his questioning and asked what had happened on the day of the rape, firing questions at her faster than she could answer.

Athena started babbling incoherently, making little sense. She repeated some of the things Delwood had accused her of during the interview, changing from one topic to another in mid-stream, pulling bits and pieces I recognized as coming from Delwood's mouth during this interview, as well as things from the previous interview that had upset her enough she had shared with me. There was no shape, no consistency no story to what she spewed, just random words that meant little and claimed nothing in hopes she would give Delwood enough he would stop interrogating her.

She repeated some of his earlier statements, one of which was Delwood telling her she had *enjoyed* having Conn as a friend. Athena repeated just the last part, "I enjoyed it."

It was completely without context, and I knew she was parroting Delwood, hoping to appease him. I knew she was referring to Conn, and the friendship she once believed they had at a time when she was depressed, and felt friendless and alone. I also knew as soon as it was out of her mouth that Delwood would fail to recognize his own words, and would instead choose to read other meaning into these words. I knew when she used the word 'enjoy" that this was not her speaking, she was just regurgitating Delwood's words.

And I realized suddenly that this was about more than text messages. I realized Delwood wanted to believe she was saying she had enjoyed being raped. Athena rambled on incoherently for a bit longer, and then she started to wind down. Suddenly she said: "But it has to be consensual, I thought it had to be consensual. I thought I had the right to say no."

The instant her words registered in Delwood's brain, he started calling repeatedly for someone to "cut the tape."

We left. I remember walking back into the sea of cops openly staring at us. One of them made a move toward me, but backed away immediately when we made eye contact. I don't think I would have stopped for him. I would sooner have ripped his face off.

Once again, when we were in the waiting area, and Delwood had closed the door behind him, he claimed that Conn is a good kid.

My daughter had been raped by this kid, and this pig had the audacity to call him 'a good boy' not just in front of me, but in front of the child he raped. He then told Athena it was unlikely she would go to jail, as if that was all that mattered. He showed absolutely no empathy for Athena, and he had no idea what being on the "wrong" side of the law meant to a child who was unlikely to have gotten so much as a speeding ticket in her life, who didn't just believe in being good, but who truly is good. He completely disregarded Conn's constant harassment and stalking, and told *Athena* not to contact *Conn*. What the hell is wrong with this man?

This was so far beyond the worst nightmare I could ever imagine. Not only was my child raped by someone she had trusted, she was raped again by the very people that should be helping her. How could this be happening? Where had the Canada I believed in gone? And yet, as bizarre as it sounds now, we still thought that somehow all this crap about text messages was some bizarre trip the police were into. I actually thought the police would have to still investigate the rape of my daughter. How could they not? The texts did not matter; no amount of texts can qualify as consent. Every Canadian woman has been told of her right to say no. It is regularly taught in schools across the country. As women's rights go, this is believed to be one of the greatest advancements of our time: No means No. Married woman have the right to say no, and if forced by her husband, it is sexual assault. If during sex a woman changes her mind, the act must stop. Consent must be given at the time, and must be ongoing. How could the Rivertown cops not know this?

CHAPTER 6
The Waiting Game

How could this be happening? Athena can't function, and I'm afraid Sandy will have a heart attack. We are a family of war zone victims, living in a land turned inside out; terrified of the future, horrified by the present. Paranoia has flooded our lives. When the phone rings, we all stop whatever we are doing, and look at each other in fearful anticipation. No one wants to answer it. We are afraid that it will be more unbearable news. When someone drives in the lane, we are terrified of what it might bring. We live in fear. Athena is not just terrified of Conn and his friends now, but the police, and being prosecuted.

⚖️

I tried to find out what "Public Mischief" is on the internet, and discovered that it is usually related to willful property damage. I know nothing about the law, and I need to learn fast. I have told friends and co-workers about the offered inducement—a word I also learned on the internet—by Officer Delwood when he told me he wouldn't charge Athena if she 'said she did it', and his praise for a rapist. Those who have never had experience with the police are disgusted and appalled. Others, who have heard horror stories about the treatment of rape victims, are not shocked. They all, however, know Athena and have for many years. Several people have concluded that if this outrage could happen to Athena, it could happen to anyone. One of our friends, a teacher, is deeply concerned about the moral responsibility of what to teach her students. Like us, she previously believed in police, but how, in good faith, can she encourage her students to trust police when this is how they treat victims?

In my search for answers I called my brother. Although he is a lawyer, he practices international law. Still, I hoped he may be able to help me with some answers. We talked more than we had in a long time, and I promised to stay in touch. He shared the stories of two rape victims he knew, both of which felt appallingly mistreated by the police, and neither of which ended in the rapist being convicted. This makes me think the problems are Canada wide, and not, as I previously believed, just a local red-neck cop issue. He strongly encouraged me to talk to a practicing criminal lawyer.

Money is becoming more and more of an issue. I rightfully put Athena's needs ahead of work, but that means our financial situation is becoming serious, and we were concerned about the cost of consulting a lawyer. Sandy looked into his benefit package from work, and discovered that his benefit package would pay for us to have one-half-hour of legal advice. This advice had to be delivered by phone, and the benefit provider would arrange for the lawyer. There was a slight issue over me talking to the lawyer instead of Sandy, but this was sorted, and a mutually agreed upon time was set for the lawyer to call me at home.

The lawyer I spoke to was from another part of the province. Unfortunately quite a chunk of the half-hour was spent just conveying the bizarre events to date. The lawyer was very surprised by the story and especially the fact that Conn had not been charged. I had a list of questions ready to ask her. My biggest concern was what to do if the police want to talk to Athena again:

Question: What do we do if Delwood wants another interview with Athena?

Answer: Say to the police, 'I have told you all I know. I have told you all I remember. I am done'. If they insist, immediately ask: 'Am I being investigated or charged with a criminal offence?'

Question: What should we do to correct the statements Athena made during the second interview when, under such extreme pressure from Delwood, she tried to fill in what she could not remember with what made sense?

Answer: Say to the police, '"I want to correct...."'

Question: How do we respond to Delwood's statements regarding what a great kid Conn is?

Answer: Ask him, 'How do you know? Do you know the family? Do you know him?'

I learned quite a bit from this phone call, but as my brain started to mull it all over, I had more and more questions. I decided to see the local lawyer who had written our wills. He is not a criminal lawyer, but I was hoping he could help me understand some basics, for instance, the difference between being arrested and being charged, and tell me what Athena's rights are.

I am very thankful to him; he realized the seriousness of our situation, and said I needed to speak to a criminal lawyer. He said he knew one in a nearby city that he has referred other clients to.

"He is not cheap, but he is good" was his assessment of Mr. Cupito, and he offered to try and contact him right then, by phone.

Much to my surprise, the phone was answered by Mr. Cupito himself, and he spoke with us for nearly an hour. He showed obvious surprise at the actions of the police, and wondered aloud if they had all lost their minds in Rivertown. He said he very much doubted that Athena would be charged, and felt the Crown would not have the appetite to charge a fifteen year old sexual assault victim with public mischief. I learned from him that public mischief is used to cover almost anything that doesn't fit elsewhere, and that it is a criminal offence, under the Criminal Code of Canada.

Incredibly, I felt a little better after talking to him, and was almost convinced that somewhere in the legal system there would be intelligent life, and that somewhere, someone with some intelligence would surface and stop this madness. I liked the fact that Cupito was willing to talk to me, that he seemed capable of listening as well as talking, and last but not least, that he had traits I believe every successful courtroom lawyer must have; a very healthy ego, complete self confidence, and some arrogance. I asked him if he would take the case should it proceed. He agreed, although he once again said he didn't believe it would come to that.

APRIL 2

Athena tried to go to school today. Conn walked by her locker and stared at her. He made a circuit and walked by again immediately. In science class Athena looked up and saw him and two of his pals standing in the doorway watching her. They stared at her for several minutes before leaving. This completely freaks Athena out every single time. She is terrified he is stalking her and will hurt her again.

Athena had a counseling session with Terry. This was not successful. Athena says she 'hates counsellors' and doesn't trust them. Her trust of adults has gone from very high, to not at all. Not surprising, when the adults who are meant to protect her have turned on her like rabid dogs. Athena said she spent the time with her counselor drawing.

APRIL 3

I have been in contact with Athena's teachers constantly since the assault, and most have been good at setting aside work for her to complete when she is unable to face school. Tonight was meet-the-teacher-night, and I finally met them face-to-face.. I was completely open about what has been happening, including Athena being arrested, but was extremely disturbed that they not only knew what I know, but in some instances, even more. It is one thing for me to tell them; quite another for them to be told by someone else. Who would tell them, and why? The only possibility I can think of is the police, but I can't believe that would be ethical or even legal.

I discussed with them the ongoing issue of Conn stalking and harassing Athena at school. There seems to be concern from all her teachers, yet somehow the problem never gets resolved. I find this incredibly frustrating, but to Athena it is far worse.

Today she came home even more non-communicative than what is now normal. She said Conn walked by her repeatedly, staring at her each time. The depth of her depression scares me. Nothing matters to her anymore; her future is a dark hole. In English, the class watched a film about a ten year old rape victim. She said she had to leave because she was crying so much. She spent lunch time in tears. I can't believe the lack of sensitivity some of these teachers have. But then, I guess some of them may not believe she was assaulted, or just may not care.

I am starting to feel a lot of hate: absolute gut wrenching hatred toward Conn and the police mostly, but also for a teacher who has such a lack of sensitivity they don't even consider the effect this has on Athena.

APRIL 4

Athena is too depressed for school. She curled up on the couch in a fetal position, and stayed there for the entire day. What I need to do is hug her. The last time I hugged her seems like many years ago, but in reality was probably before she left for school on the day she was assaulted. Now she hates to be touched in any way, and cringes when people try. The more upset she is, the more she hates to be touched. Hugs are now out of the question.

Jessie is here, but is upset because Athena is so remote. She wonders if Athena even wants her here. She just can't understand why Athena is so different now.

I don't know what to do, how to make her understand all that Athena is going through. I have never felt so helpless. I don't have any idea how to make anything better any more. I feel like my entire existence is about trying to help my family survive, and I am failing. Sandy is an emotional mess, I can't reach Athena at all, and I am becoming extremely depressed. In private, Sandy and I actually admitted to each other that we would just as soon be dead as live the life we are living now. There is no joy, only fear, anxiety, and pain. Athena is what keeps us both alive. We have to be there for her.

APRIL 5

This morning Jessie told me Athena is really freaked, and believes she has something seriously wrong 'inside' her. In spite of the feast of drugs Athena took when she was raped, she believes, and is terrified that she has a sexually transmitted disease. So, we made yet another trip to the hospital emerg. The doctor wasn't certain what is wrong, but there is a possibility she has a serious yeast infection. She was given extremely powerful anti-fungal drugs.

Sandy is showing signs of serious depression, and says he wishes he could end his life. He realizes he can't because of his responsibilities, but he wishes he could. He still refuses to see a counsellor. He is afraid that if he actually lets his emotions through, he will do something terrible. My stress level just keeps rising. I feel like I am the centre of the wheel.

It all stops here, and I have to keep strong for everyone else. When I do work, my job is so consuming I can't think about our problems, but I have very little patience, and I know I am not doing a good job. At breaks, everything floods back and I can't think about anything else.

It came out that Athena has not been telling me the extent of harassment by both Conn and his friends. She says there is no point, because no one does anything about it. She worries what Conn will do if he finds out the police aren't going to charge him.

APRIL 6

A bizarre thing happened when I was taking Athena to job shadow at the pool. She was gazing out the side window of the truck. We weren't talking, and had not been. In a completely emotionless voice, Athena said, "Conn punched me in the head."

She didn't look at me; she just kept gazing out the window. There was no indication that she even knew she had spoken out loud, but she certainly didn't seem to expect any response. Since I really didn't know where this came from or where to go with it, I said nothing. And that was the end of it. We drove on quietly.

I was shocked by her words; on the day after the assault, when she showed me the welt on her head, she had been adamant that Conn had not hit her. I decided I will wait and see if she brings this up again on her own. She gets really upset if I question her about the assault, and I don't want to put thoughts into her head. I don't understand how she could have forgotten this before, only to remember it now; I guess my biggest concern is that Athena may be having a complete breakdown.

When we got home, Sandy was on the couch with chest pains, but he wouldn't let me call the doctor.

I just don't have the energy to deal with this.

APRIL 7

Athena seems to be having every side effect possible from the drug prescribed for the yeast infection. She is severely nauseous, has terrible cramps, aching and sore muscles, and a splitting headache. I called the pharmacist who suggested she take Gravol and Tylenol to counter-act the other drug. At least this put her into a drug induced sleep.

I am so angry. I would love to kill someone right now. Only the fact that Athena and Sandy need me prevents me from choosing a suitable knife and taking the plunge. I have no doubt her infection is the result of being assaulted, either directly or indirectly. The massive amounts of antibiotics Athena took to prevent STD's have certainly lowered her immunity, as has relentless stress. I feel such hate right now. Hate for the boy walking around, bragging about this at school, and hate for the police who are condoning his act, and who seem hell bent on destroying what little is left of my daughter and my family.

APRIL 8

Delwood called at the very end of the day. His first words were, "I am charging Athena with Public Mischief."

I couldn't believe what I was hearing. I can still feel the blood pounding in my head. This can't be happening to us. When did this become my life, and for god's sake, why? I asked him why he is doing this to my daughter, and his response was something about her doing it to herself, and only then did I realize he doesn't even believe Athena was raped. Until that exact moment, I had not accepted this reality.

In my shock I said to him, "You don't believe she was raped!"

And his very disgusted sounding answer was, "She wasn't raped, she said so herself."

I asked him when she said that, (although I already knew this was the result of her saying she 'enjoyed it') and he began ranting that I don't listen; that I never listen, and I should learn to listen.

He really pissed me off, and I decided that what I say to this man does not matter; he is out to get my daughter, and nothing I say will change this.

I said, "You didn't even look into the sexual assault; you couldn't even bother to learn who Athena is as a person."

He told me again "You should learn to listen, and then you would have heard her say she enjoyed it."

I said "I heard it." But I didn't bother to say that he was the one who needed to learn to listen, and not just hear what he wanted to hear. So instead I told him he should arrest me, because I was the one who told her to lie and say she did it.

He lost it then, and started yelling at me. "Why the hell would you do that?"

"Because you told me to."

"When did I do that?"

"In the hall; you said she has to say she did it, or you would charge her. And I said, that's it? All she has to say she did it? And you said yes. You never once said she needs to tell the truth; you knew she was telling the truth. So I told her just what you told me, she had to lie, and it had to be convincing."

"You never said that. There was nothing on the tape," he responded.

Instead of answering, I asked him how he knew Conn was such a 'good boy' did he know the family?

He claimed he didn't know them. I told him he was biased, and that he should make sure he remembers Conn's name, because he will rape again, and Delwood will be responsible for that rape because he did nothing to stop him.

Delwood then told me the number of police hours that have gone into investigating Athena so far. I forget the number; all I remember is thinking how outrageous it was to waste so many hours in an attempt to convict a victim. Was I supposed to be impressed by the amount of tax dollars and police time spent to persecute my child? Or did he think that wasting astonishing amounts of time and money somehow proves Athena did whatever it is they are charging her with? Whatever his intention, it only added to my utter disgust of Delwood and what he represents.

I have no idea how the conversation ended, I believe someone hung up abruptly; it may have been me. At some point in the 'discussion' I called him a liar, and he actually told me he doesn't lie. And that, I know is a lie.

Sandy completely flipped out and I had a terrible time convincing him not to do what he really, really wanted to do. But that would end with him dead or in jail, and as much as he doesn't care about what happens to himself, Athena and I need him to be here with us. I cannot cope with this alone.

We decided not to tell Athena right away. We are terrified of what this will do to her. We will slowly let her know that there is still more fear and pain coming in her life. We were afraid she wouldn't make it through the school year; first her injury, then rape, constant stalking and harassment, and now this.

The knot in my gut never goes away. I feel physically ill all the time. There is a sensation in my head like it will literally explode. It aches so much, *I* ache so much, and I am terrified of what this will do to Athena. She has always been so proud to be a good and honest person. Her-self image has been built on these virtues, and now people we trusted and believed in are telling her she is a bad and dishonest person; a criminal in fact.

And this is all because my child did the responsible thing and went to the police for help. I feel like a fucking moron for raising Athena to trust the police.

I called the lawyer and left a message: We need to hire him.

CHAPTER 7

Depression and Darkness

APRIL 9

Sandy has hit rock bottom. I know because he has made an appointment to see the doctor. The lawyer, Mr. Cupito, called back. He does not believe the charge will get past the crown attorney. He is amazed it has gotten this far. He is refreshingly open; he seems to think out loud, and I learn a lot. He had a word to describe a cop who immediately thinks he knows who is guilty, and is then completely unable to see anything else in his unwavering arrogance and single mindedness. Apparently this sort of thing does happen.

I have been mulling over Athena's announcement that Conn punched her, and decided to call Dr. Rose; the psychiatrist Athena had seen and been tested by.

It was an incredibly enlightening conversation. It began with Dr. Rose saying, "I can tell you right now (without even seeing her) Athena is suffering from mental confusion and memory loss. The greater the trauma was to her, the more she will have confusion over events that took place. You can't expect her to have good memory after this kind of trauma. There will be a definite reduction in the accuracy of remembered details. Bits and pieces, things out of place ... He (Conn) will have a much clearer recollection as he has had no trauma."

She went on to recommend a book: Unchained Memories, by L. Terr, and she explained that this book is about memory suppression as a result of being sexually assaulted.

"In extremely traumatic situations," she said, "the brain often suppresses information because it is simply too overwhelming, and the trauma of sexual assault often causes such an overload. The information may, or may not ever return."

Suddenly Athena's comment about Conn hitting her made sense. It made sense to me that it was just too traumatic for her to accept initially; after all, she had trusted Conn. I immediately ordered the book online.

I feel so much better. There is a proven reason for Athena's sudden memory return, and in fact it completely explains Athena's inability to remember other parts of the assault. But why the hell don't the police know about this effect of trauma? How could they call Athena a liar when she, like many other victims, can't remember parts of the assault?

I won't say anything to Athena about this. She hasn't brought the assault up again and she may not even remember having the memory return and I don't want to risk influencing what she remembers.

APRIL 11

Stories of the assault are all over school. The fucking little bastard has blabbed far and wide. When Athena walked down the hall at school, a group of grade nine students yelled 'rape' after her. No one came to walk her to class, and she was all alone. Someone behind her in the hall said they were going to kill her. Cruel and hateful comments are all over her Facebook page.

Devastated, Athena cut her Facebook account. This is certainly not the first time. Athena doesn't ever engage in a conversation, she just cuts the sender off.

Interestingly, one girl, who messaged over a month ago to plead that Athena not charge Conn, recently contacted Athena again. She claimed that Conn has been seriously harassing her, and she wondered if she should go to the police about this. Athena told her no; the police won't help you.

Athena says this is her worst day yet.

"Did you tell the vice principal?" I asked.

"No," she said, "there is no point. I've told him so many times I can't count, and nothing ever changes. Nothing they do has any affect on Conn's behavior, and nothing ever changes. The school doesn't care."

I am livid. I called the school, but the VP I have always dealt with has gone home and the secretary put me through to a different vice principal. I cannot believe it. This man, whose name I do not even know, and whom I have never even met, is aware that my daughter is being investigated and may be charged with a criminal offence. Once again, the local cops have ignored the laws. This directly violates the Youth Criminal Justice Act which states that the police should not identify any youth being investigated or charged under the youth Criminal Justice Act, to anyone. How in hell does Delwood get away with this shit?

⚖

The weeks that followed were living hell. It was impossible to live, laugh, enjoy, or even be cognizant of anything but our fear. Athena and I were both in counselling with Terry, who encouraged us to do things that made us happy. I made some effort, and went for walks through the forest, but I usually just ended up in tears. Beauty was all around me, but I couldn't feel it. All I could feel was fear and pain. Athena was beyond even trying. Her depression held her like a coffin.

I noticed Athena often couldn't hear what was being said, and she complained she had lost her sense of smell. The headaches that began after Athena's first concussion dramatically increased in severity. To what extent Conn was responsible for, and how much was because of her initial head injury, we will never know for sure. But she did not suffer from hearing-loss or loss of smell before she was violently sexually assaulted.

Every year I grow a garden, and I start tomatoes from seeds. In an effort to have some normalcy, I went through this ritual. I thought I might feel some joy, some sense of achievement, but I did not. Life, living, is an overwhelming effort. Still, I put the little seedlings under grow lights to live until it became time to transplant them outside.

But the instant the grow light was turned on, Sandy and I were consumed with paranoia. Our distrust and fear of police has reached the proportions of a phobia. We were afraid they would see plants and use that as an excuse to get a search warrant and tear our house apart, claiming to be searching for illegal substances. In spite of having lived a law-abiding life, we feared we would be personally targeted by the police. We believed they would use any means to hurt our family. I carefully placed the tomato seed packages by the tomato plants where they could not be missed were someone looking in the window.

Our shed was broken into during this time. The padlock had simply been punched and broken with something like a drill bit and a hammer. Nothing was taken. Sandy spent hours searching through the shed, looking for something illegal the police may have planted in order to be able to charge us. In the past we would have called the police to let them know we had had a break in. Now we believe it just as likely the police themselves did the breaking in because we were not rolling over and baring our bellies to them. I find myself shocked by the extent of our fear and distrust.

⚖

Because of the police and the legal system, Athena has been made a social outcast. Her entire education, her future, even her life is in jeopardy. The very system that claims they are there to help reform youth is actively destroying what had been a stellar citizen. If she were the teetering on the edge of rebellion and defiance, the 'justice' system and the police would by now have pushed her over.

Occasionally Athena forces herself to get out of bed and go to school, where she is terrified, verbally abused, and threatened, and where she is relentlessly stalked by the boy who raped her.

There is no innocent until proven guilty in the teenage world. Athena is simply cast as guilty. She was new at the school; Conn had lived his entire life in that town, and had attended that school since grade nine. He constantly tells stories, many and varied, of what went on the day he raped her, while Athena says nothing; a trait I have learned is very common with rape victims. She is no longer accepted by the 'good' kids, but she never has, and never will fit with the 'bad' ones.

The constant stalking and harassment have taken an enormous toll on her. From all indications, the police have no interest in protecting her from Conn or his buddies. Daily, she is threatened, verbally abused, and told she is trash and should really just kill herself. What chance does she have?

Athena hit bottom. She wants to die: She wishes she could die. I doubt there are many worse fears for a parent than to have a child whose life is so completely unbearable she wishes for death. How often have children taken their own lives, and no one even noticed they were suffering? Here was one who was voicing her desperation, crying out for help. She claims she won't kill herself, but that only means that at this moment in time, living weighs slightly higher than death. It only means that at this moment her wish to be dead does not reach quite far enough to attempt it. It is impossible for anyone to know what straw might be the one that could push her over; the one thing that may make death better appear better than life. I was terrified that that straw would fall for her, and I might not be there to stop her.

Sandy and I discussed our meager options to get her out of the toxic school environment. Homeschooling is out. In our very rural setting our internet reception is not good enough for her to do an online course at home. We have talked about the possibility of sending her to a high school in another school board; something she does not want to do, but other than quitting school, there are no other choices.

Athena refuses to return to the school where she obtained her original head injury; we live in an area where everyone knows or is related to everyone else, and rumors the rape have circulated at her old school too. In fact, what she really wants is to quit school, change her name, move away, and never return to the place she was born and raised.

Athena has gone from being outgoing and gregarious to rarely speaking. She has bouts of anger; but mostly she is very dangerously depressed. She needs to heal, but that is impossible when the assaults keep coming; when she is being repeatedly abused by her peers, the police, and Conn. Athena and I were once very close, but that is gone. The person she was is gone. No one in our house sleeps. We spend nights worrying about things we cannot control, feeling like we are just pawns in a game we don't understand. I wonder where each of our breaking points is, and I knew it isn't far for any of us.

APRIL 12

As still occasionally happens, out of the blue Athena will say something about the assault or, in this case, her first interview with Delwood. She said Delwood asked if she had sex with Conn. She told him no, she did not have sex with Conn. What Conn did, she told him, was an act of violence, not sex. She said Delwood yelled at her and she yelled back, but she would not change her statement.

Man that guy pisses me off.

Tuesday April 13

Athena phoned me from the vice principal's office. She was crying, and talking so fast she made no sense. I was instantly freaked out, wondering what the hell had happened. I got her to take some deep breaths, and slow down. Even then it took some time to understand what she was talking about. She said she had been at a *Mothers against Drunk Driving* presentation at school, watching a very gory film when a sudden and overwhelming memory of the assault came flooding back.

Suddenly she was talking about 'all the blood' and when she saw the blood, she suddenly had a flashback of Conn coming at her with something silver in his hand when he attacked her–I eventually understood that the blood she was referring to was in the film presentation–she then remembered that she fell back onto the bed, and to try and get away, she crawled backwards up his bed. He came at her; she kicked his wrist, and saw a knife fly across the room. Then, she said, he got a really mad look on his face, and he started punching her in the head. She tried to get away by crawling further, and whipping her head from side to side, but the back of her head hit something; possibly the headboard. The next thing she was aware of was that she couldn't move her arms, although she still doesn't know why. Conn was on top of her. It was too late.

There are still gaps in her memory of the event. I asked her if she remembered anything about going down the stairs to leave following the assault. Both Shepard and Delwood previously asked if Athena remembered anything about leaving the house. But Athena still has no memory of going down the stairs. She now recalls seeing a cat at the door, when she was rushing to put on her boots, and has a partial memory of returning to the school, but she has no recollection of what happened between leaving the upstairs bathroom, and pulling on her boots. I wonder what happened that she has buried so deeply.

Athena is extremely shaken by what she now remembers. She thought this boy was her friend. It was hard enough to accept that a friend would rape her, but having to accept that his aggression and violence went beyond even that has shaken her completely. It will be a very long time before she trusts anyone again, if ever.

I decided not to tell Athena about return memories. She is not questioning why they're returning; she is far too upset by the memories themselves. I'll wait for a time when she needs to understand why this has happened, if she ever does, and then we will talk about it. I am just glad I spoke to Dr. Rose.

APRIL 14

I've completely quit pushing Athena to go to school. I couldn't take the abuse she is subjected to there, how could I expect her to? I sent an email to the school telling them Athena is very upset by the sudden return of memories of the assault. Then I reflected on how bizarre this situation is; the police have obviously told them they don't believe she was raped, yet Athena is completely incapacitated by memories of that event.

Friends of Sandy and I have been asking what they can do to help. I have started telling them that they could write character reference letters for Athena. The letters that we have received are incredible, and remind me of just how amazing a person Athena is. We now have more than two dozen letters, describing her as we have always known her, a caring, loving, honest person. Just reading the letters helps to give me hope. I thought Athena might find strength in them, but she cried when she read them, saying they remind her of how good life used to be, and may never be again.

A woman I work with is married to a police officer from a different county and detachment. I am finding I can hardly even talk to this woman; *because she is married to a cop.* I can't hide my hate for the police and this spills over to anyone related to them. In spite of the fact that this woman has never once shown any sign of being anything other than a caring person, I just can't believe anyone who is honest, caring, and sincere would actually marry a police officer. I am constantly wrestling with these new, incredibly negative feelings toward police. I no longer see police as individual people with unique personalities; I see them all as evil, corrupt, liars. In spite of this I felt I have to tell her what is going on, and I know I have to get a grip on my feelings.

When I told her what has happened to Athena, she was shocked, and asked if she could call her husband on my behalf. I agreed. The first thing her husband asked me was if Delwood knows Conn.

He then said I should complain to The Police Watchdog, but I should also complain to the Duty Sergeant at the detachment where Delwood works. He encouraged me to do it immediately, and I decided to follow his advice and not wait as I had previously planned.

When I reached the Sergeant in charge, he listened, claimed he was not aware of this case, and then made some noises of concern. Then he referred me to The Police Watchdog and offered me help in writing the complaint. I thanked him for his offer to help, but had no intention of using it.

⚖

I immediately sat down, wrote, and emailed the following complaint to The Police Watchers. I needed to have enough evidence to convince them to investigate, but police don't share information, and that makes a viable complaint very difficult. Police secrecy is one of the strongest tools preventing the public from knowing what is really going on. It puts those questioning the actions of police at an extreme disadvantage. Therefore, my complaint reflects what I knew, or surmised at this time, which is not a great deal.

Complaint emailed to (The Police Watchers):

My daughter, Athena Schuler, fifteen years old, was sexually assaulted by a boy she believed was her good friend. The attack was immediately reported to the Rivertown police. That was, without a doubt, the worst decision of her life. The hours that followed were a blur. Yet initially she was treated with dignity and respect. The first officer involved was Lana Chompsky, she then left for two weeks of training, and her partner, D. H. Delwood, took over the investigation.

Delwood had interviewed the boy who assaulted my daughter; Connor Mann. Officer Delwood either knew Conn, knew the family, or developed a highly unusual bond with Conn upon his first interview. Throughout our contact with Delwood; from the first time my daughter even met Delwood, he raved about Conn, "He's a good boy" (really? He raped my daughter!) "He's a nice boy" "He comes from a nice family." This is beyond inappropriate, it is unprofessional, unethical, and smells badly of something that should have been declared a conflict of interest. My daughter, who was raped by this "good boy," had to listen to this abuse.

What followed was a complete failure to properly investigate the case. Officer Delwood interviewed Athena on March 4. Had I any idea the degree to which she would be victimized by Delwood, I would never have let her alone with him. She came out looking as she had the day she was assaulted and said, "He believes Conn, he doesn't believe me." And, "Now I know why people don't go to the police." He did not believe her because her memory of the event was confused, and she could not remember details. I now know that this is absolutely consistent with a traumatized sexual assault victim. How is it that an officer in charge of a sexual assault case was unable to identify an assault victim?

He then decided to act as judge and jury, and set out on a mission to entrap my daughter. He tried to do this through text messages, yet what they prove, I fail to see. I was under the impression that consent had to be given at the time. He used the text messages as a reason to place my daughter under arrest for public mischief, and further victimized her until he got what he decided to interpret as a 'confession' of consent. The treatment of my daughter in this interview was indescribable: I would never have believed this would happen in Canada. As a teacher, if I witnessed any other 'professional' in Canada treat a child as he treated Athena: threatening her with jail, praying on her fear, I would have contacted Children's Aid Society immediately. She eventually just started talking; drawing on anything short of saying she consented just to make him stop. In fact he had promised that if she said the text messages were hers, he would not charge her. He lied. He says he is charging her with public mischief. This officer, for whatever reason, is out to get my child, and destroy her. He has acted as judge and jury, and completely failed to conduct a proper investigation.

I raised my daughter to believe the police would be there for her. I taught her to trust police. It took Delwood less than an hour to completely destroy her trust in police forever. I fear what will happen to her. Conn continues to stalk her, and she has no recourse. My family and friends will never view the police with trust again. I had always thought that being a good citizen meant you didn't need to be afraid of police. In the past I would have invited any officer into my home. I will never trust one enough again to do so. In fact, my advice now to any victim is not to go to the police. However, if you do, regardless of your belief that you are the victim, you need a lawyer. Police cannot be trusted. You could end up like Athena, fifteen years old, devastated by being raped by a boy you trusted, and again by the police. Every person in this country needs to know this is possible. And I will see that they do.

    Marion Schuler

I felt good sending this away. I actually believed someone out there was watching over the police and ensuring that ethics, honesty, and integrity were upheld.

APRIL 14, CONTINUED

Oh my god. Athena's Lawyer called after dinner. Incredibly, he has spoken to Delwood today, the same day I complained to the Duty Sergeant. Delwood told him that Athena will indeed be charged, and the first court date is set for May. We have no other choice, we have to tell Athena she is being charged and tried as a criminal. Sandy and I discussed how to tell her, and realized that she has lost any belief that the world will be good to her anyway, which ironically may make it easier. Another blow, but sadly that is what she expects of life now.

    Mr. Cupito, Athena's lawyer, told me to expect a cop to come to the door. We don't need to talk to that person, let them in, or sign anything, just take the papers. Athena will need to be fingerprinted and photographed. (Dear god), and that will have to take place at the police station. He said we will need to call the station to set up an appointment to do this.

April 16

We haven't told Athena she is being charged yet, and even without this additional stress she didn't sleep at all last night. She is having continuous flashbacks of being assaulted. She is constantly blaming herself for trusting Conn, thinking he was a decent person and a friend. She feels stupid and gullible, and is engaging in some serious self-bashing. I tried to make her understand that *he* is the one to blame, not her. She was caring and trusting and naive, and he took advantage of that.

When I was at work today, I walked down the hall and saw a cop-car drive past the door. My heart almost stopped. I literally could not breathe. I went to the office and asked why the police were there. I was told the police were called over a fight between two students.

I was able to breathe a bit easier until it was time for recess. I was on recess duty outside; it was my job to make sure it was safe for the children before allowing them to leave the building. When I looked out the door, I saw the police cruiser was parked in the area the children play in, which meant I needed to ask the cop to move the car before I could let the children outside.

Just the thought of speaking to a cop completely freaked me out. I could not force myself to do it. I could feel my heart pounding and I felt dizzy and short of breath again. Something as simple as asking a cop to move their car caused me to have an anxiety attack.

I asked another teacher if he would speak to the police for me.

In the past, I would never have referred to a police officer as a cop, because I believed it shows a lack of respect, and I had complete and unquestioning respect. I think it is partially this complete trust and respect I once had that makes my degree of distrust now so extreme: The more you believe in someone, the more devastating it is to learn they are not in the least what you believed they were. Yes, I must have been stupid and naive, but honestly, I much preferred my life that way. It was really comforting to believe that I was protected by honest, caring police, and discovering this is not the way the world is at all, makes me feel betrayed, angry, and afraid.

APRIL 17

Athena and I went to a nearby town for lunch together. We did a little shopping, and then both went for haircuts. It was a few fabulous hours in which Athena resembled the person she was before all this. And then a switch flipped, and she was consumed with depression. We had planned to watch a movie together as a family, but she suddenly didn't care about anything, and was once again curled in a ball on the couch. I don't understand how she can change so suddenly, and I snapped. I reached my limit.

I went into the kitchen and threw a glass at the floor, then went outside and tossed some furniture off the porch. I ripped my finger open and bled all over the deck. I am done. I just can't live this life anymore. I have completely lost my grip. I have never done anything like this before, but I have never in my life felt so utterly helpless. I sat on the step and cried in the pouring rain.

Sandy tried to calm everyone; Athena is now angry and wants to leave, anywhere would be better than here, she said. She said the only good things in her life are her boyfriend and her dog. She hates her life, she hates it here; this place is evil for her. And around and around we go. Trapped: Fish in a bowl with a stick of dynamite.

APRIL 17–APRIL 21

Athena became obsessed with blaming herself for not realizing what Conn was capable of; for being sucked in by him when she needed a friend. She sees that he manipulated her, phoning and texting and pretending to be her friend. She says she was stupid, and she feels responsible that he is still out there free to do what he wants, and she completely believes he will rape again.

Every day is a waiting game. We go through all the stages of grief; denial that the charge will really happen, anger at the outrage that it could, dark depression, and trying to come to grips with the idea that being charged as a criminal by the police does not necessarily mean you are have done anything wrong; it doesn't mean you are a bad person. And that is what we try to get across to Athena: Contrary to everything we taught you until now about respecting the law, and being law abiding, forget it. It is the legal system that is wrong and broken and is at fault, not you. You are as you always have been; an honest and caring person.

I never thought I would be teaching my child to disregard the lawmakers, the justice system and the police. But they have left us no choice. I will not let them destroy her. I will not have them convince her that she is anything other than she is: a victim many times over.

EASTER WEEKEND REFLECTIONS

We went through some of the motions of trying to celebrate. There was a feeling in the house that was a little bit lighter, a little bit less stressed; a brief respite. Only when it was over, in the middle of the night on Easter Monday, did Sandy and I discuss it. I think we were afraid that if we acknowledged it, we might jinx it, and it would disappear sooner. For no real reason, we both believed the police would not show up at Easter. And for a precious few days we felt relatively safe.

We didn't talk to Athena about it. She simply doesn't talk about her feelings or anything else for that matter. We are hyper-tuned in to her ever changing and extreme emotions, but we can't change or affect them in any way. Her deepest depression, when she is near hysteria with fear, when anger rages, it affects us to our emotional cores, but we can do absolutely nothing to ease her pain. On this weekend she, too, seemed to be a bit more at ease.

That is not to say the weekend was stress free. Athena and Jessie, who both have first aid training, believed Sandy was having a stroke. When I looked up the symptoms, it certainly seemed possible, but he adamantly refused to go to the hospital, or to let me call 911. He said he really doesn't care if he has a stroke. He has no desire to be alive; his life is not worth living. I didn't have the energy to fight. He survived the night, and life went on.

On Saturday, Jessie and Athena saw a car parked at the end of our lane. They watched as Conn got out and looked around, and then got back in and left. Athena completely freak out.

APRIL 26

Athena dropped off a resume for a summer job at a local pool, and was hired on the spot. Finally, something positive has happened for her!

Aᴘʀɪʟ 27

I received a letter from The Police Watchdog today saying they will investigate my complaint. Maybe there is hope!

In my counselling session today, Terry asked me who is there to help me through this. She knows I feel it is my job to be there for my family, but who is there for me? I didn't have an answer. I have some wonderful friends, but friends are not counsellors. I don't think it is possible, even for friends who have been with us through this, to fully understand the damage that has been done. Terry helped me to realize that I need to take care of me, and that I can only help my family if I am emotionally healthy. To do this I have to accept that it is okay to take care of myself and my look out for my own needs. I cried. I realized then how much I needed someone to tell me this. I actually need someone I can cry in front of, and not feel I am letting them down. And I needed the permission to care for myself.

I began a program on trauma. While my own trauma is the focus, what I learn will inevitably help me to better understand what Athena is going through. I believe that most of all, I am grieving. Grieving for the daughter I may have lost forever, for the life I loved that is gone, for my lost belief that I will be protected, and my lost trust in humanity.

I realized during the session that I could not find information on sexual assault because I was searching 'sexual assault' on the internet. I went to Google, and keyed in 'trauma' instead, and was successful. Trauma can be either physical, emotional, or both.

⚖

Sometime in early March, long before we had any idea that Conn would not be charged, Athena was having lunch at school with some girls she met. At that time, Athena did not believe any of these girls knew she had been raped, yet one of them told the group that Conn had cornered her and tried to force her to have sex. Athena did not share her experience, but the more she thought about it the more she felt responsible to do something about it. She told Officer Firth, the school police officer. His response, as usual, was that he would take care of it.

We heard nothing more about it until today. Jill, who made the claim, came running up to Athena at school and told her two police officers had just talked to her. The officers had asked her if she knew Conn, and she said yes. They then asked if she knew Athena, and she said yes. Jill then asked the police what this was about, and one of them told her to ask Athena. And that was the end of the 'interview'. They did not even ask if she had anything she wanted to tell them.

Athena felt she had to tell the girl something, so she just said that Conn had assaulted her, and left it at that.

When I heard this I thought it could only be one thing; the Police Watchdog must be checking to see if Delwood had conducted a proper investigation.

Sandy was not amused that the police told Jill to ask Athena. He felt their response was completely inappropriate and unprofessional. I think it is just par for the course.

⚖️

We had a couple of decent days at this time, and Athena managed a record: three days of school in a row. And then our world was blown apart.

CHAPTER 8
The Sky has Fallen

Terry picked Athena up after school and drove her to counselling. I was getting ready to leave the house to meet Athena there, and have my own counselling session.

The phone rang. It was the call we had been dreading for months. I couldn't get enough oxygen, I was hyperventilating. I was upstairs in our bedroom, and I looked out over the back field. The sun was shining and it was a beautiful spring day. It seemed absurd and even obscene that it should be so beautiful. I choked up, and I could barely talk. Tears were stinging my eyes. Even though we had been expecting this for what seemed like forever, I was completely overwhelmed. Our lawyer had firmly believed, and we wanted so badly to believe, that the charge would end up being dropped. This is the only thing that kept us going, and it seemed surreal that now it was really happening.

Officer Firth was the Judas who called. I felt disbelief, fear, sadness, and betrayal. I said to him, "You saw her that day, can you honestly tell me you didn't believe she had been sexually assaulted?"

He answered cryptically. "I was the one who started the investigation."

I took this to mean he did believe her; otherwise he would not have pushed the investigation forward. He said Delwood had asked him to serve the papers, and he had said sure. He said he didn't want to serve them to Athena at school. He was calm, and still came across like a decent person, but how could he do this? How could he sleep at night? Would this have been done if Athena had been the child of a cop? I absolutely do not believe so.

Firth told me to pick a time, a place, whatever worked for us. I didn't want him coming to our home; it would feel like we were being violated again. I didn't know where else to choose but the police station. It was a place that would conjure feelings of rage and betrayal forever anyway. I told him Athena was in counseling as we spoke, and I was to meet her at 4:00 p.m. Instead of my counselling session, we would go to the police station, so my poor sacrificial lamb could be raped again.

I was terrified for Athena. Lately the talk at home has changed from 'if I am charged', to 'when I am charged.' Still, there was always that hope that it would not come to be; that someone with some sense and integrity would step in and stop it. I asked Firth if we could bring Terry with us for support. That way, we would also have a witness to everything that was said or done. Firth readily agreed, but he is one of them, and cannot be trusted. From once having unquestioning faith, I now see the police as rabid and unpredictable animals that will turn without provocation, and enjoy ripping the life out of your body.

I called Terry and left a message, telling her Athena was being charged, and asking her to come with us. Then I called Athena. Oh my god I am so worried for her. She has been a little bit more stable the past few days, and now that will be shot to hell. What did we do to deserve this? It is so beyond comprehension that being raped can get even worse. How is that even possible?

I passed a cop on the road near the edge of town, and I started to cry. I am terrified of being stopped by the police. I am certain they would love the opportunity to charge me with anything they possibly could. I no longer believe they would stick to facts.

I have never condoned swearing, yet when I passed the police on the road, my hands gripped the wheel, and 'Fucking bastards' came out of my tightly clenched mouth. I felt both better and worse saying this: better because at least I am getting it out, but worse because I would really like to confront them, but cannot without fear that their extreme power will be used on me.

I am also riddled with feelings of guilt; to feel such hatred goes against everything I believe in. I can't differentiate anymore between hate for Delwood, and hate for all police. I struggle with this in my soul. I know it is seriously wrong, but I am completely powerless to stop these feelings.

When I arrived at the counselling centre, Terry was trying to help Athena deal with this new, expected, yet horrifying development.

Athena had withdrawn from life. She was a robot on auto-pilot, hiding inside herself once again from the world that seems determined to destroy her. An empty shell that was once the most beautiful, loving and caring girl I have ever known.

Terry was concerned about me as well as Athena, and I spent a few minutes crying and talking with Terry.

Terry tells me there are three possible outcomes for Athena as a result of being charged: there may be no setback in her healing, there may be some setback, or there may be a huge regression. Terry reminds me how strong Athena is, and I have to believe she is right. But I also know, and am terrified to believe, that we all have our limits, and I know better than anyone that Athena is teetering on the very edge; there is no room for regression.

And then we left for the police station, to move further on the downward spiral that for some unfathomable reason has become our lives.

When we arrived, Officer Firth opened the door between the waiting area and Fort Knox, and greeted us politely. I was somewhat surprised that he knew Terry on sight, having forgotten they both spend time at the high school.

I noticed that Firth did not close the door behind him when he spoke to us in the hall. He invited us in. The room that we walked through; the one I had only seen full of officers, was empty. There were only two other officers, both looking at the same computer screen. They barely glanced up. We went through to the same interview room. Athena was stone-faced. She asked Firth what she had done wrong; why she was being charged. He read the charge. She still didn't understand, but she let it drop; what did it matter. I told him how our faith and belief in police has been destroyed, how disturbed we are that they are charging a victim for reporting being raped. He stayed very pleasant, and calm. Athena and I were each given papers, no signatures required. He told us Athena would need to return to the station to be fingerprinted and photographed, and she must appear in court on the eighteenth of May.

When I got home I immediately phoned Mr. Cupito. He scoffed when I told him Firth said Athena had to appear in court herself.

"That is what you hired me to do," he said. "I'll be meeting with the crown attorney before that, and I'm confident the charge will be dropped. The process, however, will take much longer than you can possibly imagine."

We want to believe this will happen, but have had far too many shocking disappointments to risk believing it.

MAY 2-MAY 8

In the days and weeks that followed I could not carry on a conversation without feeling like my head would just spontaneously blow apart. It never left my consciousness. When I was able to sleep, overpowering feelings of horror and depression would flood my brain long before I was fully awake. I was filled with fear and sadness. If things had gone this wrong, how much worse could they get?

Sandy and I were constantly arguing. We couldn't talk about anything other than the assault and the charge, but we also couldn't talk about it without getting upset and angry. Sandy wanted to hide in his shell, and we talked about separating; but who could possibly have the energy for that? We told our friends that we couldn't get together with them, and we hoped they would understand. Day to day survival was an overwhelming challenge, socializing was inconceivable. It was absolutely impossible to think or talk about anything but the nightmare we were living in. Nothing could take our minds off of it.

Contrary to how Sandy and I needed to deal with this, Athena had completely different needs. Sometimes she lay curled in a fetal position crying for hours and hours. At times she was in frenzy, running so that she couldn't think about it. She started needing to have people around her to keep reality away; maybe to make her feel safe. We never left her alone. For one thing she was too terrified, for another, what would she do if Conn came to our home? She certainly wouldn't call the police.

She rarely slept; hell, none of us slept. But Athena was terrified of sleeping, afraid if she let her guard down, she might wake up and find Conn there. Conn had already proven he would use a weapon and Athena had recently learned from a friend of his that he had bought an illegal handgun. We lived on constant alert.

A woman at work asked me how it was going. She has known Athena since kindergarten. When I told her about our experiences with the police, she contacted her daughter at university and made her promise that if 'anything were to happen,' she would first contact her lawyer uncle, and only then consider going to the police; and only with him. She did not want her daughter to be alone with the police without legal representation. Athena's story frightened her. She is a wise woman.

In my head I tried to come to grips with this scenario: if Athena is found not guilty, it is because the judge believes she was sexually assaulted. So if the judge believes she was assaulted, then she believes Conn is guilty of sexual assault. If Conn is guilty of sexual assault, he should be charged with the crime. This just makes sense, right? Wrong. Our lawyer says that this is not the case.

To make it all worse, the civics teachers at the high school told Athena that if she is convicted, not only will she be punished, but Conn will be able to file a civil suit against her for his 'pain and suffering' in being unjustly accused. This information added another major stressor to Athena's overwhelming burden. What is wrong with this teacher that she would say this to a girl she has been told is dangerously close to a breakdown?

MAY 9

The world is a hell hole from where I am standing. Conn has been told he is not being charged, and the police have obviously told him that instead, Athena is being charged with lying to the police about being raped. Conn spread this news as fast as he could. As a result, Athena was called "trash, slut and liar" in the halls of the school by people she does not even know.

MAY 11

Today was fingerprinting day. Another of those days when I cannot believe this is my life. We went to the police station, gave the receptionist Athena's name, and then we waited. This time a woman officer I had never seen before opened the door from the inner sanctum. She didn't come out into the hall, and she didn't close the door behind her. She left the door between the hall and the police station open, so that anyone inside could see and hear her. This is transparency; this is what Delwood never did. Athena and I stood up together. I, "I would like to come in with Athena, please."

She was obviously taken aback, and began by saying, "There really isn't much space in the fingerprinting room, I'm not sure if that will work. That's not usually the way we do it, and I don't even have a chair for you...." She rambled on politely, obviously trying to come up with some reason why it just wouldn't work.

I just waited, saying nothing, and she eventually ran out of excuses. "I guess that would be alright; as long as you don't interfere."

I assured her I would not, and followed her in.

Once again I was struck by the contrast: both times Athena was interviewed the room had been full of cops. This was the second time we had come for other reasons, and there were two officers at computers, and one walking through. None paid us any attention. We walked through the room, but turned right this time in the back hall.

The fingerprinting room was really just a space in front of the jail cells. I looked at Athena. She was silent, but she was still managing to function. I stood in the doorway to the hall, trying to keep out of the way, while Athena was instructed to sit on a stool in front of a camera. While the officer was readying the equipment, she apologized that she did not have a chair for me! She was acting as if this were an every day, non-event. I guess to her it might have been, but it sure as hell wasn't to us.

I was careful to keep my mouth shut as promised, but the officer kept chatting, about the weather and the finger-printing process, and seemed trying to engage both Athena and me in conversation. I felt very weird; here we were in hell, and the devil was trying to chat us up.

This is not to say I would have preferred Delwood to be touching my daughter's hand to smear black ink onto a paper. But this event was so horrific to us; it seemed completely incongruent to have it made so casual.

I could tell that Athena was suspicious of this woman, but Athena is like that now; suspicious of everyone. She remained withdrawn, but wary. She didn't take her eyes off the officer. We were both completely civil, but only minimally participated in the ongoing attempt to chat. At one point the officer noticed me glancing at the jail cell, and opened the door for me to have a closer look, telling me to please not touch anything, not even the walls. I wondered if she was specially chosen to showcase how personable police officers can be. I can no longer just accept that she may be a pleasant person.

Finally the officer explained that she couldn't get the camera to work. Athena softly suggested it might not be turned on: sure enough. The officer turned the camera on. However in playing with the buttons on the computer, she had inadvertently turned the computer that runs the camera off, and so it still didn't work. She fiddled with it again, but again had no luck getting it to work. This happened several times, until finally she went to find help.

In the hall behind me, the one I assumed led to the back parking lot, there was some sort of altercation, and we could hear scuffling and angry voices. We pretended we heard nothing.

Another officer, a man this time, returned with the first to help with the camera. He turned it on and then off again. In a very subdued voice Athena told them again that it wasn't on, and one of them turned it on again, but the computer was still off. Then the computer was on, and in pushing buttons at random, the camera was turned off. This went on for a bit, with first one then the other machine being turned on and off, but the camera and computer were never both on at the same time. Finally, they gave up, and Athena was never photographed.

The officer remained very outgoing and friendly. Athena's entire one hand was covered with ink from being printed. 'Finger' printing is not just the print of one finger, but of several plus one entire palm. There was some dry substance available with which to remove the very worst of the ink, but only the very worst. As we were leaving, Athena asked if there was a washroom where she could wash her hands. The officer didn't just point us in the direction of the wash room; she walked us out into the public area, around the corner and down the hall. She then showed us the way out. When she left, I commented to Athena that she was very friendly. "Too friendly," was the response from the new Athena, who in the past would have thoroughly enjoyed meeting someone new and interesting.

When we got home and I was telling Sandy about our newest venture into previously unknown lifestyles, I realized two things: One, the room was full of cops both times Athena was being interviewed and empty when that was not the case, and two, the only cop who always came out into the hall, closed the door, and said outrageous things like how great a kid Conn is, was Delwood. The other cops always left the door open behind them, and carried on no secret agendas.

I spent a lot of time mulling about Delwood, and the conclusion I came to is that Delwood is a shady cop who has likely said inappropriate things and treated the public badly for a long time. I expect he has continuously gotten away with this because no one has complained until now. I also believe that now a complaint has been made, steps will be taken to ensure he doesn't do these things again.

The room full of cops perplexed and concerned me. There were far more cops than could possibly be employed in that small town. I know now that there are several women in the detachment, not including Lana Chompsky or Bonnie Shepard, who both were brought in from another area. Yet the only woman present when Athena was interviewed was Shepard. One interview was on a Friday night, another on a Thursday night, which would be strange times to hold staff meetings, and even stranger to think that Athena's interviews just happened to interrupt not just one, but two enormous staff meetings.

My conclusion? These paid police officers were spending company time to witness the interrogation of a fifteen year old female rape victim. It is impossible for me to believe they had nothing better to do, or that they were all required as a part of the investigation. Think of it; a room full of men, watching and listening to a young girl forced to describe being raped in elaborate detail. Disturbing? It certainly is to me.

MAY 14

Jessie and Athena were upstairs and on Facebook when Athena started to yell for me. She had another message from Conn. It said only 'Hey, what's up,' and there was a friend request via Conn's current girlfriend. As always, Athena freaked out, deleted the message and the request, and blocked them both. This, as always, starts her terror all over again. She acts like a deer in the crosshairs. She is terrified, and does not feel safe anywhere. As happens more often than not, I moved into her bed for the night.

MAY 15

Three months ago today; and it just keeps getting worse. Being contacted by that little prick terrifies Athena beyond belief. Today was her last day of training to qualify as a Red Cross Water Safety instructor. All day she had terrible flashbacks of the assault. When I picked her up at the end she was still so disturbed I'm not sure it registered that she passed. She is literally afraid for her life. This sparked the overwhelming emotions that she has been keeping inside to come out. Not being believed by the police has shaken her to her core. She had a complete melt down, angrily questioning if anyone believes her.

I tried to calm her by telling her the police are idiots, and I backed this by telling her some of the many things I see that don't add up; the glaring inconsistencies that the police refuse to bother with, ignore, or pretend don't exist.

I told her there are many overwhelming reasons to believe her, and for anyone who knows her, there are none that cause disbelief. The very idea that she would turn a friend over to the police if she had agreed to have sex is preposterous, not only because of how highly she values friends and friendship, but because until the police themselves destroyed it, she had unwavering respect for the police and the justice system. If she consented to have sex, and then believed she had made a mistake, she would just learn to deal with it; she certainly would not go to the police.

While she wouldn't have agreed in any case, it is inconceivable that she would consent to sex without a condom due to her intense fear of sexually transmitted diseases, and her obsession with cleanliness. Add to that the fact that Conn claimed to be gay and sexually active, plus that she is terrified by the thought of pregnancy.

She had her period. In her naivety she thought it possible that she could die as a result of having sex during this time. Who in hell would go ahead and have sex believing they may immediately die as a result? Certainly not Athena. It was impossible for me to imagine her consenting to have sex with a guy she wasn't even dating; agreeing to have a quickie and then go back to school in time for the next class. She has always considered sex a very serious matter. Finally, she has always wanted to have just one love in her life, and no more. And it certainly was not Conn.

I didn't even get into the scratches and goose-egg. These were topics we haven't talked about; two of many things that we avoid because they are a very fast track to serious distress and depression.

MAY 17

When I asked Athena how she was, she snapped at me, saying "Well, I was attacked with a knife, punched in the head, raped, charged by the police, I have to see Conn every day, everyone thinks I'm a liar, and hardly anyone will even talk to me. The girl who sat next to me in science class asked to be moved away from me. I hate life, I hate school and I want to move, change my name, and never come back. I'm just great mom."

Conn walked by her repeatedly before school, and at lunch.

I want to rip some hearts out just like the hearts of my family have been ripped out. I feel absolute hatred for the first time in my life. I have crossbow fantasies that sadly must remain just fantasies. I am starting to believe in an eye for an eye. I see myself becoming someone else, someone who hates and doesn't trust, and who now understands that the world is very different from what I believed it was three months ago. I want justice and accountability, and I am seeing a country that is spiraling away from either. Just the fact that this boy can continue to harass, stalk, and terrorize Athena without any repercussions, horrifies me. Where are her rights? Why does he have the right to terrorize her? How can it be acceptable for this creep to take away her *alleged* right to an education? I looked up the Canadian Charter of Rights and Freedoms, and wonder how the police can choose to not to protect her.

MAY 15

I got a phone call from Tybo Holder, who will be looking into my complaint against Delwood. Holder works for the *Independent* office called The Police Watchers. Interestingly, *she is a police Sergeant in the same police force I am complaining about.* Am I missing the independent part here? She told me that the police don't like her, and tried to convince me that she is somehow separate from them. She asked me where I would like to meet with her. The police station in Rivertown was suggested, but

I don't feel like putting on another show for the boys there, or worrying that we are being taped or watched on camera. Tim Horton's is out, it is just too public. Sandy is not happy, but I feel there is no option but to have her come here. She and I will talk again to set a date.

As per advice from Terry, Sandy has written a victim impact statement. I knew he has been shattered by this, but seeing it on paper really drove the degree of his devastation home to me.

Sandy's Victim Impact Statement:

I'm not sure how I can describe the impact in words. Obviously the horror, disbelief, rage and ultimately the impotence and frustration all associated with the rape itself. But the real devastation for the family and myself occurred at the hands of the police (one in particular however there seems to be others either in collusion, agreement or a lack of willingness to confront and officer obviously behaving in an inappropriate manner). Those that "serve and protect" took a victim and further victimized her to the point that I describe it as a figurative rape. Once again totally frustrated, not able to deal with the situation. I have never in my life been through a worse time. I have always through brain and brawn been able to have at least some impact on a situation, but with the badge and gun hiding the individual and giving him the ultimate authority of a police state my life becomes somewhat meaningless. I exist because I know it would be worse for the family if I did not.

My mental health and attitudes are at a bottom, I'm cynical, pessimistic … now constantly worried about money. We have taken out a loan to pay our initial legal bills, my wife has missed considerable amount of work (she has no sick time. Holiday time) so this is lost money. We had considerable expenses around transportation … to police interrogations, counselling sessions, doctor's appointments. Increased medical bills for prescriptions.

I am taking sleeping bills, pain medication, drinking more … all new to a person who prided themselves with never having to go to a doctor, never mind not taking medication. My work has suffered, I can no longer stay overnight for business which is becoming problematic.

I dread going home to find out the latest horror my daughter has had to go through ... My home, a beautiful rural property was my dream and my paradise, my retreat ... I hope that's recoverable.

I am paranoid about the police, I would not let one on my property if it's at all possible and quite frankly have avoided consciously situations where I may have had contact. I will not be able to be civil. We always had a great deal of respect, empathy and concern for the police force, apparently that was totally misguided. I make sure that everyone I tell is aware that they should never consult with the police force unless forced to do so. And then they should be seeking legal advise and protection (yes even as a victim). We have had our shed broken into ... I believe it was the police that did it. It was a professional job so either a pro criminal or a cop, 2 sides of the same coin. One is just not as open and transparent ... yes that would be the ones that hide behind their badge and gun ...

He leaves off here. He found he could not go on without "losing it".

MAY 20

I had an interesting phone discussion with T. Holder, the woman in charge of investigating for The Police Watchdog (TPW). She certainly presents herself as wanting to listen and help. She told me that TPW has no power to prevent the charge or the trial. The two are completely separate. She said again that the police don't like her, because she represents authority over them. It seems she doth protest a bit much, and this causes me concern.

She says she has looked at the interview tapes of Athena. I asked her if she could hear the inducement in the third interview; when Delwood told me he would not charge Athena if she said she 'did it'. She said it was inaudible. This means it is my word against Delwood's.

MAY 21

Today is the final phase of the Water Safety Instructor course. If she passes, Athena will be qualified to teach Bronze Cross and Bronze Medallion. She started the day feeling out of sorts, and when we arrived at the pool, was once again unable to go in alone. I explained to one of the instructors that she was recently sexually assaulted, and I got immediate support. The woman I spoke to told me she is a sexual assault survivor. She immediately commented that there were no males in the class, so that would make it a bit easier. She realized that even physical contact with other girls would be difficult, and said if Athena needed to go to a quiet safe place, she could just leave, and she suggested a safe space.

It was wonderful to have this degree of empathy, understanding, and support, and I found this almost overwhelming. We tell so few people, mostly because it is not socially acceptable to talk about. Sometimes I simply can't help it; I can't pretend that I am fine, and that all is well. It is the only thing in my life right now, there literally *is* nothing else.

Carrying the secret of sexual assault, and being a sexual assault victim, is a huge burden. Because it is socially unacceptable to tell people you were raped, there is implicit shame attached. It is completely acceptable to tell someone you were mugged, or robbed, have random sex or a communicable disease, but not acceptable to say you were raped. Having openly told a few people this fact, I see the horror and discomfort it causes them. Most people have never had someone openly tell them they were raped. Yet rape is appallingly common. The vice principal at the school Athena is attending told me *there have been three other girls at that same school raped this year.* And this is not a big high school. The highest estimates I have read say that one in three rapes are reported, although some estimates say one in ten and some are as low as three in one hundred. This means that at the very least there were twelve *and possibly forty or more* sexual assaults in that one school in this one school year.

As a parent this knowledge should cause intense fear. I would expect there would be greatly increased discussion about this horrific issue, and perhaps, as a result, less sexual assault in the future if this information was made public.

Unfortunately, Canadian law does not allow the publishing of any information that could identify victims or accused who are younger than eighteen years old. Most media sources, perhaps as a result of this ban, do not report acquaintance rape; the most common form of rape; at all. While this is allegedly to protect underage offenders and their victims, it also prevents the public from knowing the enormity of this epidemic. Because the public is not aware how common 'date' rape is, the police and the legal system have been spared from having to explain why they are failing so horrifically at resolving this epidemic. At issue is not only the incredible number of rapes, but public ignorance of the seriousness of rape. I certainly had no idea how completely it destroys lives.

⚖

Athena wanted to go for ice-cream when I picked her up from her swim course, but she asked me to come in with her to get it. I am learning to read the signs: a sudden and overwhelming fear, or sudden inability to be alone, usually means there have been more threats, bullying, or contact, from Conn. Sure enough she has gotten another Facebook message from Conn. Did she print it? No, she freaked out and deleted it. I feel like a broken record as once again I explain that she needs to print it for proof. She then began to count the number of times she has blocked him, and got to over a dozen. It seems he keeps making new Facebook accounts, which allows him to then access some of her information through common friends, as well as make 'friend' requests to her. When she realized this she became really upset. Every contact from this boy, even if it is just 'hi' makes her a victim again.

What in hell is wrong with this kid? This is not the actions of a normal person. He appears to be smart like a fox, constantly creating new accounts to intimidate Athena, and who knows what other victims. Does he realize the impact this has on her? Is it intentional, or is he so stupid he still doesn't understand the damage he has done? I reflect that the police have done everything in their power to condone his actions, so, maybe he really doesn't get it.

MAY 24

It is only three days since the last one, and Athena has gotten yet another Facebook request from this creep. This time we do print it, but what now? The police don't care, the school does nothing. Save if for posterity I guess.

⚖

Conn was constantly stalking Athena during this time and his actions seemed almost bi-polar. The friend request was followed by again spreading wild tales about the assault, and a flood of Facebook messages from so called Facebook friends calling Athena a slut, and telling her to keep her clothes on.

Many of these are from girls, and Athena told me some very concerning stories about the concept these girls have of sex and rape. Things like; 'You should be happy he liked you so much that he did that' 'You cannot be raped if you are not a virgin.' 'Rape is not a big deal; get over your-self'.. We have lost ground as women, and in many ways it seems women are leading the way backwards. This is not to say men are not responsible. As a society we are teaching our boys that the word no means nothing. Meaningless sex and violence is glorified constantly in music videos, music, television shows, and movies. We are fighting an uphill battle in the need to get across how utterly devastating sexual assault is to the lives of victims. And it is becoming horrifyingly apparent to me that our society places little value on the lives of women and girls.

⚖

I sent another email to the school VP; if I were sending hard copy notes about Conn's harassment, the world would have one less forest by now, still, nothing ever changes. The VP moved Athena's locker again to deter Conn from walking by repeatedly. But, by the end of the day, Conn had found the new location, and was waiting to stare at her. It just goes on and on, and if anything the harassment keeps getting worse.

This just compounds Athena's struggle to keep up with her school work. She is rarely at school, and when she does go she often needs to come home part way through because of breakdowns, bullying, and flashbacks. She is behind in all her classes; is completely sleep deprived, and only sleeps if someone is with her. She sees our family doctor at least monthly, and has for months now, but she is also in the emergency room at least once a month. Athena and I are both in counselling, and there have been more trips to the dentist: Athena clenches her teeth so hard when she does sleep, her jaw has been aching. It was hoped a mouth guard would also help with her constant headaches. It has not.

I clenched so hard in the night I fractured a tooth. The attempted repair did not work, and I had to have a root canal. That too failed, and finally I had no choice but to have the tooth extracted. We are constantly at appointments. I have missed more days than I have worked. Finances are a very serious problem. This just adds to our stress.

This is one point where, as Canadians, we are not equal. In my family, we have sold the future to finance the present. Money that would have gone for Athena's education is gone to pay for what she needs now, both in terms of me being able to be with her, and to pay for a lawyer. My brother has helped us hugely with financial assistance. We have a good lawyer, and good lawyers are not cheap. What would we have done if we could not afford one? Plead guilty because we had no option? Have a court appointed one, and hope for the best? Many people assume the courts will automatically refund the cost of a lawyer when Athena is found not guilty. They do not. Nor is the cost income tax deductible, regardless of innocence. The only possible way to recover the money is to hire yet another lawyer and sue, and there is no guarantee of winning. Consider this before you report a crime to the police.

MAY 26

Athena told me she cried for the first time in counselling yesterday, and for the first time she really talked about the assault. While this is no doubt a step toward healing, it comes with some side-effects; she did not sleep at all last night. Instead, she spent the night going over and over the assault. The Water Safety Instructor course is tonight, and I wonder if she will be able to manage.

Her class was in Ringwood, a drive of almost an hour one way. I dropped her off and then went to another bigger town nearby to wait out the four hours. That way I was close by if she couldn't do it. My cell phone was on.

I went to the Wing Hong restaurant while I waited. My fortune cookie read, 'Everything will now come your way.' God, do I hope this is true. I fantasized about framing this little strip of paper when the prophecy comes true, and life becomes livable again. Hope in a fortune cookie.

I drove down to the dock, and parked where I could watch the sunset, and I cried. Never have I wanted to believe in anything more than I do that fortune cookie. I am so tired. I started to think about all the people who have stayed by us and supported us. The prayers, phone calls, letters, calls from people who care, who have shown compassion and love; incredibly special people.

I needed to write my own victim impact statement and while the sun set, I started with some jot notes:

- Feelings of dread, especially around the time Athena will be coming home from school as I wait to hear how the day went.
- I am always anxious, fearful, angry, and on edge.
- This is all I ever think about.
- I get at most two hours sleep at night, and spend the rest of the night worrying.
- I feel like I am on pins and needles all the time, waiting for the next blow.
- My stomach is constantly in knots, my shoulder and neck constantly ache, actually I ache all over, especially old injuries, and I always have a headache, I have clenched my teeth so much I have fractured and lost one.
- I have no motivation, I cry so easily, I have no tolerance, and this makes my job very, very difficult.
- My marriage is at best on hold; at worst it is very broken. Neither of us has any energy left to work on it
- Our finances are a complete mess, and on one level I'm not sure I have the energy to care, on another I know it eats at me.
- I hate and distrust the police with a passion that shocks me, and it goes against all of my beliefs, and causes me more stress, but I cannot change how I feel.

I found I was having trouble staying on track. My mind kept thinking about the impact this has had on Athena. She says she doesn't see the point in writing anything; no one will care anyway, so I jot down some notes on her behalf:

- Constant rashes, migraine headaches, cramps and aches, discharges and bleeding, difficulty hearing, has lost her ability to smell, cannot sleep, suffers from horrible dreams of being victimized and helpless. She is terrified that Conn has given her a Sexually Transmitted Disease, and that he may have cut her inside while she was unconscious. She is afraid she will never be able to have a normal sex life or have children as a result.
- Athena has completely lost her freedom due to fear of Conn and how intently he stalks her. She is rarely able to go to school, and certainly doesn't feel safe when she is there, she can't walk in the town or go anywhere alone. She is terrified even when she is at home with us. She never feels safe, and doesn't believe *anyone* will help her if she needs help in an emergency.
- As a result of the continuous and varied stories told by Conn, Athena is not only harassed by him, but by his friends. She is ostracized, criticized, bullied and judged by other students who have never even met her. She is a social outcast. She often receives death threats.
- She hates her life (who wouldn't?), wishes she were dead, wants to leave this province, change her name and never return.
- In the past she was an optimist, she now lives in dread of the next horrendous event she may have to endure, and expects only bad things for the future.
- She believes Conn will at the very least try to rape again, and she feels very guilty and responsible for failing to have him stopped.

One of *my* biggest fears is of self fulfilling prophecy; what if Athena becomes the person the police and Conn are telling everyone she is?

MAY 27

Athena had an appointment with our family doctor today. She told the doctor some of the issues she is having, and has been diagnosed with Post Traumatic Stress Disorder. She is already on an anti-depressant; one often prescribed for PTSD, so the drug dosage is being doubled.

After the appointment we went to a store we really used to enjoy. At first Athena showed some mild interest in the clothes, and then suddenly everything changed. Something suddenly caused near panic; perhaps triggered a flashback, so we left the store immediately. She was upset all the way home. I tried to talk to her about it, but she just doesn't know what triggers these sudden and overwhelming feelings of panic.

MAY 30

Today Athena and I visited the school we are considering enrolling her in. It took us almost an hour to get there.

The first thing we noticed was how clean it was. Secondly, we noticed how calm it was. Thirdly, how respectful everyone was, from the students in the hall to the staff. The principal introduced herself to Athena and shook her hand.

She asked Athena "Why do you want to attend this school?"

Athena answered, "Because I want to feel safe".

The principal responded, "You will be safe here".

And we both believed her.

There is nothing more to consider. This school has promised one of the most basic human rights to a child who lives in constant terror for her life: They have promised to protect her.

CHAPTER 9

The "Justice" System

We also had an appointment today to meet the lawyer who will be representing Athena. Our appointment was late in the day, so when Sandy got home from work, the three of us drove into the city together. It had already been decided that only Athena and I would go to meet Mr. Cupito; I have been involved since this nightmare began, and Sandy and I both felt there is no need for us both to be there. In fact, one concern is that our meeting would actually be less productive simply because there would be more voices. Alright, it also has to do with Sandy being unable to think/talk/discuss the sexual assault without becoming extremely emotional. His emotions are even closer to the surface than mine are. His emotions are bleeding and raw, and we both know he may not be able to control his furious/depressed/outraged emotions.

Saying this, we had discussed this meeting non-stop for what seems like months, and had compiled a list of questions and concerns. While I am pleased that Sandy has such confidence in me, it also feels like a very big weight sometimes. Sandy ran an errand and then waited for us down the road, at a nearby coffee shop.

Mr, Cupito's office was in a large Victorian house that had been converted into space for several lawyers. It was after hours, and it appeared he was the only lawyer still at work. He met us at the door with his dog, for which he immediately earned a brownie point from both of us. We followed him up two flights of stairs to his office on the third floor. The house still had much of its original woodwork, and the third floor "attic" was open and unusual; an attractive workspace.

Initially, he spoke to Athena and I together, but he made it clear that he is Athena's lawyer, and would be spending most of his time alone with her. Anything said between them, he said, is completely confidential, and I have no right to know what they discuss. This surprised me a little given that Athena is only fifteen years old, but apparently the law is quite explicit on this. Personally, all I cared about was his ability to successfully end this insanity.

He was a talker, and not as good at listening as I had originally thought; in fact he rarely stopped talking. There is an upside to this; by listening closely, I could learn a great deal. He came across as highly competent, and very confident in his own abilities. But if he wasn't confident in his own ability, he would be useless as a defense lawyer. I believed he would be a good choice, but the final decision rests with Athena.

The first topic he raised was our expectations. He made it clear he would not plea bargain with the crown. He would be fighting for a 'not guilty' judgment, and nothing less. We were in absolute agreement about this: Athena will not plead guilty, and if this had been his solution, we would have been looking for another lawyer.

Athena voiced her concern that she may be sent to jail if found guilty, and Cupito told her the absolute worst that could happen would be probation. He also said that a guilty verdict is incredibly unlikely. He then went on to explain the law Athena is being charged under; *Section 140(1)(a) of the Criminal Code. On the summons she was given it states:*

Did commit Public Mischief in that with intent to mislead, she caused Derk Delwood, a police constable with the Police to enter upon an investigation by making a false statement to Constable Delwood that accused Connor Mann of having committed the offence of sexual assault, contrary to section 140(1)(a) Criminal Code of Canada.

He told us there are two parts to this charge, and the crown must prove both beyond a reasonable doubt. First, the crown must prove that Athena *intentionally misled the police into investigating a crime that didn't happen*, and therefore, the crown must prove that no sexual assault took place. Proving that someone was not assaulted, he told us, is extremely difficult. But even in the incredibly unlikely event she is convicted, he said, she would not go to jail.

Of everything he told her, this was the one thing she never believed, and the fear of going to jail terrified her day in, and day out. And it did until the trial was over and the verdict read.

We asked about getting a restraining order against Conn, and he told us it would be difficult to do so. For one thing, we would have to spell out where Athena works, and in doing so, Conn would then know where to find her outside of home or school, something he had not yet figured out. We agreed that was the last thing we wanted to do. It would be like handing Conn a free pass to stalk and harass her at work. Mr. Cupito suggested other options: A Letter of Trespass, which would allow us to press charges immediately if Conn comes on our property again, and it was suggested that if Conn showed up at the pool where Athena would be working, she point him out to the other workers and say, "Is that guy watching; me, or that little eight year old?" This, he felt would quickly result in Conn being made unwelcome faster than any restraining order. With regard to his stalking Athena at school, he said he would write a letter to Delwood suggesting that he keep Conn, his 'star witness,' under control.

We talked about the probability of Athena's case actually going to trial, and once again Cupito said he could not see it happening. He told us there had recently been a directive from the Justice Department which strongly recommended all reported sexual assaults be tried in court. In this city, he said, when the police don't feel they have enough evidence to convict the accused, they talk to the woman and explain this, hoping to talk her into withdrawing her charge. He saw what was being done to Athena as a bizarre way of dealing with a case that may not have enough evidence for a conviction against the boy

On his desk there were two file folders. One was enormous, perhaps ten or more centimeters thick, the other could have been empty; it could only contain a few pieces of paper, no more. He said the thick one was Athena's case file, the other, he said, was the file of a person being charged with murder.

There is a direct correlation," he said, "between the amount of paper the police produce, and how cut-and-dried a case is. If the case is clear-cut and air-tight, very little paper is needed and the file is very small. The less proof the police have, the more paper they produce."

They had outdone themselves in Athena's case.

Cupito talked about the third interview, and told us her rights had been violated under the Youth Criminal Justice Act several times. Delwood asked her if she wanted one or both parents present, and Athena said she wanted me to be with her. When asked if she wanted to consult with a parent, she said yes. She should then have had time alone with me in which to do that, and all recording devices should have been turned off. No police should have been present, watching, or listening during that time. Instead, we had been constantly monitored, and never allowed to speak privately.

Secondly, Delwood had no right to tell me to be quiet. In fact, I had every right to speak. I was there as my child's representative, just as a lawyer would be, and Delwood sure as hell would not tell a lawyer to shut up. Cupito then made some uncomplimentary comments about the cop and his competence level, and then reprimanded me for being so stupid (my words) that I didn't push Athena to ask for a lawyer or duty counsel. I certainly know that now.

The lawyer's next comment floored me. *He said Athena confessed to lying about having been sexually assaulted in the third interview.*

"I was there during the entire interview," I told him, "and she did not confess."

I went on to explain, "The only thing in the entire interview that came remotely close to a confession, was Athena saying she enjoyed it. And she had been referring to, and parroting, Delwood when he had said Athena enjoyed being friends with Conn, and enjoyed texting him."

"No," Cupito responded: "She must have confessed, *it is in Delwood's notes a number of times.*"

I was absolutely floored.

We talked about Delwood's attempts to get me to convince Athena to 'confess', and Cupito said he would watch the tape if it came to that, meaning, if the charge is not dropped before it comes to that. He still believes the plug will be pulled on this madness and it will not be necessary.

I learned the difference between court and trial. Trial is specific;

when the evidence against Athena is actually heard by a judge and a judgment made; it will be at a trial. In the meantime, the administrative stuff, like setting a date, asking for more time, entering a plea is all done in court. The same courtroom is then used exclusively on a set date for the trial, where evidence is presented and a judgment ultimately made on innocence or guilt.

I wanted to see the videos, but I am not legally allowed. How about the evidence? Was I allowed to see any of it? The answer is no. Neither Athena nor I have any legal access to the evidence, only he, as her legal representative, has that access. He told us we may apply under the Access to Information Act to obtain the evidence once this is over.

He then confirmed that the texts prove there was no agreement between Athena and Conn to meet or to have sex on the day the assault occurred. He also explained that the text messages Delwood obtained were not for a three day period, but were in fact *all* of Athena's text messages both sent and received *from everyone she was in contact with from February first to the day of the assault*. This explains the enormous amount of papers Delwood claimed were Athena's text messages. The entire interview may have been different if Delwood had bothered to tell us this.

Our legal bill is around seven-thousand dollars at this point. Mr. Cupito said he would not be charging us for every paper, every phone call. "At worst," he said, "my total bill will be less than the cost of a new car."

I could not help but wonder whether he was basing this statement on the type of car he would normally buy, or a car within our budget. But it doesn't matter; we will pay what is required to resolve this injustice. We will not allow Athena to be convicted without one hell of a fight, and it occurred to me that police have an absurd amount of power, when based on a non-existent text message; they can drive a family into fears of financial disaster.

Fighting a criminal charge of any sort will mess up your life financially for a long, long time, to say nothing of the damage to the rest of your life.

When we left, Athena said she really liked him. And so choosing a lawyer is settled.

⚖

This meeting has permanently changed my vision of the legal system in Canada; which I now as a crap shoot, a game of chance where real people are just pawns in a game, and where guilt or innocence does not determine the winner. The odds are on the best lawyer, and money is what buys the best. I believe the police see this game as a challenge to their authority, which they take very personally; and as Delwood has proven, some are willing to stretch their legal authority in order to win. But most disturbing of all is the individual caught in the game, whose life means nothing to any of the players.

JUNE 1

Today I will meet Tybo Holder from The Police Watchers. My notes are in order, and it is another day off work, and with no pay.

Sergeant Holder turned out to be an interesting woman. She came across as grandmotherly, and pleasant. Incredibly, she *again* brought up her spiel that the rest of the police do not like her. She seems most determined to convince me of her impartiality. This is lost on me. I really don't care; I can't be bothered deciding whether or not to believe she is on our side. She is my only option.

Holder told me I can't expect a great deal from this investigation. TPW does not have a lot of power, and cannot overturn a criminal charge. But I still believe that what Delwoood had done (and failed to do) is so outrageous that the overseers of the police *will* care. After all, this is Canada, not some downtrodden dictatorship where the laws are written in pencil. How could it possibly be acceptable to treat a young girl who has been violated so abominably?

I got the impression that a 'proper investigation' is a very vague idea, and there aren't even guidelines let alone checks and balances to ensure quality work is done by officers. Holder agreed with me when I said the police are out of touch with normal middle class Canadians; that police have become so jaded they simply believe everyone is lying, and dishonest. I was shocked that this statement was completely accepted by someone who, let's face it, a cop. If this is a known and accepted concept, why isn't something done to change it?

She taped some of the conversation, but mostly wrote notes. I asked if she was the officer who interviewed Jill, the girl who told Athena she

Conn had tried to force her into having sex. She told me she was not. This really surprised me, and I asked why the local cops would bother interviewing Jill two months after it was reported, and long after Athena had been charged.

Holder's response was that the police were probably just 'tying up loose ends,' and said was not an uncommon practice. I am appalled: do the police not care that this girl may have been sexually assaulted?

It appears the only reason the police got around to talking to Jill at all was so they could claim they followed up on the complaint. They were not even interested enough to ask her if there had been a problem. By not properly investigating this claim prior to charging Athena, they ignored what could have been evidence against Conn, which would have immensely supported Athena's accusation of assault. It seems obvious to me the Rivertown police are not interested in pursuing the truth, because in this case, it would support Athena's claim. That is bad enough, but to completely ignore what may have been another sexual assault victim is quite horrifying.

I told Holder about Conn's constant harassment. I told her about the day I picked Athena up from school, and walked with her to her locker: When we got to her locker, Athena told me that Conn would be walking by within a minute. He did. She said wait, he will be back. Sure enough, he walked back from the direction he had just been going. In less than fifteen seconds, he did it again. This time I stood where Conn would see me and know I was with Athena. When he noticed I was there, he looked quickly at me, and then at Athena. He looked very startled and scurried off. This went on constantly, Athena told me; and it must have for her to predict his movements so perfectly.

"Did you tell anyone?" Holder asked.

"No," I said, "Why would we bother? We have both told numerous people a ridiculous number of times that this was going on, and no one, not the police or the school has ever done anything. That is exactly why I am telling you now."

I explained Athena's brain injury to her. I talked about Conn attacking Athena with a knife, and said that Athena had blanked this event out for several weeks. I told her about the injuries I had observed and encouraged Holder to get a copy of the hospital's sexual assault records to prove that she had suffered a head injury.

I told her in detail about the inducement; that Delwood had convinced me if Athena lied, and said the text messages belonged to her, he would not charge her. Once again she said she had viewed the tape, but could not hear what was said in the hall by either of us.

I questioned why Athena, the victim, was fair game to rip to pieces without me or a lawyer being in the interview. I complained of the way Delwood treated Athena, and referred to him as the ultimate bully. I told her about the number of Rivertown police who came out to watch this bastard treat her like a piece of crap. I tried not to get emotional, but there were some things I could not talk about without crying.

I had to watch the clock; Athena had gone to school that day, and I had to pick her up at the bus stop. I had no intention of leaving Ms. Holder in my home while I was gone, which left me two options; I could ask her to wait in her car and lock the house door, or I could ask her to come with me. I invited her to drive with me. Her accepting comment made it clear she knew I did not trust her to stay alone in my home. I didn't respond. She was absolutely correct.

When Athena got off the bus, she was in better than usual spirits. It had been a rare 'good day' with Conn absent from school. "Good day' actually translates as "a day not burning in hell." Truly good days only existed prior to February 15th.

The interview between Athena and Sergeant Holder took place as mine had, at the kitchen table. We had already decided that I would not leave Athena alone at any time with Ms. Holder, so I sat away from the table, but where I could hear the conversation. Both Athena and I told Ms. Holder that this was the only way Athena would talk to her at all, and we explained that this was the result of our new distrust of police.

I was surprised at the subtle differences between Athena and my recollection of the interviews. While all of my concern was for her in the third interview, her concern was for me. She was outraged that Delwood kept telling me to be quiet, and remembers him telling me to shut-up.

Until Athena told Holder that Delwood referred to me as "mom" throughout the interview, I had completely forgotten. Not only was this disrespectful, it was incredibly patronizing of him. I suddenly realized that he has never once, on any occasion, called me by my name.

I was shocked to learn that Athena heard the entire conversation when Delwood offered to drop charges if she confessed. I had never even considered the possibility that she could hear us, and we had never talked about it. Athena said that when I left the interview room, I did not fully close the door, and she clearly heard everything that was said.

Holder expressed concern for Athena and encouraged me to keep her in counselling. I am getting tired of this assumed magic bullet, and while I completely agree that a good counsellor is an absolute necessity, having the police drop off the planet would do more to heal Athena than anything else could possibly do. It is impossible for her to even begin to heal when she is facing a criminal charge, is relentlessly stalked by the boy who raped her, lives in constant fear for her life, and is terrified that she will be unjustly convicted and go to jail.

$$⚖$$

When Holder left, we felt a little hopeful. We still had not learned that the police can appear to be with you, while grinning with their great canine teeth in anticipation behind your back.

$$⚖$$

JUNE 2

Athena is home sick. We were told that doubling the anti-depressant medication prescribed for PTSD may have severe side effects. She feels faint and is extremely nauseous. The pharmacy said to take Gravol, and after taking one, Athens promptly passed out. I was happy to see her sound asleep. For a few hours I knew she was safe, and had some freedom from her suffering. Hopefully the drugs will help keep the nightmares away.

JUNE 6

Where is the school cop? As far as I can see, he has washed his hands of Athena. She gets no protection. At lunch time the little jerk and three of his friends started yelling at Athena and Jill in the hall. Things like; you weren't raped, you wanted it, and calling them bitches, whores and sluts. Several students told her she should die; someone said she should be killed. Conn went by nine times at lunch and stared at her intently each time. He followed Athena and Jill from their class to the far end of the school. Athena couldn't face class, and after talking to the VP and to guidance, spent the last half of the day in the library. The VP told Athena that the school has not been able to control Conn or keep him in class.

I am so disgusted. How can this be allowed to go on? I sent yet another email to the school, but why the hell do I bother?

JUNE 7

I am so fucking pissed off. I met with the vice principal to discuss the bullshit he has failed to do anything about. He started by saying, "It would almost be better if Conn actually did something to Athena, so the school could nail him."

Incredibly, he failed to see the steam pouring out of every orifice in my head.

"First," I told him, "Conn DID *do* something to her, he *raped* her, and no one did a bloody thing to him. And secondly, if he does attack her again, it will completely destroy her. Just how the hell is that supposed to help her?"

I was told the three boys who yelled insults, accusations, and threats have been cautioned: they will get *an in-school suspension* if they do this again. If he thought this tap in the wrist was intended to make me think something was being done, he is a complete idiot. This harassment and verbal assault has gone way too far. I know several of these kids; they are frequently suspended, and couldn't care less.

"Conn," the VP told me, "has been talked to by guidance three or four times but he just doesn't get it."

'Why isn't the school liaison officer doing something?" I asked, and he went on to make a fatal error:

"The police told the school to go lighter on Conn because of the charge." He said.

I was absolutely shocked, but I tried not to show it. I subtly tried asking some leading questions in hope of finding out more. He suddenly seemed to realize that this was the first I have heard of this absolute bull shit, and he clammed up.

I told him then, "I have spoken to a lawyer about Conn's harassment, and was advised that it is the school's legal obligation to protect my daughter. The school board must have a lawyer on retention, so you might want to talk to that lawyer to clarify the school's legal responsibility to protect Athena."

He was looking mighty nervous by this time. Good, I thought, it is about bloody time.

He asked me then if he could have the school cop call me, likely thinking to pass the buck. I assured him that I would really appreciate it, knowing full well that I would never get a call. (And I was right.)

He then told me that when Athena arrived at school this morning she was accosted once again by the same boys. She was subjected to the same form of verbal abuse as yesterday, although there were *more* witnesses this time.

Athena came into his office then, and she told me that in addition to the verbal abuse, Conn had walked by her locker three times before school had even started, staring at her each time. She took refuge in the science room because there was a teacher there, and she thought she would be safer, but she needed to come home. To say she was an emotional wreck would be a complete understatement.

The VP then suggested it would be better for Athena to finish the year at home, instead of at school. Yup, that's great. She cares about school, always wanted a university education, she's the one being bullied, stalked and harassed, she's the one who has a brain injury and requires additional academic help, and she is the one who is told to stay home.

Meanwhile, Conn and his buddies couldn't care less about school, and once again Conn has his anti-social behavior condoned. This is like some bizarre sociological study in how to create the ultimate psychopath.

When I went to leave the school office, Conn was sitting in the outer area. I deliberately walked by him and stared. I was beyond acting socially or politically correct. I would have liked to reach out and smack him so hard his head would fly off his body. Can this actually be done? My god, I would really like to have tried.

The VP noticed Conn sitting there and quickly moved between us, encouraging me to leave through the door that didn't allow me to get too close to Conn.

Jessie showed up and the three of us went to clean out Athena's locker. Athena was finished at Rivertown high school: bullied right out of an education.

But before we were even done clearing out Athena's belongings, Conn was standing at the end of the hall, watching us. He just stood there staring as we left with all of Athena's belongings.

Later reflection:

I asked Jessie, who had witnessed a great deal of the harassment and stalking, to take note of Conn now that Athena was gone. At the end of the school year, she told me she saw Conn once during the entire rest of the term. Jessie's routine at the school did not change, but Conn's obviously did now that he no longer had Athena to stalk. Maybe he just went on to a new victim.

JUNE 9

Today we finally met with Dr. Rose to discuss the results of Athena's brain injury tests. It seems like years ago she was tested, and in fact it really was a long time; the last test was done the day before she started at the new high school. Two weeks before she was sexually assaulted and sustained another head injury.

The testing confirmed Athena has a very significant acquired brain injury. Her short term working and verbal memory scores dropped from the ninety-eighth percentile, to the *forth percentile; she is now boarder line mentally handicapped in these areas.* Her ability to sustain attention, or focus, scored in the same forth percentile range. While many scores still place her in the superior and very superior intelligence range, she has extremely serious barriers to academic achievement. There will likely be some healing during the next two years, but the extent is a complete unknown. She will need to be retested in grade twelve to determine how much damage will be permanent.

For the interim, Dr. Rose has specific recommendations for educational accommodations. The supports are intended for the time while she is still healing, and will likely change two years from now when she is re-tested.

The recommendations are the only way the playing field can be leveled for her academically, because without them, she will not succeed.

We discussed the sexual assault. She pointed out that Athena has to have extra time to think questions through. She is easily muddled and confused if she is rushed or dealing with multiple questions or directions. A police interview would be incredibly difficult for her unless the police understood and accounted for her brain injury.

I asked if the police had contacted her about Athena's injury results. No, the police had not contacted Dr. Rose. Am I surprised? Sadly, no. For me it just confirms my belief that Delwood is not interested in any facts that may help Athena; his only interested is in doing anything, legal or not (and I refer to inducement, YCJ, and Charter violations) that will help to destroy her. Once again, I don't know what Delwood's motivation is, but what he is doing to my family feels very targeted and personal.

We discussed Athena's return memory, and the emotional damage done not just by the assault, but by the police and the legal system. Dr. Rose, like everyone else we talk to, expressed shock and dismay by the way police have handled this rape case.

JUNE 9-JUNE 16

Athena found it really difficult being at home and alone. She was afraid to use Facebook, her few remaining friends were in school and she was stuck on the farm. Watching Disney movies became an obsession. I believe this was her way to hide from the world. She no longer read, and when she tried to do school work, her constant headaches, fear and inability to focus made it quite impossible. She was terrified, depressed, ostracized, and isolated. Her confidence and self esteem were completely gone. She was afraid to go out in public. On the rare occasion she went somewhere with a friend, she first had to have an elaborate safety plan in place. Calling the police was not a part of her emergency plan.

Once she was no longer attending school, she became even more terrified that Conn would come to our home to kill her. She was eating a lot of crap and doing no exercise. I started to nag her about it and we got into a fight. She said she didn't care if she is fat or unhealthy, what did it matter? Her life sucked anyway.

Eventually it came out that she and her boyfriend were having problems.

I had noticed that the tone between them had changed. I had constantly been amazed that their relationship stayed so strong despite the constant upheaval and trauma. They had been through more than many married couples would ever go through, but there was always a small thread of an issue, unrelated to the assaults. His parents kept him on a tight and ever changing leash. Plans to get together were often abruptly cancelled, or the opportunity for a date may suddenly be allowed. Athena always felt like she was "on call" feeling like she had to be available in case he got permission to spend time with her.

⚖

Out of the blue Athena began talking about being a criminal and wondering how many other people have been, or are, unjustly charged or convicted. How could we judge people, she questioned, based on their interaction with the law, when the law itself is so unjust? We couldn't know if people are truly good or bad by using legal or societal judgments; that would be just as unfair as proclaiming she was a bad person based on what the law and Conn were doing to her.

She started wanting to spend time with a family that caused me great concern: Jill, the girl who said Conn tried to assault her, and her brother. The family was rumored to have moved several times to prevent Children's Aide from taking their children. They reputedly take things that don't belong to them. There are stories of sexual abuse within the family. There are rumors of illegal drug use; something Athena has always been adamantly against. We got into what had become just another of our distressingly frequent arguments. She said these people cared about her and they accepted her, and no one else did. She wanted to go camping with them, and stay at their house.

The boy phoned, and I picked up the call. He sounded exactly like Conn had when he used to call Athena: No phone manners, just "Athena there." No voice intonation, his question sounding like a statement. I flipped out. This caused a terrifying flashback for me. I was horrified. How could Athena not see this? Never before had I infringed on Athena's privacy, but in fear and desperation I listened in on the conversation via another phone. This boy was barely coherent, he was either stoned or of extremely low intelligence. I picked up a lot of sexual innuendoes in what he was saying, but Athena hardly spoke. Occasionally I heard what seemed to be a confused giggle, and I thought it likely that she had no idea what he was talking about. When they hung up, I confronted her, and was honest in telling her that I had listened in. She was livid, and walked out the door, saying she was leaving home, and not coming back.

We had no idea how to deal with this. If Athena went to his home and was abused, who would help her? I knew the answer: no one. She will never go to the police again, and if Sandy ever learned she had been raped again, he would kill that person and then either kill himself or go to jail. I do not believe Athena could emotionally recover from another assault. She would become a statistic of drug overdose or suicide.

We were at the bottom. There was no further down we could go. I could not believe what the world had done to my child. How could police take a victim, and deliberately destroy her: Take a child who had never even had a detention, and turn her into a criminal. How can Canada pretend to care for the lives of children in foreign countries, and treat its own so horrifically?

I had no idea what to do. Even though we were completely on the same side, Sandy and I got into a huge argument. He was past the breaking point, and so was our marriage. He said he just couldn't take anymore. I went after Athena and when I found her I had to make her get into the truck. We drove and I talked through my crying. When I told her of the sexual innuendos I heard in the conversation, and how his voice sounded exactly like Conn's, thank god, she did listen. She wanted examples of the innuendos, and asked me to explain what the meaning was behind the words. I explained, and Athena stayed very quiet. But she did listen. All she has been through; and she is still so remarkably naïve.

She said the boy knew she has a boyfriend, so how could he think she would be interested in him romantically or sexually? I had to explain that simply does not matter to some people. I reminded her that Conn knew this same thing. I was crying through most of the conversation, something Athena had never seen before, and I think this concerned her greatly. I told her how much I love her, how worried we are about her, and how her actions seem so self destructive. She became more responsive. She was not interested in the boy as other than a friend, but she felt really close to the girl. This girl had been assaulted too, and a bond comes with knowing someone truly understands.

Regardless of her lack of interest in the boy, Athena told me she intended to break up with her boyfriend. I didn't think she was thinking straight. He had been her rock through all these months, and I was afraid she was doing something she *would regret for a long time. I tried to get her to wait, to think about it for some time, but the next time they were together, she broke up with him.*

An hour after the breakup she was devastated by what she had done. She said she couldn't live without him, she wanted him back. I felt like Athena was a complete stranger. Before this nightmare began she was rock solid and emotionally very stable. This was completely out of character. I had no idea what to do, how to help. She hadn't slept well in months, she was under unbelievable stress. I had been afraid several times that she was on the verge of a nervous breakdown, but it never seemed so imminent.

I called Athena's friend Jessie, who was with us so often she was like part of the family. She asked me what had changed. I suddenly remembered her anti-depressant drug dose being doubled. I called the doctor and the pharmacy.

The doctor was not so sure the drugs would have this effect, but the pharmacist was very concerned; yes, this was a possibility with the drug she was on. This was a very rare side effect, but a potentially life threatening one. He told me to cut the dose by half immediately, but warned against stopping the drugs completely. Athena needed to be weaned off as quickly as possible; but suddenly would increase the potential risk for her. It had taken about a month for the drug to take full effect, and it could take weeks for the negative affects to diminish. In the meantime she must be monitored for any signs of self-abusive behavior; and she is at increased risk for suicide.

Sexual assault victims have a much higher incidence of every self-destructive past time out there: Everything from smoking, substance abuse, self cutting, suicide, body image disorders and on and on are all of higher risk in sexual assault victims. (From: Women's Sexual Assault Centre at www.vwsac.com/impact-of-sv.htm/)

Add to that being verbally abused and called a liar by people in positions of extreme power, being charged with a criminal act, having the boy who raped and beat you continue to stalk and harass you, and the chance of emotional survival keeps dropping. Then add being socially ostracized, and the fact that the teenage years are fraught with potential risks to begin with, and it seems impossible that Athena's risk factor could get any higher, yet incredibly, it continues to increase.

I am seeing my beautiful and innocent child destroyed before my eyes. And there is absolutely nothing I can do to stop it.

Jessie texted Athena's boyfriend and told him that Athena was suffering from a reaction to the Post Traumatic Stress drugs she had been prescribed. The two eventually managed to patch things up.

JUNE 22

Athena turned sixteen today. She and her friends had talked and planned for this birthday for as long as I can remember. Sweet-sixteen was supposed to be the most amazing birthday ever. But there are few friends left to invite, and the depth of her depression made celebrating impossible. For Athena, this birthday just amplifies how wrong her life has gone. Her life is filled with pain, fear and worry. She is terrified that she will be sent to 'juvie' (the equivalent of jail for young offenders), she has lost so many people she thought were friends, she has no control over her life, has almost no social life, and lives in constant fear. She has no idea when it will finally end; and when it does, if she will be left with the stigma of being a criminal forever. There is nothing that can change the depth of her distress. Instead of being the best yet, it is impossible to fathom anything worse. We give her gifts, and have a cake; family only, and wish we had different lives.

JUNE 23

Athena and I both had counseling appointments today, but Athena doesn't feel up to it. Sometimes I think she is so depressed she just doesn't have the energy to help herself.

Today is another 'court date' in which Athena's lawyer will send someone from his law office to defer the case until he is prepared and can fit it into his schedule. Terry, our counsellor often attends court in support of her clients, and she was in court this morning when the legal representative for our lawyer spoke. She told me the judge demanded both Athena and her lawyer be present the next time court sits in Rivertown, which is in two weeks. At that time Athena will have to make a plea, and a trial date will be set. The noose is just getting tighter...

Under Terry's direction, I drew a lot in counselling today. She asked me to draw what the person responsible for doing this to me looks like; I drew a green warty toad face with scraggly yellow hair for Conn, and a blue face behind him with his tongue sticking out behind to represent Delwood. I see Delwood as the devil himself, whom I believe, enjoys destroying our lives. I made them both appear as evil as I could, because I believe they are both the epitome of evil. Terry then asked me to draw what I would like to see done to each of them. I drew Conn in prison, and someone throwing away the key. For Delwood I showed a police station, and someone pointing the way out of the station as he is fired from his job.

When I was asked to make a happy line, with happy memories, I made it into a trip to Cuba with Athena and I playing in the ocean, and searching for frogs by flashlight at night. It made me cry to remember being happy. When I am in counselling, and no one judges me, and no one gets tired of my tears, I cry, a lot. I need to let it out, or it will kill me.

Terry asked me to draw a picture of myself the day of the assault; I drew me, driving to the school, knowing only that Athena had been raped. I could feel the fear and shock and horror I felt that day.

And then I realized that *I had actually thought that day was the worst day of our lives;* that our lives could not get any worse. I completely fell apart. Athena being raped was only the beginning; it is a rare day when someone does not take another crack at victimizing her; Conn, his friends, the police, and other students. She is now fair game. I have seen this in poultry. A bird will be injured, and the rest of the flock doesn't stop pecking the injured one until she is dead.

Terry asked me what I could have done differently; what I could have done to prevent what has happened to us. I thought of two things. Athena was too caring and too trusting, but the flip side of that is also why she is so special, it is why teachers and friends have always told me they hope or wish their children were like Athena. Secondly, I wish we had never involved the police. I wish I had known not to trust them. I wish I had not taught Athena to trust them. I wish that when I arrived at the school, I had dragged her into the truck, taken her home and told the cops to go fuck themselves.

Then I realized that Athena may not have had a choice in the matter anyway. Once she told the school, it was out of her hands. She just told the police again what had happened. What else could she have done? Said I don't want to tell you to the police? All she did was tell of her sexual assault. This made me so angry I started crying again.

⚖

At home I found another kind of violation. The foxes have found our hens, and discovered they provide an easy meal. I have mixed feelings. The hens that run free are ones that are old and "in retirement". They did their life's work laying eggs for us for a year, and now they are free and without this responsibility. The foxes, on the other hand, need to eat to survive. It is always sad to see something die, but that is the circle of life. We will have to take more care to protect our retired ladies, but we really don't want to shoot the foxes. We believe in karma, and consider the taking of any life very serious.

This brought our discussion around to where Conn and Delwood will spend their next lives, and we were not terribly charitable. Athena wonders once again what she did in her past life to deserve such a terrible one this time. Sandy told her she may be just an innocent victim in the karma of others. If that is the case, it is one hell of a test. Throughout all this, Athena has wanted Conn charged, and wants him to learn and understand what he has done to her life, but she has never wished him harm. While this is the truly good Athena speaking; she also says she is afraid that karma may repeat itself if she wishes him harm, and she says she would never wish the life she is living on anyone, especially herself, again.

THURSDAY JUNE 24-MONDAY JUNE 27

Athena must physically go to the school to write final exams, and I pushed the school to make a concrete plan to protect her from Conn and his gang.

When she gets off the bus, she will go directly to the room where she is to write the exam. Because of the accommodations recommended by Dr. Rose, Athena writes in a quiet room, not in the classroom. The school will allow her to stay in this room until it is time for the bus to take her home. Even so, she went to school with dark glasses and wearing a hoodie with the hood up so she is less recognizable. There was another girl writing in the room as well. They started talking after the exam. This girl had heard that Conn raped Athena, and told Athena that she, too, was assaulted by Conn. She asked Athena if she should go to the police. Athena told her no, she should not. The police might charge her instead of Conn.

CHAPTER 10
Where is Athena?

JUNE 27-JULY 26

Where has my beautiful, caring, mature and responsible girl gone? It is like she is disappearing before my eyes. She doesn't seem to care about anyone; especially not herself. She hurts everyone she loves; I don't know if she is deliberately striking out, or if she is so far gone she just doesn't even notice. I am afraid she won't need to break up with her boyfriend; if this keeps up I expect he will break up with her. I wonder if this is intentional self destructive behavior, like cutting or drug use; hurting others so they will hurt her in return. She is showing signs of being reckless and disrespectful and is not making responsible decisions.

The biggest fear I have is that this is self-fulfilling prophecy: police and her peers have passed judgment and said such horrible things about her so often, I am afraid she may be starting to believe them herself. If she internalizes the terrible things she is told she is, and hasn't the energy to fight for who she really is anymore, she becomes what the world expects her to be.

I miss my child so much. I don't know what to do, how to respond, how to get Athena back. I hate the people who have done this to her. Her anti-depressant drugs have slowly been cut to one quarter of what she was on, but her bizarre behaviors have not changed back, and I am terrified they may not.

She makes comments like everyone hates me, and she can't wait to move and change her name. She is abrupt and angry. I tell myself that this is part of the healing process. She needs to hate and be angry, and god knows she has a right to be. I asked her if she wants to call Terry, but she is says counselling doesn't work. She says no one can change what has been done to her, and she doesn't want to think about what happened, she wants to pretend it never happened. I asked what would happen if she didn't ignore it, and she replied, "I would have killed myself by now."

I live in constant debilitating fear that if Athena is convicted, she will not survive. Hell. I don't know if she will survive anyway. I believe that if she is convicted, she will be broken beyond repair, and the great wheels of 'justice' will not even notice.

Sandy is wound so tight he is ready to snap. He feels absolutely powerless; he believes he has failed to protect his family, and in not retaliating against Conn and the police, is continuing to fail at his responsibilities. I tell him we need him, and we need him with us, not in prison. If he does something rash and hurts people, he will go to jail, and that will simply make everything worse. This is not what Athena would want, and she would suffer even more pain as a result. Thankfully he understands this, but it is at huge cost to him emotionally. There is no way to win.

And so life goes on, and on, and on. We 'survive' on little or no sleep. At best Sandy sleeps only minutes at a time, and the nights are very long. Sometimes I fall asleep, only to awaken an hour or two later. Nights are spent going over and over the nightmarish events in our minds; dissecting for the billionth time the details of each abuse to our family. Feeling like we are under siege, and knowing that we are close to losing everything.

When I do sleep, I hate waking up; waking up is like climbing out of a black hole, knowing that when I reach the top, what awaits me is even worse. Even before I am conscious enough to know I am awake, the shock of what our lives have become overwhelms me. A feeling of overpowering dread fills my consciousness. It is there every moment of every day. All night, all day, it never ends.

Athena hates sleeping; sleep brings terrifying dreams of being victimized and powerless. She dreams regularly of blood, and people watching and no one willing to help her. I slept in her bed with her until we finally decided Sandy would move to the spare room, and Athena will sleep with me in our larger bed. We live life in a trance, holed up in our paradise-come-hell; going through the motions of being alive.

Athena works at the pool, but she often feels exposed and vulnerable there. On one hand, she loves her job, but she is constantly on high alert, scanning faces; worrying about her safety, watching to see if Conn or his friends have found her.

Athena wants to move to the farthest end of the country possible. She wants to leave this area the instant it is possible. We have reached the point we are very serious about moving too. Sandy and I discuss what we will take, and what we will leave behind. We no longer want to spend our lives on the farm we have loved and called home for over twenty years. There are too many terrible memories, and we no longer feel safe. Unlike Athena, Sandy and I are not afraid of Conn; either of us would welcome an opportunity to be alone with him. For us, it is the police. We no longer trust the police, and do not believe we ever will; on any level, for anything.

JULY 27

Today Athena must appear in court. Contrary to what the judge wanted, Mr. Cupito did not attend today, and sent a representative instead. Terry came with us, thank goodness.

The court appears to be a new facility. It is a 'satellite' court, used only one day every two weeks. It is housed in the same building as the police station. When we arrived, there already were people milling about in the hallway outside the court. At the far end of the hall there are small rooms in which lawyers can meet in alleged privacy with their clients. The rooms, and oddly the court itself, have fantastic acoustics, and conversations that should be private can be heard by those waiting or sitting on the single long bench. Because there are not enough seats, someone sat on the wide window ledge, and was immediately reprimanded by a court worker.

It was noisy, and crowded; like a medieval fair. Periodically, a man wandered through the hall advertising his wares; calling out for anyone who needed duty counsel. He was wearing a suit, and running shoes.

There were police wandering back and forth, going in and out of the door at the far end of the hall, first punching a code number into the lock, and then disappearing into what must be a back entrance to the police station.

The lawyers were dressed in dark suits; their clients dressed down, most in jeans and tee shirts, some in sweat pants. Athena and I stood out from the other plebs; out of a remembrance of respect, we dressed as we would for church.

There was a constant stream of people going outside for a cigarette, and the stench of tobacco hung on the air. Outside was a group of five teens, having a smoke and goofing around, their boisterous laughing added to the fair atmosphere. I marveled at how different Athena is from them.

When court was about to start, a police officer rounded people up. We followed the crowd into the courtroom, and took a seat. Far more seats were empty than full, and the constant stream of people in and out of the courtroom never stopped.

We were told to rise when the judge entered, and I was surprised that the National Anthem was not played, and the only homage paid was to the judge. Only when she was seated, were we told to sit. The judge then began a lecture on how fortunate the community is to have this satellite court.

She then instructed us on acceptable courthouse behavior. Rule number one was to stay off window ledges that appear to be seats. Rule number two, to be quiet in the waiting area, thus preventing sounds from disrupting the court.

The court was a random, fast, and impersonal place. My immediate impression was that the judge had a definite preference for the accused to plead guilty: there was an audible change in her tone whenever this occurred; and she seemed to become more amiable.

One underage girl pleaded guilty to an assault charge. This assault apparently occurred as a result of jealousy fueled by alcohol. I was amazed when the judge did not reprimand her for underage drinking, and instead warned her to be more careful when she does drink!

Athena was the only person that day to plead not guilty. The judge then asked her a question and she responded 'ya'. Athena was very soft spoken and this was not done rudely, but I cringed. There had been many people before the judge that day who had sounded much worse, still, I was very surprised when the judge actually reprimanded her for saying this, and instructed her to say yes, your honour. I wondered to myself if this was a bad sign.

The representative from Mr. Cupito's office was not assertive. Although Cupito told us he wanted to reserve four days at the main court in the city of Southland for the trial, the judge instead scheduled the trial for two days in this satellite court. Because this court is only in session once every two weeks, the trial will start one day, then have a two week break before the next scheduled trial date. If the case is not finished at that time, we would be looking far into the future to find dates when the court and the key players are free. This meant that Athena's trial could go on for months.

Once everyone involved (except Athena and I, who are mere pawns in this game) had all checked their availability, the first trial date was set. *For December first. December first!*

We are going to have to live with this horror hanging over our heads for *four more months*, and then we *begin* the trial! We wanted this finished before school started. We *needed* it to be finished before school. Athena cannot even start to heal until this is over. Her wounds are so painful, and so deep, and they keep getting worse because she is repeatedly abused and assaulted by oh-so-many different swords. We wanted it over so Athena could start to heal; so we could all start to heal.

Not only are we looking at the stress dragging on longer, but also at the complete disruption of yet another school semester. The police, the crown attorney, the judge, none of them appear to give a shit what this is doing to Athena. The message I receive loud and clear is that Athena is the bottom of the slime barrel because she has the audacity to plead not guilty. These people, who should care about a vulnerable young girl, care only about power. I don't believe they care whether she is guilty or not; I believe this is far more about us questioning their power by not rolling over and *saying* she is guilty. I believe that their goal is to break her, because she is not willing to lie, and say 'she did it' when she did not.

⚖

Cupito's representative gave us a copy of the latest letter he has sent to the crown, along with another bill for his services. He will now need review Athena's entire file, every paper; every interview. And this of course translates into dollars.

The main points in his letter are:

1) The third interview, in which Athena was arrested, is not admissible in court for several reasons. One, because Athena,

although she requested it was not allowed time to consult privately with me.

2) In the same interview, Delwood repeatedly interrupted my attempts to assist Athena. The reason I was there was to assist my daughter, and as such, I have the same rights that a lawyer would have. I had the right to speak, and Athena had the right to my help; these rights were denied.

3) The position of Athena's lawyer is that her admission of guilt was made as the result of inducement; with Delwood telling me he would not charge Athena if she said the text messages were hers.

One interview, and Delwood managed three separate violations. Just one of these violations would have been enough to prevent the interview from being used in the trial. To have three violations in one interview is outrageous. I wrestled with this concept. How could this happen? To make one mistake I could understand, but three? Three violations do not add up to a mistake, and if it were, why didn't even one, out of all those cops watching Athena being interviewed, point this out? Did they all forget about Athena's charter rights under the Youth Criminal Justice Act? Or did they choose to ignore her rights, hoping she would either just plead guilty or not have the money to pay for a good lawyer?

It is simply not plausible that Delwood consistently upheld the rights of every person he interviewed every day of his career, until one morning–and it just happened to be the day he interviewed Athena–he woke up and decided he would no longer observe the rights set out in the Youth Criminal Justice Act. I think it is much more likely that long ago he ignored (or even forgot to observe), one Charter Right in one interview, and he was not called on it, so he tried it deliberately, and got away with it again! This must have been the case until he eventually reached the point where he ceased to bother about little details like Rights.

Even more disturbing is that to reach the point where he no longer even bothered with the rights of victims or accused, he had to have experienced no negative repercussions. Does this mean that there are no repercussions? That no checks, balances, and punishment exist for cops who ignore our Charter Rights? That can't possibly be the case: Without vigilant monitoring and serious repercussions for violating our rights, our Canadian 'rights' are not worth the paper they are written on; our protection then would be no better than that third world dictatorship you saw in the news last night. I simply can't believe that could be the case in Canada. I believe that The Police Watchdog will be as outraged as we are and that they will impose some form of discipline.

My next shock in reading the letter Cupito wrote to the Crown was the fact that Conn was released unconditionally the day of the assault. Conn was not charged with sexual assault, and there was no restraining order. He was given a green light to stalk and harass the girl he sexually assaulted.

Chompsky told us the day of the assault that Conn would have a restraining order not just to protect Athena, but to protect other potential victims. Not only was Athena completely without protection from Conn from day one, so were other potential victims. This says one thing to me: *there never was a sexual assault investigation.*

I am so fucking angry. I feel completely betrayed, used and lied to. Police are not the solution, they are the fucking problem. We aren't allowed to protect ourselves or our loved ones, but they sure as hell don't protect us. They come after the fact, and if you are still alive, they try and find something to charge you (the victim) with. Welcome to Canada.

Okay, I tell myself. Deep breaths get calm. Cry.

To actually have this confirmed in writing, still shocks me. Now I understand why Delwood was so abrupt the very first time I spoke to him; why he seemed resentful when I asked what had been done to date. This was the reason we weren't told there was no restraining order; why Athena was not treated with compassion or respect in the interviews, and why he kept going on about Conn being such a good boy. *He never did investigate the rape.* He immediately went after Athena. In his mind she never was the victim; she was the criminal. For some reason I can only speculate on, he chose to let Conn go based on alleged consent that did not even exist.

The next item is equally surprising, and further supports my theory that Delwood did not investigate the sexual assault. Cupito speculates that Delwood was investigating Athena, not Conn, when he applied to obtain Athena's text records, and that Delwood mislead the JP by saying the text records were required to investigate the sexual assault. Delwood then applied not just for the three days of texts he told Athena and me he would be applying for, but for the entire month of February; and he ordered *all* of her texts, not just texts to Conn. He also ordered all her phone records. The letter points out that this violated not only Athena' right to privacy, *but the privacy of every person she communicated with for the month of February.*

Cupido's states again that there is no reasonable prospect of a conviction, and suggests the crown drop the charges. The letter also states that there are a lot of witnesses listed in the file, which, if they are all called, will mean that the trial will last at least three full days.

Cupito also suggested that Delwood keep Conn, his 'star-witness' under control.

JULY 28

Sandy and I spent the night talking about our fears, our depression, and how badly we need for this to be over. If only it could be done by Christmas, so we could start the New Year with new lives. I literally ache for this to be over. In some ways, Sandy and I seem to be handling our emotions a little bit better, but when I think of it, one thing I have learned (thank you again Terry) is that every day is different. How we feel today is often completely different to how we feel tomorrow and the next day. This nugget of wisdom gives me hope and the courage to keep going. When Athena is drowning in depression, I remember this, and it helps me to keep perspective. Today Athena may be wishing she were dead, but if we make it through today, surely she will feel a bit better tomorrow....

But today, Athena's emotions are raw and close to breaking. Today she is without hope. Jessie came to visit and told me Athena was 'bitchy.' I tried to explain to her that the trial is not until December, and in spite of what the lawyer has said to her, she is terrified she will go to jail. She has no trust that truth or justice will prevail. Jessie expresses amazement that this is happening in Canada, not in some third world country. She thinks this must be an isolated case. Sadly, I no longer believe this is isolated. Reports of outrageous police acts appear disturbingly often in the media, and I fear that what is reported is just the tip of the iceberg.

Athena is having real problems with the concept of time. She gets dates wildly out of whack with events; not able to differentiate if an event happened a few days ago, or weeks ago. I don't know if this is stress related, or from her brain injury. Life has not been good to Athena.

She spends so much time curled in a fetal position, but today, in what has become a really rare event, she let me hug her. Since the assault she hates to be touched, and will recoil when anyone tries. When she was finally ready to talk, it was about her phone, which she believes has been hacked. Her boyfriend researched the symptoms of a hacked phone, and Athena's phone has a disturbing number of the symptoms. I called the phone company about this, and once they heard the details, they suggested we trade her phone in. When I told Athena we were going to town to trade in her phone, she was instantly relieved. Believing her phone is hacked makes her feel violated again, this time from within her own house. If trading in her phone will ease her overburdened mind even a bit, that is what we have to do. We didn't even think of not replacing it; all three of us needed the peace of mind that came with being able to call one another for help immediately if needed.

AUGUST 4

Athena came home from work very upset. A photographer from one of the local newspapers came to take pictures of the pool staff. Names of the staff would be listed under the photo. Just the thought of her name and photo being in the paper, identifying where she works, terrifies Athena. The fact that Conn had not shown up at the pool is a good indication he doesn't know where Athena works, and she did not want to hand him this information on a silver platter. Every day, all day, she worries that he may learn all on his own.

She told her boss she could not have her picture or name in the paper. But opting out and not explaining to the rest of the staff made her feel alone, but her co-workers don't seem to know her history, and she really doesn't want them too. Unfortunately these 'secrets' create chasms that can't be bridged. The fact that her life is so different isolates her. She is struggling to survive, and for Athena, survival is a serious challenge.

AUGUST 5

After Athena and I had counselling sessions, we went to pick up some groceries. Athena would not leave the truck, preferring the thirty-two degree Celsius heat to being near people. She is deeply depressed, and I tried to talk her into going back on antidepressants. She won't even consider it. She says the drugs stop her from having any emotions, even compassion.

AUGUST 6

Friends that I have not seen for months came for dinner tonight. Alex has been one of the few people Sandy actually confides in, and while the two of them have met for lunch, I have not seen Alex's wife Heather because they live a distance away.

It was beautiful out, and we were sitting out on the porch when we heard a loud crack. It sounded like one of the horses had kicked the barn wall. Sandy and Alex went to investigate.

Sandy's horse, Diablo, had shattered one of the oak boards in the fence. It seemed as if he was trying to get our attention. Gretchen, our other horse, was in serious distress. She had gotten herself trapped under the wall of one of the horse stalls. It looked like she had been rolling, and had slipped under. She was stuck on her back, with one hind, and one front leg on either side of the stall wall. Sandy and I roped her legs together and dragged the thousand pound mare to safety.

She must have been in this position a long time. She was unable to stand up, and was in obvious distress. Finally we got her on her feet, and helped her stagger out of the barn before she fell again. We spread straw beside her and rolled her onto it to make her comfortable.

The vet came and gave her a sedative, we sprayed her to keep the flies away, and that was the extent of what we could do for her. She would either make it or not.

AUGUST 7

Gretchen seems somewhat better. Al, the vet, came again. He fed her twenty-five liters of electrolytes, water and oil through a stomach tube, and gave her another tranquilizer to make her more comfortable.

🜪

Athena is very fearful tonight, and says she is terrified that Conn or his parents are out to kill her. Although she doesn't know why these feelings come on, I find they are usually the result of Conn making some form of contact, either directly or indirectly. If I wait a day or two, Athena will tell me. I believe she blocks the incident from her conscious mind at first, because contact from Conn brings such uncontrollable fear. After a few days she calms a little, and her terror subsides a bit, allowing her to consciously deal with her fear. Only then will she remember and be able to share with me that Conn has made contact. She has yet to make the connection between him contacting her and her resulting terror.

AUGUST 8

Gretchen is dead. She drank a bit of water earlier today, and managed to stand. But when I went to check on her again, she was dead. Diablo is really upset, and we worry about how he will do on his own.

How can things go so wrong, and keep going wrong.

AUGUST 9

I ran into a girl from the first high school Athena attended and it made me realize just how much Athena has changed. On her first day of high-school in grade nine, Athena went with a bright pink streak in her hair. She introduced herself to everyone she met. By the end of the first week, pink hair was everywhere, and she had a ton of friends. She was gregarious and extroverted. She would not think twice about getting up in front of the entire school and speaking. I wonder if she will ever be that person again.

Terry says it is impossible to go through what Athena has gone through and not change. All we can do is pray she will be alright in the end. I miss her so much, it rips my guts out.

CHAPTER 11

Perfect Storm

AUGUST 10

To say I am shocked wouldn't come close to describing how I feel right now. A package came in the mail from The Police Watchdog. The verdict: *improper investigation is not substantiated.* The response is *on police letterhead. This* is what constitutes an independent and impartial review? Investigated, written and determined by a police sergeant? What an utter bunch of trash.

If I disagree with the verdict, I can apply for an appeal. I will only be granted an appeal if I present a good enough case. I will, of course, be appealing.

When I first looked at the response I was completely overwhelmed. The report, not including the cover letter, consists of twenty legal sized pages. My first thought was 'we're screwed.' There was just so much paper. I couldn't help but think they must have tons of evidence. But trying to make sense of this document was mind boggling. It was as if I were reading about someone else's complaint it bore so little resemblance to what I knew had occurred.

I kept reading it over and over. Suddenly Mr. Cupito's words came to mind: The more evidence, the more succinct, and hence the less paper produced. This was anything but minimal paperwork and clarity.

With this in mind, I persevered, and eventually bits and pieces started to fall into place. It was like trying to focus in the near dark; bit by bit ones' eyes get used to the lack of light, and images start to come into focus.

First I saw that there were four police officers cited in the report, though interestingly, there wasn't a word from the school officer. The various people all put in their two cents, and they certainly' circled the wagons to support Delwood.

I started to notice errors. The report didn't follow any order, and times, dates, and events were thrown together in a stew of words. Details were out of place, and as a result, many events came across dramatically changed from what I had experienced, and what I had told Sergeant Holder. Times, events, and even conversations had been blended together. The same fragmented bits of information showed up on several pages in slightly different variations. Several event dates were incorrect.

For example, when Athena was being fingerprinted, I was determined to go in with her and after silent stand-off with the officer, I was permitted to. This event, modified to a fair degree, showed up instead as a part of the third interview of March 30th, and had me in a stand-off with Delwood, which did not happen. On March 30th, when Delwood came into the hall to get Athena, I simply stood up and followed them both in, and no attempt was made to prevent me.

When Delwood used inducement, telling me Athena had to say 'she did it,' the most vital statement Delwood made, had been omitted. When I turned to go back into the interview room, Delwood's final statement, "and it has to be convincing" had been left out of the report. To me, this last statement tells all; he knew she would be lying if she said "she did it" and in order to compensate for that and have it appear to be honest, she would need "to be convincing."

Why had Holder left out the most important part of this event?

There are things I was purported to have said, that I did not say, and very important statements I did say that were also omitted. Since I had been present the only time Athena spoke to Holder, I heard everything Athena said to her. When I read what she is alleged to have said, I was shocked, both by the condescending tone Holder used, and the extent to which Holder had twisted and changed Athena's words. The words and the statements Holder attributes to Athena did not even resemble what I heard.

In the report, the police give an alleged size difference as the reason for pursuing an investigation against Athena. They estimated Conn at between five feet, two inches and five feet, four inches in height, and state (correctly) that he is very slight. Athena they estimated at five feet, eight inches or taller! I called the doctor's office when I read this, because every child under sixteen has their height measured and recorded at every visit to the doctor. One week after the assault Athena measured in at five foot four and a half inches. This is a maximum difference of two and one half inches. And the police are allegedly trained at this stuff!

They ignored the fact that Conn was very active and in great physical shape, and commented that Athena was "athletically built," in spite of being told that she had been unable to participate in any sports (except for her swim lessons) since her head injury, and was not in good physical health.

They state that there was no physical evidence of an assault, and then mentioned that there was blood in her bra. In an attempt to disregard the blood in Athena's bra, Holder says this could be transfer blood from menstruation. Since the police were not interested in conducting a sexual assault investigation, this was never tested or confirmed. How would menstrual blood end up in a bra unless there was some form of struggle? The report fails to mention that Conn bit or sucked her breast very hard, and there was no mention of the lump on her head we found the morning after the assault.

Holder couched many of her comments with terms that render them arguable: "there was virtually no sign of a struggle," and "there was virtually no evidence that Conn had overpowered Athena." This says to me that in fact, there was some. Otherwise, would she not categorically say there was no evidence of a struggle?

The tone of the report is appalling. Athena is repeatedly mocked for informing the police of her brain injury and short term memory impairment, as well as for being intellectually gifted. It is written in a manner that belittles Athena, and makes everything she said come across like the words of a moron without a clue.

As for me, I appear to be public enemy number one. There were a remarkable number of personal attacks on me: "Athena had to compete with her mother's interruptions in order to try and tell the truth." and, "At times it was obvious (To whom? All the cops there for titillating entertainment?) that Officer Delwood was having difficulty controlling the interview due to Marion's interference. Interestingly, I had every right under the Youth Criminal Justice Act, to speak without being told to shut-up. How could Holder ignore the law, and say that Delwood had the right to prevent me from providing guidance to my daughter?.

Instead of solid evidence, the report consists entirely of verbal, unsubstantiated hearsay that had been massaged to suit the police. Given that we had a total of four phone conversations with the police, an amazing amount of what they call evidence is said to have occurred as a result of phone calls, and it is clear that whatever a cop says, is believed by TPW. Sadly, this was one of my concerns, that the police do not need to substantiate what they say, and they have made many, many statements which are not, and cannot be substantiated, yet Holder accepts every statement made by police as being a fact. Impartial report? Bull-shit.

Everything Athena or I say is discounted. There is not one instance where what we say is accepted as the truth or even worth investigating. The words of the cops are accepted as God's Word.

When Bonnie Shepard, asked me if Athena was afraid of Conn, I told her Athena was now afraid of everything, and went on to explain that she was unable to go into the swimming pool, she could not walk alone at school, or go into a store alone. I told her she was terrified all the time. Shepard's response to me was "She does seem traumatized."

Yet this is how it was written in the report: "Marion stated that one of the other investigation officers, Bonnie Shepard had commented to her during the investigation that she believed that Athena was telling the truth about the sexual assault and she agreed that Athena did appear to be victimized by the assault." These were not the words, nor the meaning I had conveyed to Holder. These misconstrued statements are throughout the entire report.

One paragraph talks about Athena's interview on the day she was assaulted: Chompsky stated that "Athena did not sway in her responses." And then several sentences later, still in the same paragraph, and referring to the same interview, states that "Chompsky noted inconsistencies." So, which is it? No examples are given.

There was a lot of concern as to whether Athena wiped the semen off on a sheet or a blanket. I would think that after being sexually assaulted not many people would really care or remember which they used. But this was made a great deal of in the report, and much is made of Athena not being able to say which for certain it was. In spite of this, neither the police nor Holder bothered to contact Dr. Rose, who could have explained to them that this inability to differentiate between a sheet and a blanket was also consistent with her brain injury.

The piece d' resistance is this: "Conn was interviewed, and he seemed to show sincerity." Apparently the key to getting off on a crime is to look sincere. You don't need evidence; you just need to seem sincere.

So based on this, the cops decided Conn was innocent. Based on his apparent "sincerity" they did not do a sexual assault investigation. The names of a number *of famous criminals who were interviewed and let go after showing sincerity, only to repeat some atrocious crimes again come to my mind.*

Conn admitted to consensual sexual intercourse with Athena. (A smart move on his part, but what would anyone expect him to say, 'no, she didn't consent'?)

From the report: "Further, Conn related that he and Athena had been close friends and had planned the sexual encounter in part, using instant messaging technology. Given that Conn had offered alibi evidence in the form of text messages...."

When Conn failed to produce this text, wouldn't it be prudent to then question its' very existence? And then, when the texts were obtained, and there was no text substantiating his claim of sexual consent, wouldn't anyone else on the planet realize they had been duped?

And incredibly, there is not one mention in the entire report of the numerous Charter Right violations, or the violation of Athena's rights under the Youth Criminal Justice Act, regardless that this was one of my main concerns. How in hell could such vital breaches not even warrant a mention?

At one point I gave a great deal of consideration to including the report in this book, but I later learned I do not have legal ownership of the document, and trying to obtain any permission from any part of the legal system proved to be an exercise in being screwed around repeatedly (one request I made took over five months to get an answer to). I also found when I did share the report, it was so overwhelmingly confusing that, like me, it caused complete mental overload.

When I think of this report, the term 'bullshit baffles brains' comes to mind.

I went through the report at least twenty-five times. I started by sorting the information onto a separate sheet of paper for each topic. On one sheet went anything from interview number one, then number two etc. Eventually I ended up with a clearer picture of what the police had for evidence: A big fat nothing. Still, I was still working in the dark. I had no access to the documents, no right to ask questions, and no legal training. I simply tried to cover some of the bases, and I still believed that somewhere, someone with justice and integrity would emerge to correct this atrocity.

I spent many days going over and over the report, sorting information, starting my response and request for an appeal. At times I became furious at the incompetence and blatant bias that brought us to this point. I also spend a ridiculous amount of time angry at myself. If only I had known, if only I had done something differently. No one should have to go through this pain.

AUGUST 17

Athena went horse-back riding last night, for the first time in several years. She enjoyed it, and it seemed to be really good for her.

I woke up this morning feeling "hopeful". How amazing is that?

AUGUST 19

Another smack on Athena. She had been told she would be hired at the indoor pool this fall, but she called the pool today and they have already hired fall staff. The pool manager sent letters out to all the students who did their Water Safety Instructor course at that pool, inviting them to apply. When she called, Athena was told she was inadvertently missed because she had taken the course at a different location; yet she had done her practical hours at this pool. She is devastated. Why does nothing ever go right for this child? She is crying and won't eat, back in the fetal position. She is done with her summer job now, and fall is looming.

The pool manager had guaranteed Athena a job when she was done the course because she was so impressed with her ability to work with children. I can't help but wonder if between guaranteeing Athena a job, and the jobs being open, she heard something about Athena being charged, or she knows Conn's family, and if that could be why she wasn't hired. This is a very tight knit and closely related area. I wonder if this will be the way it will be for Athena now.

AUGUST 22

I am so angry I could spit fire. Mr. Cupito wanted to know what was in the forensic report from the sexual assault centre, and since I wanted to as well, I offered to obtain it. Sandy works in the general area of the hospital, so, as arranged, he picked up the report. My main interest was to see what was documented with regards to Athena's head injury. Incredibly, *I learned that the Sexual Assault Centre did not even check Athena's head.* By now we should be so used to shock we are immune, but we aren't. It is unfathomable that things can go so wrong so consistently.

The document is obviously a standard one used for all sexual assault victims. It consists of thirty-three pages, incredibly few of which were completed. So what the hell were they doing with Athena for so long? One page has the front and back of a head photocopied on it. The intention is for the nurse to map the victim's injuries on the drawing. On the side of the page someone has handwritten a large N/A on it: Not Applicable. I am beyond horrified to realize that Athena was right; they did not check her head. Why was I told they would go over her entire body and document every injury?

They have no idea the amount of grief this has and will continue to cause us. How much did their failure to check her head weigh in the decision to charge Athena? What concrete proof do we have now? While I still believe the police have completely screwed this up, having had the welt on Athena's head documented would have been independent proof of Conn's violence. It is now down to Athena's word that Conn punched her, and Sandy and my word that we saw the evidence.

I had believed without question that there was proof, and that the police had ignored it, but I was wrong. I am so outraged, disgusted and so bloody depressed. I never doubted that this document would clear Athena' name and prove that Conn had injured, and then raped her. I can't believe that these *professionals* completely failed to check her head. The nurse did put a check mark beside "headache" on the report, and they *still* didn't check her head.

This makes absolutely no sense to me. I now know that trauma victims are notorious for having memory blocks. So how many victims leave the assault centre without being thoroughly checked, only to have a return memory in the future of other physical damage not found simply because no one looked? Of all bodily injuries, an injury to the head, particularly under a full head of hair would be the least likely to notice. Unless a nurse actually felt the head to detect tenderness or swelling, they would never find it. And of course, a concussion itself can result in the victim having no recall of the injury. To my mind, failure to have done this simple check amounts to negligence.

If only I had known. If it can go wrong for Athena, it does. My opinion of the sexual assault centre plummets. Dear god, why does everything have to go wrong?

And then I realized; no one checked her for a concussion. Until right now I simply assumed that some form of physical check-up had been done, similar to what I would expect at the scene of an accident, assessing her for bangs and bruises. Sexual assault is, after all, an act of violence.

Did they ask her if she needed her head checked? Maybe, but there is a very good chance that someone in shock might not be coherent enough to articulate this, assuming a) they actually remember the attack, and b) someone actually asks them the right question. Given the mental and physical trauma of being sexually assaulted, a significant number of victims would not remember. Why on earth do they not just check everyone's head?

Obviously, my impression of what was going on that day was completely wrong. I believed that we were being looked after, that we had put Athena in the hands of people who knew what they were doing, who were there to take care of us. I believed that we just needed to trust them to do their jobs. Instead, going to the sexual assault centre and having a rape kit completed has likely destroyed any chance of Athena of being believed; because they did not check her head.

I should have been doing much more than just providing emotional support, I should have been protecting her from those people who are allegedly there to help her. And it hit me: how can any of them be trusted. Cops, sexual assault workers, they all repeat their mantras over and over, "We believe you," "You have done the right thing." And it was all lies. They spewed out completely empty words that they didn't mean. Words they were taught to say, but can't be believed.

Sandy says this entire tragedy is the "perfect storm," with absolutely everything going wrong.

CHAPTER 12

Running on Empty

AUGUST 24 SEXUAL ASSAULT REPORT CONTINUED:

I am disgusted to think that no one; not the police, the sexual assault centre, not Services for Victims; no one told us what to do if we noticed signs of injury. Of course, we still may have not bothered, thinking Athena had been searched inch by inch for injury; and I had called and left messages at the Sexual Assault Centre several times, and never did get a call back. Now I wonder if the Assault Center had been told by police not to bother.

What fools we were to subject our child to such humiliation, only to make the situation worse than if she had not gone to the assault centre at all. They had tried to check her vagina, but even that was an issue because of what was 'likely' menstrual blood, and they completely ignored the rest of her body. How traumatic for a rape victim to go through this to begin with, but to go through it and have the entire humiliating event actually go against you is astonishing. While they neglected to check the rest of her body, the pages that show her external sexual parts were thoroughly documented, and did show redness, a great deal of irritation and tenderness in the vagina, and even outside. No wonder she complained about being so sore.

This would seem to be at odds with the good time sexual encounter the police claim happened, especially since her menstrual flow should have provided lubrication to protect against such rawness and irritation.

I think about the freezer of stored evidence at the sexual assault center. All those people who wanted evidence kept while they decide whether or not to go to the police, and now it seems to me to be such a waste. Athena is right, no one cares.

There are some minor bits and pieces of value in the report, but overall, there is ridiculously little; certainly not enough to have justified putting Athena through such an invasive and humiliating assessment. Hindsight is 20/20. I know now without any doubt that I should have insisted Athena get in the car and come home with me the day she was assaulted. We would have been much better off just throwing in the towel, and at least Conn would not have had his actions actively condoned by police and society.

Athena's clothes had been taken, but it appears they were never processed for evidence. If they were, that part of the report was withheld. Missing too is any reference to there being blood in Athena's bra, yet this fact was in the TPW report. I wonder what other physical evidence was given verbally to the police, but not included in the report I obtained from the hospital.

The report says the "Client remained quiet during the examination process." At the time I believed she was in shock, now I believe she was suffering from a concussion as well. Regardless, she would simply have accepted the assault team doing whatever they did without question; believing they were doing right by her. I should have been in there with her. The guilt I feel right now is consuming me. I really feel like I failed my daughter through stupidity; I should have known better not to blindly trust people.

Now I know I should have documented every single detail. I should have asked questions of every detail, and once again I should never have let the workers be alone with her. I should have taken Athena back to the hospital to have the goose-egg looked at and documented by the hospital. I should have taken pictures of the scratches, and had them seen to as well. And most of all, we should not have trusted any of them with our child's life and welfare.

⚖

Today is the final blood-test to ensure Athena did not contract an STD when she was raped by that filthy little pig. (Sorry, just needed to get that out.) Supposedly this will be the last test, and will ensure she is 'clean'. Something I am not sure she will ever feel again. Her body has turned against her since the assault, or maybe she has turned against her body.

Since she was assaulted she has constant and severe headaches, and difficulty hearing that she did not have before. She has completely lost her sense of smell; she has trouble breathing, and has ongoing and increasing pain in her lower abdomen. She has gained a lot of weight. She still suffers from serious depression, but will not even discuss taking drugs to combat the symptoms. She only vaguely remembers some of the things she went through when the dose of her depression drugs was doubled, but what she remembers frightens her so much she is not willing to risk it happening again. I have told her there are other drugs that may work better, but she is too frightened of the possibility to go there.

AUGUST 25

Sandy has an appointment to see a stroke specialist today, and he is required to take a family member (me) with him. The doctors believe he has suffered at least one small stroke, so we need to learn how to help prevent it from happening again. It seems like the stress of this will kill us all eventually, yet we somehow seem removed from it too. Under normal circumstances, Sandy having a stroke would be a huge and frightening event, and would be foremost in our worries. Right now we are so burned out it hardly registers. We have no more emotion to invest; we are all running on empty.

AUGUST 26

At our appointment with Cupito today, Athena spent the better part of three hours going over the assault in miniscule detail. I was really surprised when I heard this, because when I first saw her, she didn't seem upset at all. Usually even thinking about the event results in either anger or severe depression.

I realized her reaction was just delayed when she suddenly and completely fell apart.

I spent about an hour with Mr.Cupito as he discussed his game plan, and provided me with another bill for his services. The bottom line is another twenty-two hundred dollars, bringing the total to over thirty thousand dollars. What would happen if we could not raise this kind of money?

I picture a cartoon of two parents and their greatly distressed teenage daughter. The bubble over dad's head reads: "We know you were raped, dear, but we just can't afford to have you report this crime to the police...."

We talked about the amazing fact that the charge has not been dropped. I responded, "I wonder if Delwood is just trying to save face."

Mr. Cupito's response was, "He's more likely trying to save his career."

Is it possible that we are living in hell because Delwood is trying to protect his frigging career? The thought absolutely disgusts me. What kind of a person would do this to a young victim just to avoid eating crow?

Mr.Cupito wanted to know *exactly* what was said in the hall when Delwood wanted Athena to say 'she did it.' I think, by the way Cupito was suddenly speaking to me, that he assessing my ability to be a witness.

I began by qualifying any parts of the event that were vague or arguable, and that quickly earned me a lecture. Eventually, after some minor verbal abuse, I got the hang of telling the story in a court-acceptable style. This means no comments about what I thought, wasn't sure about, or speculated on. I found this remarkably difficult, but did my best.

AUGUST 31

Athena's friend Linsey lives on what was, until very recently, a dairy farm. The family is going out of dairy farming, and has sold their cows. As sometimes happens when a herd is dispersed, a few of the cows have been held back for various reasons and not sold with the majority. One of the cows has calved, and the little bull calf seems to be blind. Usually the bull calves are sold to a farmer who raises the calves as veal, but the family is concerned this one will not do well unless he has some tender loving care. So the calf was offered to Athena. Although in past years we farmed and raised cows, calves and sheep, Athena was too young at the time, and does not really remember. She has, to date, not been interested in farming at all.

But she is excited at the prospect of raising this calf. Sandy and I discussed the idea, and decided it may be therapeutic for her. Being responsible for another living being is a huge, but rewarding undertaking. Loving another living creature, we pray, will be a step toward healing.

It is not without it complications: we no longer have calf-sized stalls, feeders or the special giant bottles required to feed this forty-five kilogram baby. We made some temporary modifications, and learned that Atticus, as Athena has already christened this black and while Holstein calf, can already drink his milk from a bucket. We will need to buy milk replacer, the bovine equivalent of infant formula, which comes as powder in twenty-five kilogram bags from the feed store. Atticus will start with just a couple of liters a day, and will build up to drinking eight or nine liters per day. During this time he will also start to eat hay and grain. Eventually we will begin to decrease the quantity of milk until he is on a diet of just hay and grain.

While he is still drinking milk, Athena will need to feed him twice a day, about twelve hours apart. She has decided she will feed him at six o'clock morning and night. In addition to this, she will be responsible for cleaning his pen of the sloppy and smelly calf manure, and giving him fresh straw to sleep on. Calves cannot be toilet trained, and produce an astounding amount of waste, so this will be a big job. Atticus will gain about forty-five kilograms a month, and will be ready to butcher in about six months, at about three hundred and twenty kilograms. As with any animal we have ever raised, we promise him a good life until it is over. A promise very few living creatures, including people, can expect from their time on earth.

Athena is fine with the fact that her baby will not live a long life that ends naturally; she has grown up with this philosophy. This is the reality of being a meat eater. We will front the money for the costs: first the cost of the calf itself, but also the milk replacer, calf starter grain, and later a mix of grains called calf grower. We agreed to provide hay in exchange for her doing all of the barn chores, which consists of feeding the horse, chickens, and barn cats; and cleaning out the horse manure. When the calf is butchered Athena will be responsible for the cost of butchering. She will then sell the meat, and pay us back what she owes. The rest is her profit. We committed to buying half of the meat for the freezer, but the other half will need to be sold. A horse stall has been cleaned out, and Atticus has come to live.

SEPTEMBER 2

Athena has a medical CT scan today to try and determine what is causing her headaches. Our doctor is working through Athena's long list of ailments with patience I greatly appreciate. We are really fortunate to have Dr. Grace as our family doctor.

Athena is nervous and worried about starting school and this is aggravating her depression greatly. I tried to get her to talk about specific concerns so we could think about some coping strategies. She is feeling very alone, and that is the most difficult thing for her to deal with right now. She doesn't know anyone at the new school, and she has come to believe she is not a likeable person. She is so different from the girl she was. Even after her head injury when she first was bullied, she had a level of self-confidence very few teenagers possess. Within the first two weeks at her last school she had already started making friends. This ended abruptly when she was raped. Now her self-esteem is non-existent.

⚖

After countless hours, my letter to TPW requesting an appeal is finished. I feel like it has been a real time crunch to get it done in time. Besides the very short time frame the TPW allows for an appeal to be filed, I am still working completely in the dark. I have tried to learn as much as I can, but I am severely hampered by what I don't know. This case smacks so much of cover up, I hesitate to believe anything I read. I still don't know what was actually in the text messages, and I don't know how they could be interpreted, and I don't know if anyone else texted anything using her phone.

Mr. Cupito has clarified three vital things: there was no plan to meet at all on the day of the assault, there had not been any texting at all between Conn and Athena for a week prior to her being assaulted, and the only consent Conn claimed to have was in the non-existent text message.

In writing my TPW letter, I wanted to cover all the bases I could and make it as self explanatory as possible. I wanted to be able to send it to the media and possibly a civil lawyer and have them be able to follow the events and the issues; hence, the detail.

The entire TPW system is set up in favour of the police, not the complainant. Only by providing the complainant police records, reports, and access to interviews would the playing field be leveled. In writing this appeal I had to decide how to counter comments made by Holder. For example, Holder not only stated that Athena confessed, but that she had offered to write a letter of apology to Conn! This was completely inconceivable to me. I was at that interview, and didn't hear this, still, I had to address some of these bizarre comments, because this was the story the cops were using. I would have focused on the physical differences as the police had, but Mr. Cupito was absolutely adamant that this was a non-issue. He had seen far more extreme physical differences between the rapist and the victim in courtrooms, and the size variation was not even mentioned, let alone been an issue. Interesting that the slight size difference is the only point the police have.

And so, with very limited information, I sent off my letter.

⚖

Dear TPW

I have received your response to my complaint. I am writing to appeal your findings, and have further information to add, as outlined below. I most certainly do want my concerns to go to the next level, hopefully an independent review, as I am not satisfied with the investigation done by the police to date.

Just to review the situation, my daughter, Athena, was sexually assaulted February 15, 2011 by a boy she knew as a friend. She went to the police for help, believing that was the right thing to do. Instead, Officer Delwood, the officer assigned to her case, decided during his first and only interview with the boy, and without meeting my daughter for another two weeks, that my daughter was lying about being sexually assaulted, and further, deliberately set out to mislead the police into an investigation. Athena has been charged with Public Mischief.

My complaints were as follows:

1) *Officer Delwood showed obvious bias toward the boy, and hence did not conduct a proper sexual assault investigation.*
2) *My daughter and I were treated with disrespect- I described Delwood to the police officer that investigated for the TPW as "the ultimate bully" using his power to intimidate and degrade.*
3) *This has completely destroyed the previous confidence we had in the police, and in fact, the police have failed to protect my daughter not just in the case of her assault, but from the boy, Connor Mann who has been allowed to continue stalking her.*

Delwood decided, during the one and only interview with Mann that he was innocent, and the report from TPW on this issue completely fails to convince me otherwise. In addition, I have further evidence to prove this bias existed. From the TPW report, page six: "Mann seemed to show sincerity". Seriously, what kind of policing is this? The reason given was that Mann gave an "alibi," saying that he had consent to sex given to him in a text message. In fact, Conn was released after "being unable to retrieve any messages. Delwood cautioned Conn not to communicate with Athena directly or indirectly, with a strict tone in his voice and they left." (pages nine and ten)

So in spite of Mann being unable to produce the evidence to prove his "alibi," he was released unconditionally. Page six: "Given that Mann had offered alibi evidence (that the police admit they could not substantiate) in the form of text messages between he and Athena and that investigators believed Mann posed no additional threat to Athena (he residing in West County and she in East County)...."

Just the idea that a text message could qualify as an alibi shows a complete lack of understanding of the law regarding sexual assault. I could text you every hour for a year saying

I would have sex with you and that gives you absolutely no right to have sex with me. Prior consent is not admissible. For Delwood to consider this unsubstantiated text an alibi is ridiculous. For Conn to believe that this gives him the "right" to have sex should have made many warning bells go off for the police. How far would Conn push what he chose to believe was consent? Well, I know the answer to that one: To the point of force and rape. Yet once again, Delwood, for some as yet unknown reason, chose to ignore the evidence against Mann.

Conn and Athena attended the same small high school. The garbage about being in another county is just that. Delwood did not put a restraining order on Mann because he believed him innocent. Yet from the first day Athena tried to return to school, two weeks after Mann assaulted her, until the school admitted they simply could not keep Mann away from her, she was relentlessly stalked and harassed by Mann. I spoke to the police about this the first day it occurred, and twice more following, yet the police did not take any action. In fact, I learned in June, after countless emails, phone calls and meetings with the school, that the school had actually backed off from enforcing the provincial act against bullying, at the direction of the police. So much for "Every individual is equal before and under the law and has the right to the equal protection and equal benefit of the law without discrimination ... (15.1 Canadian Charter of Rights and Freedoms)" And how about "to be presumed innocent until proven guilty according to law in a fair and public hearing" (11.d of Canadian Charter of Rights and Freedoms) I would think that any objective and responsible officer would have reconsidered his stance that Conn "posed no additional threat," but Delwood was blind to anything but his unfounded and adamant belief that Mann was innocent. The school admitted they could not control Conn, and could not keep him in class. Athena missed far more days than she attended, was terrified to go to school, and in the end at the recommendation of the school, Athena finished the year at home. This almost cost her the entire semester. With her brain *injury she is simply not able to achieve academically without structure.*

We feel that we have no choice but to send Athena to another school now. She will spend almost four hours a day on a bus. What sort of justice is this? Mann could care less about school, Athena is a student who wants to achieve, and she is forced to leave the school. How do you suppose she feels about the police now? She has twice needed protection, and both times it was denied. What is required to qualify for protection in this province? I no longer have any idea. I have extensive evidence of Mann's harassment of Athena, and will produce it if required.

During the time Athena and I spent with Officer Chompsky, she repeated several times that Conn would have a restraining order against him to protect Athena, and that he would not be allowed to associate with people younger than himself. This did not happen, and we were not informed. Yet under (our legal rights), it appears to me that Athena should have been informed. Unless, as was the case, Delwood had already decided Conn was innocent, and had started to investigate Athena instead.

Why didn't Delwood apply to obtain Conn's text messages? Why did he completely breach Athena' right to privacy and obtain all of her text messages to everyone, not just Mann, over a period of more than two weeks? This would seem a serious invasion of privacy to others Athena had contact with. Or is privacy just an illusion in this country? Why were all her phone calls investigated as well? Why were Mann's messages and conversations not requested as well? This was not to investigate a sexual assault; this was an attempt to get Mann off the hook using my daughter.

Delwood did not investigate Conn, he investigated Athena, and at huge cost to the police force. Delwood was happy to share with me (and Athena' lawyer) the incredible number of hours that were spent in order to find enough "evidence" to charge a fifteen year old rape victim instead of her assailant. And yet, it is my understanding that there is no text agreement to even meet on February 15ᵗʰ, let alone have sex, which shows Mann lied during the interview. And if there were, it would still be a moot point. Only Delwood, and perhaps his supporters at Riverview police, seem to be ignorant of the fact that consent has to be at the time, and ongoing.

Delwood applied for the production order to obtain Athena's text messages prior to March 4ᵗʰ. This means that Athena was already under investigation when she was first interviewed by Delwood. Why then were we not informed? Why was Athena denied her right under the Youth Criminal Justice Act to have a parent present? I expect Delwood will deny this allegation, and say that he was still investigating the sexual assault of my daughter. This is further questionable as under the Victim's Bill of Rights, Athena should have been given the opportunity to be interviewed by a police officer of the same gender. In spite of the presence of Officer Shepard, Athena was not given this choice. She, in fact, did not even know of Shepard's presence until I told her. Delwood therefore either ignored her right under the YCJA, or her right under the Victim's Bill of Rights. Either way, Delwood completely ignored Athena's Charter Rights in this interview. Somehow I would expect that a proper investigation would involve the inclusion of one's basic rights.

Let's tackle that much mocked topic of Athena' injury. I am absolutely appalled at the way TPW has responded to what is, in fact, a disability. One of my complaints to TPW was the manner in which we were treated by Delwood. I complained of serious disrespect and referred to Delwood as the ultimate bully, using his extreme power in a very negative way. The TPW report is remarkably more of the same. It appears there is a far bigger problem if this is considered acceptable treatment of the public, and more exactly, someone with a disability. Our provincial education act mandates that accommodations be made at school so that Athena has an equal opportunity in spite of her disability. I would expect there is some requirement for *accommodation in treatment by the police. I have been in touch with the Acquired Brain Injury Association. This attitude cannot continue in a country that claims to have equality.*

Can you imagine in one day losing ninety percentile points in your ability to focus? How about losing about ninety percentile points in your short term working and short term verbal memory? What if your brain was now rewired so that say, you had difficulty distinguishing between a sheet, and a blanket? How would you respond when faced with severe trauma, and a further head injury? That is what happened to my daughter. It is devastating. It is a huge issue in everyday life, let alone in a sexual assault situation. And Delwood would not even pick up the phone to talk to the psychiatrist. He actually chose to charge Athena instead. He spent a ridiculous amount of time trying to prove her guilt, and absolutely none to pursue the sexual assault investigation.

On page two, Holder becomes a little confused in retelling my "statement" about the sexual assault charge. I don't believe Athena gave consent for a number of reasons (below) but for the sake of argument, let's pursue Holder's train of thought. If Athena were unable to remember giving consent due to short term memory impairment, then she could not have intentionally mislead the police into an investigation. *Should the police not have cared enough to find out? Instead of a simple phone call, they have chosen to destroy a young woman's life. There are absolutely no reasons given in the report as to why Athena' disability was ignored; there are however a lot of extremely ignorant and juvenile jabs at her handicap. I am very disappointed and appalled at the level of discrimination demonstrated by the TPW investigation and police towards those with disabilities.*

Moving on to the third interview, the one in which Delwood arrested Athena for Public Mischief, conducted on March 30th, 2011. Holder found absolutely no problems with this interview, yet this interview has been disallowed in court due to the number of human rights issues.

Delwood informs Athena of her rights under s.146 of the YCJA, and asks if she wishes to consult with a parent. She says she wishes to speak to me alone, and yet he completely ignores her request to exercise that right. It is interesting to note in the TPW investigation report on page fifteen, Holder states that Athena did not ask to speak to me in private. That is incorrect. Were this the only error in this report, or even one of a few, I would understand, yet the TPW report is riddled with errors, omissions, bizarre insertions, and blatant twisting of facts.

We see more of the bullying attitude in the TPW report in response to my complaint about the interview. The entire reason I am allowed in this interview is that I an acting as my child's advocate under the Youth Criminal Justice Act. I am, in fact, taking the place that would otherwise be held by a lawyer. I have the right to speak on my child's behalf, yet I am continually told to be quiet by Delwood, and to once again quote the report, I presented "an aggressive presence" in the interview (page thirteen). This report is full of put downs against me, and in my defense I must say, I actually thought I was very controlled. I would hate to see what they would have had to say had my husband been in that interview. Delwood abused his power as a police officer and an authority figure, and demonstrated an apparent disdain of women. Especially intelligent ones.

The final issue was that of inducement. When Delwood takes me out of the room, what does he say we are doing in the hall? Having tea? He was, in fact, convincing me that if Athena said "she did it" he would not charge her. There is no point in going over my previous account of this incident; I have only to add that Ms. Holder failed to include the second, and most revealing, part of Delwood's statement: As I turned to go back into the interview room following "tea" with Delwood, he added to his previous words of "All she needs to do is say she did it" (page three) with "... and it needs to be convincing." (Oddly, this statement was missing from the report, although I specifically told Holder about it.)

While I realize now I should have seen that this interview was about more than text messages, I did not. Whatever legal garble came out of Delwood's mouth at this interview, I did not comprehend. I was still under the impression he was investigating the sexual assault of my daughter. Following this very disturbing interview, I contacted out family lawyer to ask what public mischief was. The answer was that it covered pretty much anything that didn't fit another law. When I took Delwood's offer of "saying she did it" forward to Athena, I told her she had to "lie, and it had to be convincing." I couldn't tell her to tell the truth, we'd been over that a million times. I had this insane idea that this was some weird hurdle we had to get over in order to get back to the real issue: The rape of my daughter. I certainly was not even thinking of her saying the assault had not taken place.

It was not until Delwood phoned on May 2nd to say that he was charging Athena that I realized he didn't believe she had been raped. Hence my shocked "You don't believe she was assaulted," on the phone to him.

Where did the inducement go? On page fifteen, I believe I am actually blamed for my daughter not having the charges dropped in spite of Delwood claiming he had obtained a confession. "It was decided that diversion or the youth restorative justice program would not work because restorative justice can only take place when the offender admits guilt, (which, according to Delwood she did) accepts responsibility for his/her actions" (according to the TPW report, Athena actually offered to write Conn a letter of apology, page nineteen). She was never given the option to participate in a program, how could anyone say she "was not doing that?" The next part, I believe explains it all: … "and Marion Schuler was still insisting that Conn Mann be charged for sexual assault." So, because of my refusal to believe Athena if guilty, she is being punished. An odd form of justice, to be sure. While Athena would not have gone with the program, and was actually shocked when she read what she allegedly said in this interview This completely supports my feeling that this has become a personal vendetta against me by Delwood.

Have you been unfortunate enough to have a loved one be raped? It was, and continues to be, so glaringly obvious to me that Athena has been victimized that I simply cannot believe the investigating officers didn't see it. I am also surprised that the community officer at the school felt so sure that Athena had been assaulted that he moved the investigation forward, yet the remaining officers did not feel this way. How is there such a huge dichotomy of views? For the first few weeks Athena could not leave my side. She could not go into a public washroom alone, talk to a stranger, be in a crowd or be alone. She cowered if someone came near her in public. It is now six months later and I still have to sleep with her many nights. She hates to sleep; it brings terrible nightmares of being assaulted and helpless. She no longer trusts authority figures, and this has been an issue with counselling. She believes there is little to live for, and often wishes she were dead, although thankfully she says she's "not stupid enough to do it." Once healthy, she is continuously ill, often with "female-type" issues, or fears of STD's. She suffers from severe depression. Her self confidence is gone. I can't remember the last time she really laughed. She is terrified all the time. My counsellor says she will likely never be the same. She has been diagnosed with Post Traumatic Stress Disorder. But never mind, she wasn't assaulted-so how is it even possible for her to have PTSD is no trauma was endured? Surely she deserves a graduate degree for her research skills on acting as a sexual assault victim, and an academy award in acting for her carrying off this act for six straight months.

But why, if she is such an accomplished actress and faker, has she done such a terrible job at lying to the police? I would think if she were truly lying, she would have her story down pat and unwavering. The fact is, she is not acting, and she is confused about what happened. That is not the same as lying. This is very common in assault victims.

Delwood ignored many factors that I raised, and except

for poking fun at them in the report, I have as yet to be given a satisfactory reason as to why he ignored these issues:

- *Athena was menstruating when the assault occurred. One of the first things she asked me was if she could die from being raped while having her period. I do not recall exactly where we were when she asked this, it is possible it was in front of the school officer, Officer Firth. What fifteen year old would choose to have sex for the first time when having their period? Not only that, but Athena is still uncomfortable with using tampons. Even cold logic would dictate that someone who is still so young and uncomfortable with inserting a tampon would never choose to have sexual intercourse while menstruating.*
- *Athena told Officer Firth that Mann ejaculated outside of her body. We did discuss, in Officer Firth's presence, that this meant less chance of STD's, as Athena was extremely concerned about this. She knew Conn was sexually active and gay, and was aware that this greatly increased the risk of STD's. Why would she risk having sex without a condom when she was so concerned? Although she hates taking drugs (she is actually afraid of taking any drugs, even prescription) she chose to take additional drugs offered at the assault centre because Mann had told Athena numerous times he was actively gay.*
- *In an effort to find a motive for Athena consenting, and then turning on her friend and lying to the police, Athena's boyfriend has been named. Yet, if she did have sex and did not want her boyfriend to find out, why on earth would she go to the police. Given that her boyfriend goes to a school well over an hour away, and they have no mutual friends, the chance of him finding out were about nil. Delwood never even asked where he lives or goes to school. He did not care. There*

is an effort to attach great importance to the fact that Athena was worried how her boyfriend would react to her being raped. I cannot imagine too many women that would not have this concern. Yet Delwood chose to see it as sinister. Is any woman who shows this concern considered a liar, or is this selective, based, say, on the officer's first and only impression of the rapist? I also take objection to the addition in the report that Athena is sexually active with her boyfriend. Why should Athena' sexual activity be focused on, and Conn's not? Why would she openly share this information with the police unless she had nothing to hide? This truly is shades of the 1950's police reaction to rape. Blame the girl for being raped.

• *Athena did not tell people she had been assaulted. This is typical of trauma victims. One lunch hour a girl Athena did not really know, and who certainly did not know of Athena' assault, said she had been cornered by Mann and he tried to force her into sex. Athena told Firth about this on March 22. When the police finally spoke to the girl, on April 27th., they asked her if she knew Conn Mann, then if she knew Athena. When the girl asked what it was about, they told her to ask Athena Schuler. That was the end of the interview. Delwood did not ask anything about her problem with Conn, he wasn't at all interested. Jill did ask Athena what this was all about. There have been two other girls that have asked Athena if they should go to the police about Conn. Athena has told them no; they could end up being charged, like she has been.*

I could go on for days about the utter garbage in this report that apparently is intended to prove that Delwood did his job. To me it simply supports my new understanding of what policing in this province is really about, and it's not about honesty, integrity and openness. As much as Delwood denies

*he would say "Conn is a good kid" "Conn is a really nice kid"
and "Conn's mom calls every day, think about how she feels"
he did, and not just once. Every time we talked to him. We did
not know it at the time, but having now (unfortunately) dealt
with a couple of cops, he is the only one who always comes out
into the hall, and closes the door behind him ... and it's not to
offer tea.*

*So, Canadian Charter of Rights and Freedoms, Youth
Criminal Justice Act, Victim's Bill of Rights, Human Rights
violations, likely some privacy violations (I will have to look
into that one) ... a great deal of disrespect, ignoring evidence of
a sexual assault, failing to provide basic protection ...*

*I think it would be impossible to honestly say that Delwood
did a "proper" investigation.*

Marion Schuler

SEPTEMBER 6

Athena's first day at another new high school. After spending her entire
life in one house, and attending only one elementary school, it seems
outrageous that she is just starting grade eleven, and will be attending her
third high school. Yet we still live in the same house she was born in. At
the last minute another bus was put on her route, so she now has a shorter
bus ride than expected. She gets on at 7:45 a.m. and is home about 4:10
p.m. There is also a wonderful thing called "the late bus" which allows
her to stay at school late for homework help, clubs etc. The late bus will
bring her to a town fourteen kilometers from us at 5:40 p.m. Since the
school is about an hour drive one way, this is a great help.

Athena has been worried sick about starting at another new school.
She was concerned about how to find her locker, where to get on the bus
to come home, what would happen if she was late finding her classes, how
she finds out her timetable. She is stressed about things that she would
not have given a second thought to in the past. She doesn't know anyone
at the school, and she wanted me to come with her on her first day, so I
drove her to help ease her worries. This also meant that I could take the
psychiatrist's report and last year's Individual Education Plan in to the

school. The special education teacher made time to see me, and once again I was impressed by this school. We chatted briefly, and I gave her just a really quick and general overview of what Athena is going through. The teacher suggested that I meet with Athena's guidance counselor and a vice principle, and so a date is set for early next week.

Athena came home in an 'alright' mood. She felt really alone and is uncomfortable at lunch because everyone eats in the cafeteria at very long tables. They all know each other, and the social etiquette, and she knows no one and nothing of the school etiquette. Because she is repeating grade ten math (remember after her head injury she failed by four percent, and the plan to do a "recovery" program failed because of Conn). Her lunch period is with grade nines and tens, with whom she shares only one class with in addition to lunch.

SEPTEMBER 7

Athena's godmother is temporarily working out of the same town Athena is attending school in, so they met for lunch today. Athena was greatly relieved to have someone to go to lunch with. It seems in all schools eating alone is the equivalent of having 'loser' stamped on your forehead.

Athena was taken out of class to meet with a support team of school teachers and counselors. At first I was very impressed, but later upset to discover this is because she has been charged by the police.

Athena continued to suffer great anxiety at the thought of eating in the cafeteria, and started to eat her lunch in the library. Once this was discovered and she was told it was not allowed, an arrangement was made for her to eat in the guidance department. It was supposed to be only when she was having anxiety attacks, but she constantly suffered anxiety attacks, so it became an everyday occurrence. Unfortunately she had to sit in the open, where she was seen by everyone passing by. This certainly didn't help quash her feeling a big "L" on her forehead, and she felt like she was on display. So she stopped eating lunch, and went to the library instead. She found the students were friendly enough, but they were already in established groups, and since her head injury, interacting with groups of people has been impossible for her. She feels overwhelmed and confused by group dynamics. Because she felt so inept, she avoided groups altogether. She met a few people; mainly those who did not belong to groups. Fitting in was made even more difficult by extreme stress and frequent flashbacks.

Athena must have seemed very odd to other students; she often had to leave in the middle of class because of anxiety attacks or overwhelming flashbacks, she could not talk about her life, no longer had a sense of humor and never laughed. She lived in fear that Conn would find her and hurt her. She both dreaded and was terrified of her future. She felt, and indeed she had, no control over either her life or her future. Her future was a dark and dreadful hole; her life was not one anyone could possibly want.

SEPTEMBER 10

I had a meeting today with a guidance counselor and the vice principal. When I explained what is going on in Athena's life, I was met with the usual shock. The guidance counsellor asked "So, when is the boy getting charged?"

When I told her he is not being charged, she asked again, "Will the boy be going to court soon?"

Again I replied, "No, he is not being charged, Athena is."

She seemed completely unable to get her head around this bizarre concept, and asked, once again, in slightly different way, "When will the police press charges against the boy?"

She simply could not believe what she was hearing. She thought I didn't understand her question, when in fact she was just too shocked to accept what I was telling her.

The vice principal interrupted her at that point, and in an annoyed tone of voice told her, "The boy is not being charged, Athena is."

The guidance counsellor quit asking, but still looked confused by what I know is an outrageous and unbelievable story.

The VP made one very interesting comment during the meeting: If a student from that school has an acquired brain injury, and the police for some reason wish to interview them, the school makes certain the officer knows of the brain injury. The reason the school does this, the VP claimed, is that brain injured victims respond differently to people without this disability, and their responses may look and sound different. This could result in police wrongly interpreting reactions and responses to questions, and could cause the police to believe the student is not being open and forthcoming.

Of course I left wondering if this could be the key to why my daughter was charged.

The school seems very pro-active, and very concerned about Athena. Supports have already been put in place for her academically as well as emotionally. I am shocked by the level of support. I am bringing a terribly broken child who will require incredible amounts of support just to survive, let alone heal, and they are accepting the challenge without question. When I voiced my appreciation, I was told that this is what they do. Everyone who needs support at this school will get it. This is so different from the other two high schools, where there was no help, not even protection from the boy who sexually assaulted her.

SEPTEMBER 15

As always, I can't help but notice the anniversary of the assault. It has been seven months. Seven months of hell. I reflect on the legal system, and how it rewards those who plead guilty. But what if you aren't guilty? The police do such a crap job of determining who to charge, there must be many, many others who are charged when they are obviously not guilty.

We tell Athena constantly that the outcome does not matter, and we mean it. But to people such we used to be, it does matter. For us now it is a terrible conflicting combination: horrifying, shameful, and irrelevant all at once.

We know we must convince our child that the justice system is a meaningless sham, and we must do this in order that our child will survive. It is not easy to convince someone like Athena, who has always had complete faith and belief in the law, but with her fear and distrust of police, she is getting there. In Canada a conviction does not necessarily mean that the person committed the crime. It could also mean either their lawyer did not win, or they rolled over. The entire system is set up to reward those who plead guilty.

SEPTEMBER 20

After talking to my brother about the outrageous actions of the police, he convinced me to send a copy of my TPW appeal to a very well known criminal lawyer. I had written the appeal with the thought that I may use it for other purposes, such as this, or to send to the media, so I added an introduction, (below) with the appeal to TPW as an attachment:

Dear Sir,

There is not a person who knows of this case that has not expressed outrage and disbelief that this could happen in 2011, and in Canada. On February 15th, 2011 my fifteen year old daughter was sexually assaulted by a boy she thought was a friend. The very day the assault took place, and without even meeting my daughter, the officer in charge, Delwood, decided the boy was innocent. The "alibi" given by the boy, and accepted by Delwood, was a text message allegedly agreeing to have sex. He failed to produce the text, yet was released without any conditions. We did not realize the sexual assault case was not being investigated for many weeks. We now know that Delwood set out immediately to "prove" my daughter Athena lied about being assaulted. Evidence was ignored, as were a remarkable number of her Human Rights. The assailant, Connor Mann, harassed and stalked Athena following the assault to the point she could not attend school. The police refused to respond.

Athena suffers from an acquired brain injury. Her short term visual and short term working memory scored in the forth percentile; borderline mentally handicapped. Yet she is also identified as intellectually gifted, as scores that are not affected by the injury are still in the ninety-eighth percentile. Her ability to express what happened that day is confused, and she is unable to remember some details. The police refused to contact the psychiatrist that diagnosed Athena's disability. I filed a complaint with The Police Watchdog. In the response from TPW, the entire idea of Athena having brain damage is ridiculed. Given the current media focus on acquired brain injuries, I find it impossible to believe the police are unaware of the devastating reality of brain damage from injuries. I believe that Delwood showed bias toward Mann, and failed to conduct a proper investigation.

The lawyer defending Athena in the Public Mischief charge is constantly amazed the case is going forward, and says there is no evidence to substantiate it. He contends that Delwood is now fighting to save his career. At the expense of my daughter. This has almost destroyed Athena, and my family.

We taught Athena to respect and believe in the police, and instead of their help, she has been further victimized. I am hoping you will help us in a civil suit against Delwood, and/or the police to ensure justice for both my daughter, and future victims.

Thank you for your consideration,
Marion Schuler

CHAPTER 13

The Kindness of Strangers

SEPTEMBER 21

When I checked my email this morning there was a response from the partner of the lawyer I contacted yesterday. In my new ever-paranoid state, I Googled his name to verify who he is. The lawyer I contacted is a criminal or defense lawyer, and his partner practices civil law. I realize now this is the type of lawyer I actually need. If I want to sue someone, it is a civil suit, and hence a civil lawyer. I do feel a bit stupid not realizing this before, but hey, I used to be an upstanding citizen from an upstanding family, and I didn't think I needed to know this stuff. How fast life can change.

Through email we arranged a time to talk on the phone.

From this man I learned that there are only two possible charges that can be brought against the police: Negligent Investigation, and Malicious Prosecution. The first three criteria are the same for both:

1) The person who is suing must be the person charged with an offence, which means Athena would have to be the one making the claim

2) The charge against her must lack reasonable and probable grounds

3) The outcome of the charge against her must end in favour of the accused, i.e. Athena has to be found not guilty

To qualify as malicious prosecution, the first three criteria are the same, but with one addition; the primary objective in laying the charge was not that of upholding the law; the police must have acted in malice.

He explained that in Canada it is very hard to win a suit against the police, and that even if successful; settlements are a fraction of what we hear about in the United States. He told me that the most successful suits in Canada are several hundred thousand dollars, and only recently have legal costs been added separately onto settlements.

We agreed to talk again when the trial is done, and I have obtained a trial transcript. I am adamant that I want Delwood to pay for what he is doing to us, and I conclusively believe that he acted in malice.

I am very grateful to this man for taking the time to explain all of this to me.

⚖

I also received a letter today from The Police Watchdog, accepting my application for a review. I was told that I can provide more information if I have any, and that it will be some time before the review takes place. Apparently, the information will be assessed by a 'review panel'.

I want to feel hopeful about this, and I think I do. It is impossible for me to believe that blatant bias, telling Athena she will not be charged if she lies and says she "did it", completely ignoring legislated rights, and treating people the way we have been treated is acceptable in Canada. Yet in saying this, I can't believe the Police Watchdog investigator considered what Delwood did to be a proper investigation.

⚖

Athena was having the odd 'good' day at school, but there are huge challenges. While the school is in some ways very supportive, I am constantly pushing teachers to observe the educational accommodations set out by the psychiatrist. Sadly, the recommended accommodations are generally interpreted as giving Athena an unfair advantage, instead of an equalizing measure. No matter how many times I explain the reasoning, I still get resistance from her teachers, but without these accommodations, I have no doubt Athena would fail, and quit school in frustration.

The high school years are such a critical time in a child's life, that to condemn Athena as unable to succeed would undermine her entire future. Yet, I am constantly intervening when teachers make comments claiming they need to mark Athena harder to be fair to those students who do not have an acquired brain injury. If Athena does not recover, she will not be attending university; and if she does recover, it would be another tragedy to have eliminated the possibility of university by not providing what she needs while she is healing. In all but one case, teachers seem to balk if she does well, and believe she did well entirely because she had an unfair advantage. The general belief appears to be that because she is academically accommodated, she should prove her need by barely scraping by. But in fact, she should do well, many of her psychological test scores are still in the gifted range in, and had she not suffered the injury, she should be achieving marks in the mid eighties or higher.

At the time I met with the psychiatrist, there was so much going on in our lives that Athena's brain injury took a back seat. Suddenly we are seeing the full extent of the damage, and the scope and depth is shocking. It was once a guarantee that Athena could accomplish anything she set her mind to, but that has completely changed. Her memory actually seems to have gotten worse since she was last tested, and she seems even less able to focus. She is having difficulty in all of her classes.

On an interesting note, we learned that the high school where Athena sustained her initial brain injury now exempts students who have had concussions from writing tests. That Athena was failed in math at that very same school, and given absolutely no help really upsets me. Her head injury and the lack of concern by the school where it occurred is what started us on this nightmare. Am I bitter? You bet. The complete lack of support was the entire reason we moved Athena to Rivertown high-school, and had she not moved, she would not have been raped.

SEPTEMBER 25

I am feeling somewhat hopeful for the first time in a very long time. I know Athena is feeling fairly safe at that school, and except for being very, very lonely, she is getting by. The bus ride is a social challenge, and she is still unsure of where she should sit. She makes a lot of comments about the bus, but overall says the people are friendly and it seems 'like a family'. She is, however, very disturbed by the use of the word rape, both on the bus and at school, where the term is used completely out of context to give a statement emphasis. She says the word is almost exclusively used by girls, and the example Athena gave me was, "He totally raped my binder," which interpreted means, "He scribbled all over my binder".

Every time Athena hears the word rape it fast tracks her to a flashback, and she is incapable of stopping it. It really emphasizes the chasm that lies between her and her peers. She has experienced so much horror in the world already, and they are like ignorant babes in the woods.

SEPTEMBER 26

When talking to the Special Education Resource Teacher today I commented that Athena is feeling quite safe at the school. Unfortunately, I spoke too soon. Athena came off the bus in terror. She had already heard from people on the bus that a guy named Connor Mann had started to make Facebook friends with a number of people at the school, but now he has posted a message on his Facebook page saying that he and some buddies have obtained second hand school uniforms for Athena's school. For Athena this means only one thing; that Conn will be disguising himself and trying to get into the school to hurt her again. Since she learned that Conn owns a hand gun, her fear now includes him hunting her with a weapon. When she heard this, she immediately went to the vice principal and told her, but she felt that the principal did not take the situation seriously enough. Athena explained that Conn may do to someone else what he did to her, and she could not allow that to happen. Athena is constantly plagued by feelings of guilt and failure in addition to everything else because she has been unable to do anything to stop Conn from assaulting someone else.

SEPTEMBER 27.

Here we go again. Athena is too sick for school. How much of this is her fear of Conn? What a freaking bastard. I am so pissed off; I wish I didn't have a conscience, and then I really could kill him. Alas, I can not; all I have are my dreams.

Athena and I spent a lot of time talking today, trying to work through her fear. I couldn't go to work, because she was too terrified to be left alone. I finally got her to realize that this new school will take it very seriously if Conn shows up there. They have a security guard on staff, and he has been told what Conn looks like. It is a small school; he would be noticed, and he would not get away with it.

SEPTEMBER 28

Athena went to school, but the stress is glaringly apparent. She's wound tight enough to snap.

SEPTEMBER 29

The school called to ask if I could pick Athena up early. She completely broke down. One upset was that she failed an English test, but her overwhelming terror was caused by an intruder alert at the school. Although we were never told one way or the other, Athena was terrified that Conn had come to hurt her. She is very, very near the breaking point.

SEPTEMBER 30

Athena and I met with Cupito today, and as usual, I learned some remarkable and disturbing things:

Until now Mr. Cupito had only read the police report describing what was said in the third interview. Since we last saw him, he watched the third recorded interview himself. *He found if he wore headphones he could hear quite clearly what was said in the hall outside the interview room when Delwood took me out and told me that if Athena said 'she did it' he would not charge her.* Mr. Cupito confirmed that just as I had told him, Delwood did not actually come straight out and tell me to lie, but it was certainly implied. So, why was The Police Watchdog's Ms. Holder unable to hear the inducement? I expect she didn't want to.

Because the conversation in the hall could be heard so clearly, there is now a chance that I will be called as a witness to this event. If I am called to testify, I will get to see the tape, something I am adamant I want, not just for this interview, but for them all. Sadly, the law prohibits me from seeing them except for reasons like this.

Cupito himself had been surprised when he watched the interview, because, contrary to what Delwood had written in his notebook, Athena did not confess. Not once.

My conclusion is that Delwood lied about the confession in his notes. So is it because of Delwood's lies the crown attorney has pursued this prosecution? My god, the hate I feel for Delwood is unbearable. I feel more hate for this man than I have felt in my entire life. How many other innocent lives has this man destroyed?

As a result, Cupito will talk to the crown and suggest that although the third interview can't be used in court, he should watch it and see for himself that Athena did not confess.

I voiced my concern that the judge may be adversely influenced by the knowledge that this interview has been removed from the trial. Will she know it existed at all? If so, will she think it contained something incriminating, and that is why we had it removed?

As it turns out, the crown has pulled the second interview themselves. And I wonder if that is because there is nothing in it? Or because it presents a picture of a cop with no morals or integrity? The lawyer tells me it doesn't matter; the judge cannot use the information as a part of her decision either way. Still, I believe people can be swayed by what they are led to believe.

Mr. Cupito has also watched Conn's interview, and he made several comments. Conn *did not* say in his interview that the sex was consensual, (contrary to what is in the report from The Police Watchdog). In fact, it appeared to Mr. Cupito that Conn had no idea what the word 'consent' actually meant. According to Cupito, Conn's interview was very poor, and Delwood did not push him at all. Conn told several versions of what happened, and his story was extremely inconsistent. The only time Conn claimed to have any form of consent was when he said the two of them had planned in a text message, to meet and have sex that day. And that ship sailed when the texts were received and it was proven not to exist. The lawyer is completely confident he can shred Conn's story on the stand.

Athena had one request: She wants to see Conn cry. Mr. Cupito said he will do his best.

OCTOBER 2

Another melt down. Athena spent all day trying to study for an exam. For hours she tried to memorize, and the harder she tried, the more confused she got. She wants to succeed, but just can't, and ended up angry and severely depressed. Again I tried to talk her into going back on depression medication; once again she adamantly refused to even consider it. She says she would rather feel the pain than be emotionally numb the way the antidepressants made her feel.

It's devastating to see her like this. We have been told students are only allowed fifteen days of absence at this new school, and we are already on day three. She has upcoming medical appointments, lawyer appointments and a criminal trial. God knows how many days she will end up missing. It all just adds to the stress.

☖☖

When Athena returned to school, some sort of social worker was assigned to talk to her. Athena, perhaps because of her recent terror at the school, told her story to the worker. The social worker's response, according to Athena, was, "Document everything, and if you do get killed, I hear heaven is a nice place."

Athena refused to meet with her again and this just reinforced her reasons for not talking about the assault: No one cares.

I wonder, and hope, that this was a miss-communication on someone's part, and not the actual way it occurred.

OCTOBER 5

Thank goodness Athena and I both had counselling today. Athena seems a little better after, and I have a bit of positive perspective back. I have been fairly disturbed by the idea that Conn didn't know what consent was, and needed Terry to help me get my perspective back. It really doesn't matter if he doesn't know the term; he had no right to commit a violent act, no right to force Athena, no right to hurt her. I spend a lot of time thinking about how poorly we raise sons in our culture if they do not even know such basic right from wrong.

OCTOBER 7

Sandy's birthday. Somehow special days just make us more depressed. Athena discovered Facebook messages to her boyfriend from a girl that seem to cross the line. The problems between he and Athena appear to increase all the time. I think about how much they have been through together. At times I am amazed it has lasted this long, and I am really worried what her emotional state will be if they break up. In many ways he has been her rock.

Sandy is having issues at work, and I just wish I hadn't been born.

OCTOBER 8

Thanksgiving. We are trying to be thankful, but it isn't easy. Athena now believes that if there is a god, he has turned his back on her, so she finds it easier not to believe at all.

Athena's boyfriend was supposed to spend Thanksgiving weekend with us, but in the end showed up for only a few hours on Sunday night. Next weekend's plan to get together was also cancelled. They seem to be constantly making plans and then more often than not he cancels them, often at the last moment. I see the writing on the wall. He needs freedom, and she needs someone who comes through for her. I see a breakup looming, and he won't understand why it happened. Athena says she has given up trying to talk about the problem because he gets defensive, and Athena avoids confrontation like the plague. Sandy is worried sick about how Athena would handle a breakup.

OCTOBER 11

I picked Athena up from school before noon to take her for a pulmonary test at Southland hospital. This is another of the ongoing physical issues that have cropped up since she was assaulted. She constantly feels like she can't get enough oxygen, and she may pass out. I know at least some of this is stress induced, but it takes a very real toll on her body. I expect we have all lost several years of our lives. The test shows no pulmonary issues, and it is likely brought on by extreme anxiety.

OCTOBER 12

Terry talked to Athena today about the trial; what to expect and what the protocols are. She has asked Athena to think about whom, if anyone, she would like to have with her for support. Terry has offered to be there, and says that the staff from Hope House would also like to come and show support. Without any hesitation Athena said she would like them to be there. The women who work with Terry have followed this story from the beginning, and want to show how they feel about police charging a sexual assault victim instead of an accused rapist.

Athena will also ask some of our family friends, as well as her own friends if they would come to support her.

OCTOBER 14

Athena had another breakdown during a test at school, and the guidance counsellor called again to ask about the injury, the assault and the charge against her. As always the school wants to know if she is getting that magic bullet: counselling. They can't understand how she can be so fragile if she is getting counselling. They don't understand that she can't even begin to heal until the legal system stops victimizing her. I guess they just have to believe there is something that can cure the pain. I don't believe there is.

OCTOBER 18

Our German Sheppard/Boarder Collie cross dog, Timmy, has been having more and more problems with mobility. He has been on pain and anti-inflammatory drugs for a several years now, but they are no longer enough. The last few days he has gone outside only to do his business, but today he could only get up with a lot of assistance. He stopped eating yesterday, and he is very obviously in pain. It is time.

I knew it was coming, but I am really going to miss him, and it just seems like there is no end to pain in our lives. I am far more upset than I expected to be. Tim is a very nervous dog, and he is afraid of the vet. I want him to go peacefully and without additional pain or fear, so after talking with the vet, I went and picked up some pills from the clinic.

The vet called when he was about to leave the clinic, and I immediately gave Tim the pills to sedate him. By the time the vet arrived, Tim was very sedate, and he went easily into death. I think I am so upset because Tim was never a happy dog. He came to us from an abusive home and was always nervous and worried, but he was loving and obedient, and a perfect companion. It bothers me even more because he was still in full control of his mind; only his body has failed him. Still, if I were in his place, I would be thankful to have my suffering ended.

Our vet is a gentle man who genuinely cares about his patients. I know he hates to put an animal down, and he does it with total respect. I held Tim when the time came, and I know that there were tears in the eyes of everyone there. Tim will be missed greatly.

God I'm tired of all this pain.

WEDNESDAY OCTOBER 19

It really will take some time to get used to Tim being gone. In some ways it is calmer; I realize now how much I worried about him, and how vigilant I always had to be to make sure he was not in too much pain; that he could get up and down the steps safely. His beloved teddy bear is a reminder that stayed behind. We buried him on our property along-side Gretchen the horse and our beautiful dog Spike, who Tim had grown up with. I have no idea how Athena feels about this. She won't talk about it, and did not want to be here when Tim died. I can only guess that denial is a safety net for her right now that prevents her from falling even further down, and I wonder how close to rock bottom she really is, although I guess none of us know until we hit it.

Athena talked openly for once about how much it distresses her to hear the word rape used jokingly at school. It took a long, long time to get her to calm down. I wanted so badly to hug her, but hugging is still far too close a contact, and causes her more upset.

She was finally exhausted, and fell asleep in our bed.

OCTOBER 20

Meet the teacher night. While the teachers seem concerned, two of them commented that they had to mark Athena harder because she has open book exams, and they believe this gives her an unfair advantage. I tried to explain that it is almost impossible for her to remember where in the book an answer is, let alone memorize specific information. They really don't get it, and I'm really getting tired of fighting it all the bloody time.

OCTOBER 21-OCTOBER 30

I am having sudden and overwhelming anxiety attacks, and I know Sandy's emotions are already like fractured glass; one touch and he will shatter. I can't really imagine how stressed Athena is.

Several of Athena's friends got together to watch horror movies in celebration of the Halloween season. We tried to talk her out of it, but she just wants to do something normal, and wouldn't be swayed. They had a good time, but as we expected, it left Athena very disturbed. Horror movies and Post Traumatic Stress Disorder do not go well together. She is afraid to be in the dark, to sleep alone or to shower downstairs if we are not there. Several days later, just as things were starting to calm down from the horror flicks, her English class watched the movie "Frankenstein." They had read the book, which was not too much of an issue, but in this movie version, Elizabeth has her heart torn out while she is still alive, and in an attempt to overcome the pain, tries to set herself on fire.

More school and more sleep were missed over this event.

Unfortunately she woke up the next morning with a severe stomach ache. I freaked out because she is missing so much school. I knew there were stomach bugs going around, but she was also scheduled to go on another field trip the following day to the art gallery. Although Athena is trying really hard to be successful at school, it is a never ending, uphill battle.

In the end she stayed home sick that day, but went on the field trip the next day. She found the art very disturbing. The main art exhibit seemed extremely violent to her, and she came home very distraught. Her emotional state is so fragile, and (I pray) we are at the peak of the Post Traumatic Stress. We are always terrified that she may get worse, and if she did, what the hell we would do. There is always that haunting fear that never ends, never goes away... she says she is 'not stupid enough' to try and take her life, but what if it is just a matter of degree? What if she reaches the point where death looks brighter than her life? Would we know? Would we recognize it before it was too late? Although we pretend it isn't possible, inside we are always on high alert, because we know it is.

OCTOBER 31

Athena slept alone last night for the first time in weeks.

It has been impossible for Athena to remember even the simplest of directions, decode information of any depth, and memorize literally anything. If we ask her to do something, it has to be one step at a time. Giving her more than one inevitably means she gets muddled and confused, no matter how simple the instructions. We decided to take her to Dr. Rose again; in case the blows Conn gave her did more brain damage.

The first words from Dr. Rose were, "Athena can't have lost more of her short term memory or she wouldn't remember her name." She believes the problem Athena is having is the result of the incredible and ongoing trauma in her life.

Dr. Rose is very perceptive. As she and I were talking, I noticed her watching Athena, who did not seem to be mentally with us. Dr. Rose says that whenever Athena is at school or in public places, she vigilantly scans her environment, searching for potential danger or threats. She is always on high emotional alert, terrified. In the rare times she does feel safe, she shuts down, completely exhausted, and that was what we were witnessing.

I realize that I see this constantly at home, but had no idea what was going on. It certainly explains why she has so many problems with school. The need to feel safe must completely override her ability to concentrate on anything else.

Dr. Rose also picked up on the helplessness Athena feels, and encouraged her to find her voice to say how she feels about Conn, Delwood, and the legal system. When she commented that many victims feel guilty when their assailant is still out there and may harm someone else, Athena broke down and cried. Apparently this is a common, if futile, feeling. Athena does feel responsible that she could not stop him, and we all believe he will rape again. Dr. Rose told Athena she is not the one who is responsible, and that led to a discussion about the police.

As always, there is a great deal of incredulity that the victim is being blamed for the crime. I promised I would let Dr. Rose know the outcome, and we left with new and reinforced academic recommendations for the school that will hopefully help Athena to survive the school year.

CHAPTER 14

The Trial of Athena

As the trial date grew closer, the stress grew exponentially. We were far beyond functioning, stressed to point where, if one more thing happened; any one of us would have snapped.

We tried to encourage Athena to sleep on a futon in our bedroom, but that wasn't close enough. She had to be with me. She was sixteen years old, and so afraid to be alone, she could not sleep if she were not. She was terrified that "someone" would come in and kill us during the night, and the logic that Conn and his family were unlikely to do this since she was the one being prosecuted, made no difference. Her fear was so profound, logic could not touch it. When she would start to fall asleep, she would suddenly jerk awake from horrific nightmares, and that would end any chance of sleep that night. She would try not to fall asleep, so she wouldn't dream. The nights were very long.

Sandy handles stress poorly and tended to over react to everything and anything. This would set Athena off, who was already walking on the razor's edge. I felt like I was always in the middle, trying to soothe everyone until I just could not take any more, and I wanted badly to break something.

The exceptional stresses and complete lack of sleep made school impossible for Athena. Work for me was a rare event; dependent on Athena's emotional health as well as my own. Somehow Sandy managed to get to work most days, but he was walking on the edge. He was unpredictable, irrational, and snapping angry.

Athena and I met with Mr. Cupito several times before the trial. Athena *approved of him from the beginning; she then had a brief like/dislike relationship with him when he pushed her to prepare for trial, but by November she was very confident he had been the perfect choice. He seemed to be able to calm her fears and concerns when I could not, something that hadn't even crossed my mind when we hired him, but turned out to be a godsend.*

Cupito is an interesting man. I expect people meeting him for the first time might underestimate him; and it is not that he doesn't appear competent, but that he is even more competent than he appears. He takes his time in court, makes notes to himself seemingly at his own bumbling speed, asks innocuous questions, and then goes for the jugular. I was told by a number of friends who came to the trial that the judge was unduly quick to reprimand him. It was believed she did not like our lawyer. I was told this contrasted completely with her treatment of the crown attorney, who, I was told, got away with the ridiculous in court.

As I write this, our first trial date is over. We don't have the verdict, and to our utter dismay will not until January 24th, 2012. One hell of a wait, and there goes Christmas. It will be one month short of a year before Athena's case is settled. My thoughts on small town satellite courts are simple: they should be eliminated. While our first trial date was December 1st, the second day of trial was not for another two weeks. Court is held in the small town of Rivertown once every two weeks, which means a trial held there could take months. How accurately can a judge remember what went on if there are numerous other trials, and several months between the start and the verdict? How could it possibly be in the best interest of anyone to draw out a trial for this length of time? And most of all, if other satellite courts function as the incestuous little family unit this one appears to, they need to be gone.

DECEMBER 1

First trial date. An event I never in my life expected to be writing first-hand about. We didn't bother pretending to sleep last night. Athena's facial muscles are so visibly tense she looks like her face is about to shatter. She is terrified she will be sent to prison. Cupito has told her this cannot happen, but Terry says that given the unprecedented bizarreness of all that has happened so far, it seems anything is possible. Considering the assault was ignored, Athena was charged, and the nightmare has continued in spite of what everyone believed would happen, proves that we cannot count on anything, and Athena needs to be prepared in case the worst does happen. We are charting new territory in the unbelievable department. And sadly, the worst case scenario seems to be Athena's lot in life.

We have decided that Sandy will stay at home and keep the home fires burning. Having had a stroke already, however small, is testimony enough to the extent of his stress, and I could see him having to be carried out of the courtroom either because he has a massive stroke, or he loses his very tenuous grip on his emotions and is charged with contempt or assault. We opt for a tidy house and supper ready when we get home. His presence at court would be another worry for me, overwhelming for him, and a huge issue for Athena if he did lose control in court. This is one small concern we can control.

Athena's older sister, a few close friends of Athena, and some of our friends are coming to support us. A number of Terry's co-workers from Hope House will be there as well. These counselors often attend court and trials in support of the women they assist, but usually the women they are supporting is the victim, not the accused. In this bizarre case, the victim has become the accused. They are deeply concerned by this, and are hoping their presence at the trial will make this clear to the legal system.

Just prior to the start of the trial, Mr. Cupito decided he might call me to testify, both about the goose egg on Athena's head, and the inducement offered by Delwood. Being a witness meant that I would not be allowed in the courtroom where I would hear other evidence, and possibly be influenced by it. And so I was banished to the hall for the first day of the trial. Terry stayed with me, and for far too much of that time Delwood was there.

I am eternally grateful to Terry for her support. It would have been unbearable to be banished to the hall alone while Athena was inside, being maligned, hearing the lies stringing from Conn's mouth, and being terrified of what these people will do to her.

For so many hours I had no idea of how Athena was fairing. I tried to mentally send good thoughts, but I also tried not to really think about her emotions: it simply would have been too overwhelming. When Terry first offered, I asked her to stay with Athena instead, not realizing that Athena would be sitting at the very front of the court in the accused chair, beside Cupito, her only support.

Although the Crown had initially given a long list of witnesses to our lawyer, in the end, they called only one: Conn. Obviously none of the other witnesses sited could provide anything that would help them to convict Athena, or they would have been subpoenaed to testify.

So the trial went on with one witness, Conn, and one piece of evidence: the text messages, which supported Athena's innocence, not Conn's. Mr. Cupito continued to marvel that the trail went on.

I believe this trial was not about justice, but about power. As a country we like to pretend that one is innocent until proven guilty, but that is not the reality. The system rewards those who plead guilty, and goes out of its way to punish those who do not, and this is certainly proof of the punishment doled out when one has the audacity to plead not guilty. Add to that my complaint to The Police Watchdog, and it is my belief that objectiveness went out the window and was replaced by outrage that Athena refused to lie and say she did it.

The judge asked if there were "other Charter Rights issues", which was exactly what I had been concerned about. When she was told there had been Charter issues, what else was she told? In the past, I would not have believed a Canadian judge would be influenced by what she was told. I am not so innocent now.

The trial broke for lunch at some point, and as our friends and family came out of the court room, most were in tears. Apparently the first item on the trial menu was watching the video-taped interview of Athena telling her story to Officer Chompsky the night she was raped. Several told me it was better that I had not seen it; every one of them was deeply disturbed by what they saw: They said Athena was forced to tell the entire story, and was then made to start all over and tell it all again. The second time she was told to include as much detail as she could remember. (*Interesting to note that The Police Watchdog report used this against her, saying she had included too much detail*) Between the first and second telling of the event, Chompsky left the room for several minutes, and Athena just sat there hunched and hugging the teddy bear she had been given at the sexual assault centre, looking completely devastated and exhausted. I was told that the Court Recorder was in tears watching the tape.

Several people told me that when watching the taped interview, they saw what appeared to be a bruise on Athena's left cheek. One couple said they watched to see if it was just a shadow, but it moved with her when she changed positions, and it appeared to be raised.

Athena's sister, who had come to provide support, is a physiotherapist. She later told me that a swollen mark like this is consistent with a blow to the head, and blood pooling under the skin. She said it often takes a few hours between the time the injury occurs, and the time the blood has pooled enough to become evident.

Those watching the tape said Athena's interview was very consistent, and again, this directly contradicted what The Police Watchdog report claimed. The overall feeling by those who watched was that this confirmed every negative thing they had ever heard about the heartless treatment of rape victims by police.

Athena did not speak at all during lunch, and sat silently on her chair.

After lunch, while Terry and I were again exiled to the hall. Connor Mann, his father, step mother and mother arrived and were shown to one of the little interview rooms. Delwood went in and talked to them for a long time before either of them testified. I didn't think that was ethical or even legal, but hey, when it comes to those who enforce our laws, it seems the rules are made to be broken. The Mann's then took turns walking past Terry and me to go outside for a cigarette. As soon as one returned, another left. They were loud, and extruded a party atmosphere with a disturbing amount of laughter.

Delwood was called in to testify, and Conn was taken down a hall between where we were seated and the room he came out of. His parents walked past us again on their way into the court room.

I could hear voices coming from the courtroom, and at one point I heard Delwood spit my name out, as if he was ready to choke on it. I suddenly realized this was the only time I have *ever* heard him say my name. I guess he couldn't call me 'mom' when he was testifying at a trial; odd it would be considered acceptable in a formal police interview.

The reporter from the local newspaper was there, but not a word would ever show in the paper. Legally, the details could have been made public, providing the youth involved were not identified. But good lord! The public would then know how appalling the 'justice' system really is, as well as get the (accurate) idea that their daughters aren't safe in this little town. It also would have deterred anyone in their right mind from reporting a crime here.

After he was finished testifying, Delwood came into the hall and sat at the end of the (fairly long) bench Terry and I were on. He looked like hell, and I wondered if he was on leave because he didn't go into the cop-cave at the end of the hall. My hope was that he had been suspended as a result of his multitude of violations of Athena's Charter rights, but I had no way to find out. He completely ignored us, but would periodically put his elbows on his knees, and rub his head with his hands. I could taste my hate for him, and it seemed so tangible I am sure he must have felt it. At times I watched him openly, and he showed no reaction.

It was a very long and incredibly stressful day. Finally I was called back into the courtroom and 'all present' were told by the judge that they may not speak of anything that had occurred in the court that day. Then the day was over.

By and large, we did not speak of it. We were still in survival mode, and details didn't matter; only the end result mattered.

Having said that, there were a few outraged comments made to me by those attending:

The charge against Athena had to be amended to say she lied to Chompsky instead of Delwood because *everything Delwood did was thrown out of court as a result of his violating so many of Athena's Charter rights.* The only thing that Delwood had touched that was still used in court, were the text messages, which, as mentioned before, were there entirely by our choice. <u>Everything</u> *Delwood had done was tainted. Everything.* And yet he is still employed as a cop. What is wrong with this picture? You and I are paying this man to screw people around, waste our tax money, and undermine the rights of Canadians.

Several people commented that the judge showed an open and immense dislike of Athena's lawyer. They thought the judge coddled Conn.

I was told that during a recess one of the court workers slinked up to the crown attorney, and the two flirted openly in the courtroom. It concluded with the crown attorney agreeing to give her a ride home at the end of the day. The friend who told me about this is a professional. She expressed great surprise to witness this open breach of professional conduct. This reinforced my vision of this small town court.

I was told by several people that Conn and his parents came into the court room smiling and making little waving gestures to Conn on the witness stand. They appeared the think the entire thing was a joke. Our friends were quite aghast at this behavior, and even more surprised the judge said absolutely nothing to them about their behavior. One of the more outspoken of my friends was ready to 'tune' them herself. She was, however, spared having to do this when Mr. Cupito began to question Conn, and his plethora of stories fell apart. Long before he was done testifying, Conn lost any semblance of credibility, and Athena got her wish; Conn did indeed cry on the stand.

In fact, when the Mann family left the court room, every one of them was in tears.

Athena was completely exhausted. The only thing she said was how stressful it was to see Conn. She curled up in a ball on the way home and cried. I asked if watching the tape of her interview was difficult, but she said she didn't watch it. She said knew exactly what was in it, and it is always in her head.

⚖

As impossible as it sounds, the stress just continued to build during the two weeks we had to wait for the next court date. Athena was frighteningly depressed and withdrawn; going to school was out of the question.

If you recall the last thing we were told in court was that no one was to talk about the trial, yet the day after the trial, Conn began telling students at school that Athena texted him and told him she was going to lie in court. Did he think he was on trial? What is wrong with this kid? In any event, he couldn't or wouldn't keep his mouth shut, so once again, more versions of the assault made facebook headlines. At this point, Athena was beyond caring. She was far too just worried about her future and her freedom.

DECEMBER 15

Day Two of "HER MAJESTY THE QUEEN VS Athena Schuler"

Three of Athena's closest friends came with us on this second day of trial. Jessie had stayed overnight, and two others were dropped off by their parents in the morning. Sandy and I spent the night alone in our bed; a very rare occurrence. Once again we left Sandy to tend to our comforts at home. The counsellors from Hope House were waiting at the courthouse, as were friends; some there for the first time, some returning. From the entry-way to the courthouse, we saw that Conn, his father and stepmother were sitting in the waiting area. At that point, Athena was appearing remarkably confident.

Delwood walked through the middle of our group. He looked ill. Someone said they heard he has cancer. I felt a sudden attack of guilt; I have repeatedly wished this man all the pain in the world. When I later shared this with Terry, she told me I have no reason to feel guilty; I am not responsible for his illness, and I have a right to my feelings. I realized I could no more control my hate for him than I could make lightning strike him.

Mr. Cupito arrived, and Athena and I met with him in one of the small interview rooms. He said I could attend the trial today; there was no need for either Athena or me to testify. Today he would finish questioning Conn, and the trial would be over.

He said Conn was close to being the worst witness he had ever seen: He lost all credibility when he contradicted himself repeatedly, and was caught in numerous lies. Cupito said, "The crown started with nothing, and has less than that now."

He said he was amazed that we were still playing the game. It was his belief that another judge would have called the trial off. He told me that Conn admitted the sexual sounding text messages were jokes that he himself started, and that he repeatedly changed when, where, how, and the number of times he said Athena consented. Interestingly, he never once referred to his original claim that he was given consent via a text message.

Cupito then clarified the issue with the text messages; on the day Athena was raped and interviewed, Chompsky asked Athena what she and Conn had talked about in their text messages. Athena told her they mostly texted about school, and when he could phone. And in fact, that was what most of the texts were about. Chompsky later asked if they had sent any messages that were sexual in nature. However, before Athena could answer, Chompsky excused herself and left the room. When she returned, she immediately began asking other questions, and never returned to the topic of texts.

Cupito stated that the crown has absolutely no evidence to support the charge against Athena. And yet here we are. I mentioned the term 'malicious prosecution' and Cupito did not dispute this.

I felt better than I had in a long time as we left the conference room. Athena and I went back into the entry way, and realized court had begun. At one point a police officer came out to ask us to quiet down–the acoustics here are better suited for a music hall than a court–there are two sets of doors between us and the courtroom, and we were far from loud.

Delwood again entertained Conn and his parents in one of the conference rooms. What was he doing there? It is my opinion that he was coaching Conn as to what to say on under oath. What other reason could there be?

Suddenly an officer appeared and told us the court was ready for us. Before Athena left to sit in the hot seat beside her lawyer, several of us give her quick hugs. Judge Sheila immediately chastised us, saying that hugging is not acceptable behavior in a courtroom.

Things then got confused as someone else, charged with theft, suddenly showed up for their own trial. Then there was a discussion about a person, subpoenaed for some other trial, who was stranded somewhere. We sat through the theft trial (of which I remember absolutely nothing), and then had a brief recess. I had another character reference letter to give to Mr. Cupito, and a copy of Dr. Rose's new report on Athena.

Mr. Cupito and I stayed in the courtroom and talked during the recess. For the first time, he suggested I contact the media. He suggested that we should give serious consideration to suing Delwood, Conn, and Conn's parents. He had always said to wait and we would discuss a civil suit when everything was finished. But that has changed abruptly. I tried to convince him to do the civil suit for us, but he said he just isn't qualified. However, he said he would be willing to interview Conn in a civil suit, as he already has experience and knows what to expect from him.

He told me I should order copies of the trial transcript, and offered to arrange that for me. He told me it is cheaper to order the total number of transcripts we think we may need at one time, and I asked him to order three copies.

He also brought up another possibility: he knows Athena wants Conn held accountable for his crime, and told me that she can go before a justice of the peace, produce the evidence we have against Conn, and ask that the crown charge Conn. *Cupito believes that with the statements Conn has made under oath in the courtroom, the crown will have no choice but to charge him with sexual assault.*

He then said the crown attorney spoke to him before the trial and said that after his last court appearance, Conn went to the hospital, believing he was having a heart attack. The crown asked our lawyer to go easier on him this time.

To say this pissed me off would be an understatement of astronomical proportions. There had been absolutely no concern for Athena at any point in time. She has consistently been treated worse than slug slime. She has been to the hospital more times than I could count as a result of this kid, there was no one in the court, *perhaps* save a cop, who didn't believe beyond any doubt that this boy had raped Athena, and the crown attorney is concerned about the little ******* **** ****. What is it about this kid?

While we were talking, I became vaguely aware that Delwood, *who had been sitting on the other side of the courtroom with Conn's parents,* was walking closely behind me. He made a loop around Mr. Cupito, and then spoke to the court cop. Suddenly the court cop expressed concern about a brief case resting against the wall, which turned out to belong to Mr. Cupito. I wondered if that was really what Delwood had been checking out when he walked right behind us, or if he had been trying to hear the conversation between Mr. Cupito and myself and used the briefcase as an excuse. I hope he heard us speaking about suing him; let him stress it out for awhile.

And then we were told to rise as the judge re-entered the court. Conn was put on the stand and Cupito resumed his cross-examination. Conn looked very nervous and this time, so did his parents. Athena sat at the front with her lawyer, hunched over the table, looking down. The only time I saw her lift her head was when Conn admitted he locked the door once he and Athena were in the house. I realized the significance of this but the judge chose not to. Our lawyer did not ask if the door was locked when they arrived, but I later asked Athena, and she confirmed it had not.

Conn then back-paddled and contradicted him-self several times when questioned as to when and where he obtained sexual consent.

And finally, under oath, Conn admitted if he got Athena into his mother's house, he intended to have sex with her one way or another.

And the questioning was over. The crown gave his closing statements, and it was obvious the crown attorney knew he had lost, but would not give up without, well, being an asshole. It seemed clear he knew Athena had been raped, and couldn't care less. He made as many verbal jabs and stabs at Athena as he could, *and then he began discussing his unique interpretation of the Criminal Code under which Athena was charged.*

He wanted to believe that it is a crime for any person being interviewed by police to omit any information. Because, at the end of the day, this entire nightmare was the result of this: On the day she was raped, Athena did not say she and Conn had sent text messages in which they joked about sex. Athena did, however, tell Delwood the very first time she spoke to him. Delwood then forgot, or ignored this rather important tidbit of information completely, and charged her with a criminal offence. And the offence as this crown attorney sees it is that Athena didn't say they had sent text messages that joked about sex in the first interview. Rape vs. a temporary omission by a girl just raped. **This** *is what we call justice in Canada?*

The law Athena was charged under is remarkably clear. It states that *it is illegal to mislead the police into investigating a crime that has not been committed.* This means that Athena had to have lied about being raped, not about the existence of text messages, and as a result of Conn's admissions, it is clear that Athena was raped. Yet the crown has come up with an outrageous interpretation of the law, which means that if you forget to tell police that you stopped at the mall on your way home and let them believe you went straight home, you could be charged with a criminal offence.

I don't know about you, but my days of coming forward to help police died a solid death upon hearing that the crown will go to these lengths to charge a victim, and ignore a violent crime.

Fortunately there exists a set of checks and balances to prevent abuse of the law. Canadian law works on precedence, which means that this particular section and subsection (Section 140,) (1) (a) of the criminal code would have to have been interpreted as the crown was claiming and a conviction made at a previous trial. If it had been, then precedence had been made which would allow the same interpretation to be used in Athena's trial.

Incredibly, the judge allowed the crown time to research the interpretation of the law. (So this crown attorney charged a child rape victim under the Criminal Code of Canada, dragged her through the courts, and is *only now* interested in finding out what the law he charged her with actually means? Holy shit.)

This also means that the final verdict will not be read until *January 24th, 2012*. I felt like I had been hit with a ton of bricks. January 24th was over six weeks away. I don't know if Athena can make it that long.

When I could finally hug Athena, we just stood and cried. This nightmare wasn't going to be over until after the New Year. By that time, it would be one month short of a year since Conn raped her. I could hardly believe it: God truly does hate us.

Mr. Cupito and Athena met again to discuss the trial, and I stayed in the hall. Delwood went again into a meeting room with Conn's parents. Mr. Cupito then called me in to join him and Athena, and I left our friends talking together in the hall.

When I came out, my friends told me Delwood had left the room after slightly more than half an hour, and as he left he said to the Manns, "I will see you next time, Merry Christmas, and you guys know how to contact me if you need to talk to me."

Strangers eh? Bull shit.

CHAPTER 15

Persecuting Athena

Sandy is incredibly paranoid. Since experiencing how unpredictable the police can be, and knowing that reporting a crime can destroy your life, we have lived in constant fear. But during this time, our fear of police reached extreme proportions. Sandy believed the police might retaliate against us because we have fought this thing so hard. I was at least as paranoid as he; I was surprised I was still alive, and I made sure that if anything happens to me, enough friends were aware of my fears, and knew where to point fingers. Whenever I drove in Rivertown, I was the most cautious driver there. I had no doubt the book would be thrown at me if I were stopped for anything; or nothing. Athena had the worst nightmares she has ever experienced, and would constantly wake me up, arms flinging and crying out.

I contacted a friend whose daughter is trained to do hypnosis to see if she could help Athena, but she was afraid to put Athena under hypnosis. She felt Athena was so severely traumatized the procedure could actually cause more damage.

I often wondered what it would be like to feel calm; not to have a racing heart and feelings of dread at all times.

⚖️

Conn continued telling more and more outrageous stories. I wondered: Do the kids he tells these stories to never question the numerous versions he has told of this one event? Honest to god, I want to fill his mouth with cement.

Oh yea, and the last thing the judge said before adjourning, was that we were not to discuss the trial.

Athena and her boyfriend officially broke up during this time. Sandy and I had seen it coming, but he seemed completely unprepared when it actually happened. Sandy was flipped out, and worried that Athena would soon regret her decision. She did not.

⚖️

When I finally got fed up waiting to hear from The Police Watchdog, I phoned to check the status of my complaint. I was cut off twice, and after being put on hold the third time I called, I was told the file needed to be found, and someone would call back.

The call eventually came, and I was told my appeal was scheduled to be heard within days. I asked if I could submit new information to be considered, and was told I could. I considered what I had learned since my previous submission. I believed what had come out in the trial was both relevant and important to substantiate my complaint, and so I sent another email to The Police Watchdog, incorporating information I had learned as a result of the trial, and from Cupito. I ended my submission by saying how I felt about this audacity:

This feels more like the persecution of Athena than the prosecution of Athena.

DECEMBER 2

Athena decided not to go for counselling today. School this week has been really tough. In one class she is studying the Holocaust. Horrifying at the best of times, it aggravates Athena's terrors to the point she can't function. Why do we expose teens to so much horror?

I feel like I am badly in need of counselling; my time to let my fears and depression and anger out. And as usual, I leave the counselling session feeling drained, but like I may actually make it through another week.

Terry has consistently recognized the financial devastation this has caused us. She has asked me a number of times if I need anything, and when a local store donated a number of bags of cat food, she sent some home with me. I always feel there must be someone who needs it more, but I also really appreciated it, and used it thankfully.

Today the hall outside her office was filled with new, white, laundry baskets, and the laundry baskets were filled with non-food items. Donations for the basket had come from all over the county. The baskets themselves were wrapped in cellophane, and tied with a bow; enormous gift baskets. She told me one of them was for us, and told me to choose one.

Looking from the top, I saw one that had paper towels, toilet paper, tissues and some tea towels. I chose that one because I thought it would be more modest; some of the others showed quite expensive gifts, and I know there are others who need it more. I cried when I accepted the basket, and I am crying now writing this: The incredible generosity of people who do not know us, who have no idea of what we are going through or how badly we need to know that there were still caring people in the world. It comes at a time when the world is so very dark for us, at a time when our belief in humanity could not be lower.

The true meaning of Christmas is in this basket, and it touches us profoundly.

The very best, though, came when I brought it home. Athena was visiting with some friends, and Sandy and I opened it without her. What I had thought was 'modest' was not in the least. Sandy and I cried together. There were socks, and P.J.'s, insulated gloves, scented candles, a gift card, jam, shower gel and body cream. There was a cute little tea pot, a picture frame with space for 8 photos, dishes, a book, a warm and fuzzy blanket, a beautiful handmade quilt, and an electric tooth brush. The list went on and on, and it suddenly felt like Christmas; like peace on earth, and goodwill. It felt like someone in the world actually cared.

We made a list of the items, so that we would never forget, and we decided what we could give to Athena from the basket. Amazingly, she had asked for an electric tooth brush, but it had not been in the budget. The toothbrush, the picture frame (exactly what she likes) hair curling solution, body wash and lotion, and several other items we wrapped, put her name on, and wrote on the gift tag that they were from Hope House. The rest of the gifts we put back into the basket and stowed away.

We decided not to tell Athena about the gift basket until Christmas Day. On

Christmas Day when she opened her gifts from Hope House, we told her about the amazing generosity. Then the three of us went through the rest of the basket together. It was the highlight of our Christmas. To all those who contributed, thank you. It helped to renew our faith.

DECEMBER 23

The results of The Police Watchdog review have arrived, and I am in complete shock: They claim Delwood conducted a proper investigation! Inducement, violating Charter rights, deciding based on a non-existent text message that a rape did not happen, charging the victim; obviously the police can do whatever they want. They are untouchable, and clearly know it. I am really, really disturbed that they hold such incredible power, and yet are completely unaccountable.

I think the most difficult for me to accept is how little our Charter Rights really mean. That the police can completely ignore legislated rights and still be said to have done a proper investigation, tells me that no one is monitoring the police, and there are no consequences for them. If a cop can get away with breaching our rights with no repercussions, then our rights are not worth the paper they are written on. In fact, by not reprimanding police who ignore the rights of Canadians, police are actually encouraged to do just that: ignore our Charter Rights. To be worth anything, we need to treat rights as sacred laws that are stringently enforced and the violator severely punished. Rights require constant monitoring for compliance and serious consequences for those who do not comply. If rights are not enforced, they don't exist. They are merely a suggestion. If we do not make the police accountable, we will soon find we are living in a police state; if, in fact, we are not already there.

I am in tears writing this. This is serious beyond words. Woman are in serious shit when a sexual assault victim cannot trust the police. Athena was, and is, as respectable a person as you will find anywhere in the world, and yet she has been dragged through criminal court. *Because she was raped and went to the police for justice.*

Welcome to Canada: The country that claims to have human rights, but observing them is completely optional. We may be slightly above a country that stones a rape victim to death, but we should be outraged that a rape victim in Canada can be treated as Athena has, and that it is completely condoned by the system that is allegedly there to help her.

Not one of my friends; and certainly none of my family would voluntarily go to the police now. I have always believed in people. Yes, there are some bad people, but I used to believe the majority are good. I believed in goodness, and I believed in being a good person. I thought that by being a law abiding citizen all my life that this could never happen. In my heart I do not believe in stereotyping people at any level. But now, when I see a police officer, I am filled with loathing and disgust. I despise the person *because of what they do for a job.* And I fight with this emotion constantly. It is against everything I have ever believed in and valued, but I can't control it. I will never trust a police officer again. They are playing a game completely stacked in their favour. The rules exist only for you and me. They are free to do whatever they want, without consequence. Canada: Proud of its police state.

So, what do you do if someone you love is raped? Do you have a spare thirty thousand? Are you willing to risk the stigma of being arrested, charged, and possibly convicted of a criminal offence? If not, you can risk going to the police. What do you do? Get a good counsellor, and walk away. How utterly appalling that this is the safest solution and the one that will cause you the least pain. On the learning curve that is my current life, I have been shocked by the number of people who have told me they would not have gone to the police; they would have taken the law into their own hands. When I first heard this, I was quite horrified, now I think they are smarter than we were. One thing is for sure, we pay far too much money for police protection we don't get.

I see that the police have a really neat gig going. We aren't allowed to protect ourselves, and we are forced to pay them to protect us. Yet they don't, and in reality, usually can't protect us, because they aren't there when a crime is committed. Still we are forced to pay for this alleged protection. When there is a crime, they show up after the fact with the ability to protect themselves, and clean up whatever is left of the first victim. They then try to find something they can charge that victim with. If you do not yet believe this statement, it just tells me you aren't watching the news.

I have no respect and no trust in the police now, and they themselves are entirely responsible for my new attitude. Police need to realize that fear of police is the opposite of respect for police.

$$⚖$$

Christmas. This was once my family's favourite time of year.

Maybe we should have seen how emotionally devastated we were, but we didn't. We thought we were stronger; strong enough to actually enjoy Christmas. Strong enough to visit with friends we had put off seeing for almost a year. It started well enough; we celebrated the first advent, and decorated the house. We called and made dates with friends we had badly neglected. We decided to entertain in our home.

It was wonderful to see people again, and it all held together until Athena's friend Jessie suddenly needed a place to stay on Christmas day, when, after a disagreement with her family, she was told to leave. Every single day from then until the New Year we had friends or family coming to visit.

The sudden and unexpected arrival of Jessie was the straw that broke the camels' back. We had no idea until then just how precarious our emotional stability actually was. Sadly, having one more person as a semi-permanent guest pushed us over the coping line. We all began to show serious signs of breaking: Athena began to shut down, Sandy started to get very testy, and I felt like I just couldn't take any more. At night it felt like my heart would pound itself out of my chest.

An image came to me of being on a plane, and being told that if the oxygen mask falls, I must put it on myself before attempting to assist others; the idea being that I would be of little help to anyone else if I die first from suffocation.

I felt like I was suffocating. I was barely able to function and could not help my family in the state I was in, let alone another human being. I could see the strain the situation was having on Athena, and her mental wellbeing was paramount. My family simply did not have the strength to help others. I had to ask Jessie to find accommodation with someone else. That caused me more stress, but the survival of our family had to take precedence.

Our world fell rapidly apart after this. The verdict date was getting closer, and we were all growing more and more anxious. I have never been more stressed in my life. I can't describe the stress Athena was under. She lived in absolute terror that she would be convicted and be sent to jail. Mr. Cupito had told us the trial outcome was a done deal, and Athena would be found not guilty, but we have no trust or belief in the legal system. We wanted to believe his words, but in reality, we couldn't.

Athena celebrated New Years Eve with very close friends from the first high-school she attended. She had as good a time as she could; I think the others did as well, yet there was always that elephant in the room. A couple of her friends knew she had been assaulted, and charged with public mischief, but the others did not. Mario, a boy she had just started to date, knew nothing.

For the rest of her life Athena will be forced to decide whether to tell or not to tell her story. To wonder and worry about how it will be taken; if she will be believed. To wonder if the person she decides to tell will still want to know her after.

One night Athena had some friends over. They watched movies and went snowshoeing in the moonlight. Sandy and I sat in the sitting room, and we could hear them in the living room. I could tell by Athena's voice that she was trying to be upbeat; and I could tell she was working hard at it. I wondered if the others knew how close to a breakdown she was.

The next day she hit rock bottom. I knew she was terrified she would go to jail, but until that day I hadn't realized just how deep her terror was. With this went other fears; that she may never be allowed to get a drivers' license; never be accepted to any university or college; she wondered if she was now on the 'no fly' list; she wondered if she would be able to have children. She believed that if she was convicted, her life would never be good again. She believed she would always be treated as a criminal.

In an attempt to stay sane, we made appointments with Terry for counselling. We talked about our fears, and how we wanted more than anything in the world to just get this over with. I become really angry when I think that this trial could have been over in two days at a real court. Instead it will be more than *two months* from the start of the trial to the verdict. Sandy voiced concern that if Athena is pronounced guilty the sentence may not happen till another court date. I can't even think about this it causes me so much stress, and I hope to god no one says this to her, I think that would finish her.

⚖

My mind constantly goes over the trial, and my concern about the verdict. My brain these days is a broken record, going over and over the same mind numbing details. I am seeing such a remarkable resemblance to how rape victims are treated in some middle-eastern countries, and I would never have believed I would see so many parallels in Canada, but there they are, glaring in appalling similarity. I think about the outrage that resulted in the "Slutwalk", and believe that this is even more of the exact same mentality.

I have decided that if Athena is found guilty, I will stand up in court and say the following:

"It is astonishing the lengths gone to to blame the victim while the rapist goes free. What's next? Shall we stone her to death?"

I have written this on a blank card and will keep it in my purse where it will stay until I either use it, or can throw it out after the verdict is read.

Why will I do this? Because if Athena is convicted it is because the judge believes that by joking about sex, Athena has asked for it; and she has gotten what she deserves. It seems to me this has been a bottom line.

I have worked and reworked the sentences I will say. I want them short; because I know I will be quickly shut down by the judge and the court police. If Athena is convicted, I will risk being charged myself because I will then have what I need to get the media to pay attention to this outrage. And these two sentences reflect exactly how I feel about this atrocity.

⚖

Exactly one week before the trial verdict, Athena received another death threat. The phone rang, she picked it up, and a female told her she would be dead in seven days; the day the verdict would be read. Athena screamed and dropped the phone when she heard this. She believed Conn had again convinced some girl he knew to do this.

Athena was still terrified the following day. I wanted to know if Athena was a target, or if this was just a silly and random prank. Unfortunately there are not a lot of ways to find this out, and the only possible way I could think of was to ask the police if there had been other reports of telephone death threats. It took some mental debate, but we do live in a different county, and hence a different police force from the one in which Athena was charged. I decided I would just make a little inquiry, you know, "Just wondered if you have had any reports of telephone death threats?"

It seemed sensible at the time. I fully expected the police to brush it off, and that would be the end of it. After all, how many times had we reported threats in Rivertown *all* of which were ignored?

I just wanted a yes or no answer; yes, we have had other reports would mean it was not personal, and no would not tell me a great deal. If no one else had reported such a threat, I would interpret it as possibly being personal, but it could also mean that no one else had reported the call.

To my utter amazement, my call was taken seriously. The police seemed to fly into action. I tried to downplay it; I really didn't want to get into the whole story, it was far too complex. No, I was told, this was a serious matter and an officer would be out. I said we were on our way to an appointment, but would be back in a couple of hours. I gave a cell phone number as requested, and Athena and I left for the appointment.

Before we were half way there, a police officer called. He was sitting in his cruiser *at our house*, waiting for us. Appointment cancelled by cell phone, we turned around and returned home. He was indeed waiting for us, but in the meantime he had looked around, and assessed our home. This was extremely unnerving. Had I known the police would actually show up at my house, I would not have called, but it never occurred to me they would be concerned, let alone come to my home. I did not want a cop on my property or in my house.

He ended up in my house anyway. He showed profound concern, and wanted to know if there was anyone we knew who might do this. Athena and I looked at each other, and I told him there was, and that this was not the first threat against Athena's life, just the first time it had been taken seriously. He asked for the details, I asked him how long he had, and if he was really sure he wanted to know. He said he did, and called in to the station to ask that he not be disturbed.

Two and a half hours and the entire story later, I said "But it could just be a coincidence that the trial verdict will be in seven days."

His response was, "I doubt it."

He then went on to give a list of suggestions: We had tried star sixty-nine to capture the phone number, but the number came up as not listed. He gave us a different code to use if we received another call, and told us to then call the police immediately if that happened. He suggested we install motion detector lights outside, and showed us where. He said not leave Athena alone. He thought Athena should not use Facebook, and he looked at Princess, Athena's Blue Heeler, and said we should get a big dog, one that looks intimidating.

We were both shocked by being taken seriously. He asked if we wanted him to talk to Conn, or if we thought that would aggravate the situation. Athena and I discussed this, and decided that direct contact was a concern. For one thing, it would probably require the police in Rivertown being informed and getting involved, and we know how completely unsupportive they are. We decided we would take the chance that Conn or his minions might call back. We would then have a police record of it, which would mean we would finally have the proof to have him charged and could do it through the police in our county.

⚖️

The next day Athena, although warned not to, was on Facebook. She saw a post from our next door neighbors' daughter, saying she had received a death threat. We are in the country; houses are on one hundred acres or more, so next door actually means some distance away. It was odd that the calls were to these two homes. Athena and I brainstormed; our neighbors had the same first 3 digits in their phone numbers as us, and we lived fairly close. The two girls, Athena and our neighbor, did not attend the same school, and there was a four year age difference between them, which is huge when one is pre-teen, and one sixteen.

There was one possible connection we thought of; the family had ties to the town Conn lived in through church and a church youth group. In the past, Conn had used girls, even ones in his church group, to convey hateful and threatening messages to Athena. He looks much younger than he is, and seemed to 'date' girls several years younger than himself (being gay must have been either a passing fancy, or he plays in both fields).

Was it possible he had convinced a girl from this church group to call Athena, and the girl decided to also call our neighbor after recognizing the first three phone digits and perhaps knowing the girl across the road? It seemed like a stretch, but nothing else made any greater sense. I called our neighbor, and found out that it had actually been the mom who had answered the phone. When the threat was made to her, she believed the caller was a young girl, and thought it must be someone her daughter knew. She responded by reprimanding the caller, who then hung up.

I tried to call the officer who had come out, but he was off duty, so I was going to leave a voice message, but his answering machine put me through to another officer. I did not want to tell the entire story again, so I just asked that a message be left for the officer to call me when he returned to work. I said I did not need to speak to anyone else.

I never did get a call back from our local police. I will always wonder if it was because he was 'counselled' by the police in Rivertown, or if he simply did not get the message I left.

⚖

The rest of the week passed, and somehow we survived. This emotional pain was different than physical pain. I have been badly injured; but I only remember that the pain hurt like hell, I can't actually feel it. When I remember going through this horrific time, I still feel it, and it still feels like I am being ripped apart.

CHAPTER 16
The Verdict

The day finally arrived. We were at the same time terrified, and desperately in need of closure. We longed for the end, dreamed of the sudden and complete relief we would feel when it was over. We clung to the hope that we would hear the verdict, and the enormous weight we had been suffering under would be lifted. We envisioned celebrating and crying with joy: Sweet anticipation of having our shredded lives returned to us.

Instead, the judgment came with a backhand slap for Athena. It seems the 'justice' system cannot get enough of beating this child up. It was shocking to hear the judge bully and insult Athena after everything she has been through. And after hearing Conn's statement under oath, no person with a fraction of an open mind would believe him to be the innocent victim. The verdict is *not guilty* yet the Judge stated that she did not believe Athena had been sexually assaulted. Based on what? There had been no need to produce evidence of the sexual assault; Conn's testimony left no question to anyone else that he had indeed raped her; yet the judge actually said she did not believe Athena had been sexually assaulted.

I had been worried about this judge and her apparent bias from the start. This confirmed my fears. She said she believed that Conn was easily led by Athena's lawyer, and said she believed Conn's testimony. I had to wonder: Which one of the ever changing seven or eight times Conn said he obtained consent she believed? And if she did indeed believe him, did this mean she believed him when he admitted to pre-planning the rape? This seemed outrageously contradictory.

And it gets better: *The judge actually commended the police for their hard work in bringing this to trial.* Yet the Judge knew the police had violated Athena's rights so completely entire interviews were thrown out, and the charge against Athena had to be changed to reflect this!

The judge criticized Athena for not taking the stand and testifying. But why would she? She would have, but in the end, there was no need. Conn had made so many damning statements and changed his story so many times he couldn't remember what his story was. His testimony alone was all that was required to bring the trial to a conclusion.

Yet, instead of charging the boy with either sexual assault or lying under oath, the judge chose to very systematically and deliberately demean Athena. Judge Sheila read out several sexual-sounding text messages in court. Yet Conn had admitted they were just joking around in the texts *he* always started. So, did she believe him or not?

Why was the judge reading these texts aloud in court at all? Two reasons, I believe: The first was simply an attempt to degrade, belittle and bully Athena. Yes, even joking about sexual things is in bad taste, and as we have learned, can be extremely dangerous. Yet joking about sex in text messaging is not an illegal act, and theoretically rape in this country is. It is also consistent with an acquired brain injury victim that they may not understand joking about sex is both socially unacceptable and potentially dangerous. But more importantly, I believe Judge Sheila did this to make it difficult, if not impossible, for Athena to sue the police, the crown attorney, and Conn.

The sexist slant on this is remarkable. Conn admitted he started all the sexual jokes, but he is not ridiculed or reprimanded or held in any way responsible for his actions. Athena regularly tried to change the topic in the texts and wrote "Ha ha" after some, yet she, exclusively, is held responsible for the texts, and for being raped.

The implication is completely clear: Athena deserved what she got because *she* should have known better than to joke about sex. I thought we valued Canadian women, and enforced laws to protect them. I was so wrong. We seem to be heading the opposite way, returning to much simpler times when we just blamed the woman.

How contradictory is it to be told you are guilty, yet be found not guilty? Does this not completely defy innocent until proven guilty? If this is acceptable behavior, no one can ever expect to be considered innocent again after being charged by police, regardless of the verdict. Why would we even bother with a trial? Given this judge's response, her job is obviously redundant; guilt was decided when the police laid the charge, and obviously no evidence was required.

There is not a person who attended court that day with us who will ever trust or believe in Canada's "justice" system again. The degree of outrage, disgust and disbelief at what they heard is not something easily forgotten. Most of those who attended had witnessed the entire trial, just as the judge had, and were incredulous that the judge could, and would say the things she did. Where did such apparent bias come from? I believe this is indicative of the incestuous nature of this little satellite court, and a judge who is so pro-cop that she accepts anything they say without question or proof.

We went away in shock. Glad it was over, but angered and appalled beyond belief. Athena was adamant she would be petitioning the court to bring about a charge against Conn, as Mr. Cupito had suggested. I fully supported her decision, but Sandy was less convinced. He was exhausted; he just wanted his life back.

⚖

During this time reality started to sink in that the stress we had accumulated would take a very long time to dissipate. Far from a sudden recovery, if anything, Athena's health further disintegrated, as did her emotional state. Both Sandy and I worried constantly about her, and rightly so; the degree of her fragility was frightening. Her health had steadily declined following the sexual assault, but in the months following the trial, her physical and emotional problems became even more acute. Several times every month we ended up in the hospital emergency department. There were constant doctor's appointments, specialist appointments, and Athena was on an ever changing menu of multiple medications. When she managed to go to school, I spent the day worried sick while I waited to hear what had triggered flashbacks, intense fear, and crippling depression that particular day. As often as not, she was unable to attend school at all, or I would have to drive an hour there and an hour back to pick her up when she completely broke-down.

One day she got very angry at me. She told me that every time I looked at her I saw a rape victim. I expect it was true. I worried about her unceasingly, and it was because she was trying to survive not just a rape, but a complete shattering of her belief in humanity, and the profound and terrifying fear that comes when you know for a fact there is no one who will protect you from harm.

I worried because her very survival seemed so precarious. When she said this to me, I worked to change the way I was treating her; I worked to see her not as a fragile and broken victim, but as a person who is healing. I worked hard to find a new way to respond to her that was productive, and it took time. Eventually we started to rebuild ourselves and our relationship.

Athena continued to be adamant that Conn be charged with sexual assault. From the way her lawyer explained the intention of this legal process, it seemed virtually guaranteed the outcome would be positive.

Mr. Cupito told us the process would go like this: Athena would go before the justice of the peace and present the JP with evidence of the sexual assault. We did not need to have the transcript at that time, he said, Athena would show and give other evidence first. The justice (or JP) would then pass this on to the Justice Department, and we would then have a visit from crown attorney Mike Baird, who would likely inform us there was not enough evidence to pursue a sexual assault charge.

By that time, the trial transcript Mr. Cupito had ordered for us would be in our hot little hands. It had been ordered the day the verdict was read, and we were told it would take four to six weeks. We would show Mr. Baird the transcript of Conn's testimony under oath, and voila, the Crown would have no choice but to charge Conn with sexual assault.

Nice idea. It took several phone calls to the courthouse just to determine the process. It did not appear that "Bringing about a Private Charge" is a very common process, and what I was told was very vague. One detail that was not at all vague was the fact that the court and court workers could not help us navigate the process in any way.

This is what the court clerks told us of the procedure: Athena would be required to complete the appropriate forms. She would then take them to the court house when a justice of the peace was available. That justice would then assign her a date to return and present her case in the form of evidence against Conn.

Athena was solely responsible for requesting the charge. I would not be involved except that <u>I must</u> be present in the court as guardian of an underage child.

The process is called a private prosecution and there are specific forms that pertain to this process. No, they could not fax or email the forms. The forms must be picked up at the courthouse. My friend works at the court house in another county, and was good enough to pick the forms up for me, otherwise we would have had no choice but to drive the hour to the main court house in Southland, drive home, have Athena fill the forms out, and make another trip back to the court.

So, forms obtained and completed, Athena and I took the day off work and school to submit them, after having previously ensured a justice of the peace would be available that day.

When we arrived at the court house, we were told we needed different information to identify the charges we were requesting be laid against Conn, and the big book of charges was produced. The clerk did help by at least turning to the pages regarding sexual assault. I could help at this point, and together Athena and I decided on the charges we believed Conn should answer to. Since she had been physically beaten, and a weapon used, we requested he be charged with the following:

Sexual Assault s.271 CCC

Aggravated Sexual Assault s.273 (2)(b)CCC

Sexual Assault with a Weapon s.272(2)(b)(a)CCC

Sexual Assault Causing Bodily Harm s.272(2)(b)(c)CCC

Note: CCC refers to Criminal Code of Canada, and s. refers to the section of the code, followed by the subsection. This is the actual way the charges are written and identified.

At one point the clerk complemented Athena for pursuing a charge against her assailant, saying she wished more people would take this action.

The information on the forms we handed in was typed out on yet other forms, and we were then sent to wait outside a courtroom, where we were called in turn.

When we entered the court, there were a number of people present; the ubiquitous court cop, a justice of the peace, a court recorder, as well as several other people. One of those people was the crown attorney who had prosecuted Athena. He was sitting at a long table looking through a pile of papers. Athena went forward to the stand while I stayed in back. As soon as Athena said her name, the crown attorney's head shot up from his papers, he jumped up, and rushed out of the room. I wondered who he was going to tell, and imagined him calling Delwood.

We were assigned a date to return for the hearing. Again Athena was told that she would be responsible for the presentation, but that she required an adult present. She was told to bring any witnesses she could provide. We then left, with Athena finally feeling some sense of control over her life.

We worked diligently to put together a package of information that Athena would refer to in the hearing, and made a separate copy for the justice of the peace including copies of information Athena would be referring to. Jessie went with us as a witness and I was a witness to the head injury she sustained during the assault. Sandy was also a potential witness, but we decided if they didn't believe me, they were just as unlikely to believe him; and conversely, if they did accept me as a witness, we could always bring him in later, when Conn was actually on trial.

We were intent on showing several things. One was that Athena did not have plans to have lunch (or sex) with Conn on the day of the assault. The text messages proved this was not true, but we did not have access to the texts messages. If you remember, Athena had a lunch date planned with Angela on the day of the assault, but Angela texted her that morning saying she was not coming to school and had to break the date. Athena then planned to have lunch with a new friend at Tim Horton's. I phoned this friend's mother. She clearly remembered the discussion at home before school on the day of the assault. We would have liked to have the girl come with us as a witness, but she would not be in the country on the date of the hearing. I asked if she would write down what had occurred that day, including the fact that she had been invited by Athena to join them at Conn's house for lunch. Jessie was to get this letter from her at school, and bring it with her to the hearing.

We also set out to show that the alleged size difference was negligible, and to prove that Conn has a history of aggression. We found valuable information on the website for Conn's hockey team which showed he had the greatest number of penalty minutes on the team, indicating a tendency for aggression. Online, the local newspaper provided us with the fact that Conn, who had been portrayed by the police as small and weak was actually a pitch hitter on his baseball team.

We included information on Athena's acquired brain injury, as well as details of the physical injuries she had sustained when she was raped, and evidence of the constant stalking and harassment.

In all, there were about fourteen pages of information and evidence, and we sited three witnesses.

CHAPTER 17

Kangaroo Court

The month of February 2012 was one of the worst months to date for Athena. Not only was it the anniversary marking the date her life ceased to be worth living, but her physical pain was growing daily, and her ability to focus and function in school decreased even further during this time. She was on stronger and stronger pain medication, constantly being tested in an attempt to determine the source of her pain, and at least once a month she required emergency treatment at the hospital. She suffered severe anxiety attacks, was frightened all the time, and very, very depressed.

FEBRUARY 15, 2012

Dear god. One year ago today Athena was raped. What were we doing at this time? Still at the sexual assault centre, I believe, thinking we were being well cared for by professionals; being told over and over, "We believe you," and "you are doing the right thing." What bullshit, and how utterly disgusting to find that people can be so dishonest. To say these things at a time of such need and not mean a word of it: It was all just lies, smoke, and mirrors.

This has been a year in which we all lost our innocence. I wonder if it is because we trusted and believed in the police so completely that we have fallen so hard. If we hadn't had such ridiculous faith in the police, we wouldn't now feel so incredibly violated. If we had even an idea that they could be so heartless, dishonest and self-serving, it would not have been such a shock. We were too trusting. We believed we would be protected from evil; instead we went to the devil for help. We actually believed the police were there to help us.

What naive, stupid fools we were.

FEBRUARY 21

Another 1:30 a.m. trip to the hospital in uncontrollable pain. Athena was given a shot of pain killer, yet another new and stronger pain medicine prescription and a referral for an ultrasound and scope.

FEBRUARY 22

We spent the morning at the hospital, Athena having an ultrasound and a scope. Even with the stronger prescription, her pain is barely controlled. She is completely sleep deprived. Sleep is elusive enough without the addition of pain, but this has rendered sleep impossible. I tried to talk her into putting off tomorrows hearing, but with no success. She is determined to see this through as soon as possible.

FEBRUARY 23

Today is the hearing *to bring about a private charge* against Conn. I'm really worried about the amount of pain Athena is in and we are trying to find an elusive balance between having enough pain medication to control the pain while allow her to be fully functional, and not groggy or incoherent.

Following the hearing, Athena has a doctor's appointment in Rivertown. The appointment is not until this afternoon, so hopefully there will be no problem getting there on time. We were told to be at the court for 9:30 a.m. I can't imagine the hearing will take more than an hour, and I think the drive to the doctor will be about an hour from Southland, so hopefully we can make it with no problem.

At the courthouse we will be meeting Janna McDonald, one of the counselors from Hope House, the same organization as our regular counsellor, Terry. Neither Athena nor I have ever received counselling from Janna, nor have we previously spoken more than one or two words to her, but Janna attended Athena's trial to show support, and so is fully aware of what Athena is going through. Since we met Janna last November, Hope House has received government funding which allows her to be at the court full time providing support to women who have been victims of violence. She has told us she will be supporting two women on that day, one of whom is Athena.

FEBRUARY 27, AFTER THE KANGAROO COURT

Jessie, Athena and I made the hour trip to Southland in relatively good spirits, in spite of Athena still being in considerable pain. While this made Athena's job today far more challenging, she felt very positive; believing she would finally see justice. We never really considered the possibility that we wouldn't succeed. We believed that with the admissions Conn made in court, the court would have to charge him. No, would *want* to charge him. Their job is to bring about justice, and that could only be achieved by charging, and subsequently convicting, Conn.

By the appointed time of 9:30 a.m. we were sitting in the waiting area of the courtroom, waiting to be called to present the evidence we both had worked so hard to compile. We met up with Counsellor Janna, who asked us if we were requesting a restraining order against Conn. We had no idea that was an option, but we decided on the spot that we would indeed be requesting it.

The court told us there were other cases to be heard first, and then Athena would be called. While we waited on the long, uncomfortable bench in the long, narrow hall, a man appeared and introduced himself to us as Mike Baird. I immediately recognized his name: Mr. Cupito had said he was with the Regional District office. Sounds of warning went off in my head: Cupito said Baird would be the crown representative who would contact us following this hearing to say there was not enough evidence to charge Conn, at which point we would show him the transcript, proving that there was plenty of evidence.

Instead, he was already at Southland courthouse, looking for us.

Athena and I introduced ourselves to him and I introduced Jessie by first name only. Baird immediately knew who Jessie was, and commented on her being a potential witness. Interestingly this was not because she had witnessed Conn's constant stalking, but because Athena had phoned her when we finally got home after she was assaulted. Until he announced this, I had not even known about this phone call. It was instantly obvious to me that he had thoroughly read and learned everything that was in Athena's file.

He asked if Athena had a lawyer with her. We told him, no. We had been told this was not necessary; that she could do this herself. He then claimed he was there to help her.

He took Athena and me to an interview rooms, and he started to talk. He made a comment about the case, and told us outright that he knew little about it. He showed us Athena's file in his open briefcase; open because there was too much paper to allow it to close, and said he certainly did not have time to read this much information. Those warning bells were starting to get mighty loud. This statement directly contradicted what I had just heard in the hall when he was instantly able to place Jessie, knew her last name, and knew that she and Athena had spoken by phone the night of the rape.

Why did he want us to believe he was not prepared when he so obviously was?

Athena hated him on sight, and they immediately got into an argument when he would not let her speak and constantly cut her off. I could not believe how Athena bristled. She was like a cat on the defensive; hair standing, claws out, ready to fight back. This was yet another new Athena that I had never seen before. I wondered if it was the pain medication, the pain itself, or a manifestation of her distrust for people in positions of authority that has arisen as a result of the *justice* systems' treatment of her.

Athena asked about getting a Peace Bond against Conn. He asked us if we had ever signed anything against Conn at the police station. Although we had complained several times to the police about him, the police had never even raised the subject of signing a complaint, so no, we had not. His response was that because we had not signed something with the police, it could not be done. He spoke with an obvious edge of contempt in his voice. He reminded me of a serpent.

Once again I silently cursed the police. How were we to bloody know we should have signed something? What is wrong with these cops that they never even mentioned we could do this? Once again they withheld protection from my family.

When Baird left the room for a moment, I tried to calm Athena down. I encouraged her to give him a chance, and warned her about burning bridges. She did not trust him, like him, or believe for one moment he was there to help her.

When he returned he announced that I would not be allowed in the hearing, as I was a potential witness. We were also told that Jessie would not be allowed in for the same reason.

I was not happy with this turn of events, and told him we had repeatedly been told by the court workers that I was required to be there, as she was a minor. He skimmed over this, and refused to change his mind. I had no option but to let it go. But I knew that Janna would be there to provide support, and I knew her single concern would be Athena's wellbeing.

Baird spent some time alone with Athena, and when I saw her again she said he was extremely rude and demeaning to her, but that his manner changed immediately when I showed up. He told her he would be playing both sides of the field, since she did not have a lawyer. Something was starting to smell very rotten. How could he play both sides of the field? This struck me as a blatant conflict of interest.

When our meeting with Baird was done, we returned to find Jessie waiting on the bench with Janna. While we waited, Janna commented on Athena's trial. The one thing that had really upset her, she said, was when Delwood said under oath that Conn came from "a good family". She felt this was not just irrelevant, but totally subjective: Any number of children from "good" families got into trouble and what determined a "good" family anyway. I had not heard this before, and it peeved me off for oh so many reasons. I want to see this in writing, and I just can't wait to get transcript to check it out. I would like to know just what the context of this statement was. If Conn's family is considered a "good" family, mine is stellar.

It was over an hour later when Baird called Athena to the courtroom. Once again he told me that I would not be allowed in, nor would Jessie. I introduced Janna and told him her role was to provide support for women who had suffered violence, and said that she was a counsellor from Hope House. He said she would not be allowed in either, because she too was a potential witness. I informed him that she was *not* a potential witness. She had never provided counselling to either of us, and even more importantly, she could not legally be a witness because she had been present throughout Athena's trial.

Without batting an eye, he changed his story: the justice had deemed the hearing 'in camera' he said, and so no one was allowed in. And he took Athena, all alone, into the courtroom. Sixteen years old, and not allowed to have an adult present. Sixteen years old and no one to witness what was done to her.

If only we could go back and change the past. I should have seen the signs; I should have realized this was just more of the same abuse. The technique is used in torture cells around the world; divide and conquer, isolate an individual from the group, and there are no witnesses. It frees those without moral conscience to do as they please, and I expect it pleased them to verbally and emotionally abuse her. Why else would they have done it?

Jessie, Janna and I sat outside the courtroom. There was a sign on the door warning that no one was allowed in. From inside I could hear Athena crying, and Bairds' voice, going on and on. Occasionally I would hear an attempt from Athena to say something, but Bairds' voice would cut over her attempt. I could not distinguish the words being said.

Suddenly Athena came out of the courtroom. Her face was puffy and red, her eyes swollen from crying. I tried to hug her, but she backed away and angrily told me not to touch her. She sat on the bench with her arms wrapped around herself and cried inconsolably. She would not tell us about the proceedings; she had been instructed not to, and so she would not. The only thing she said was that Baird was a complete fake; pleasant to me and in front of me, but a mean bastard (my word: Athena would not use this word) when I was not around. She said that 'the only human' in the room was the woman cop, who had repeatedly brought her tissues, and had eventually and firmly told Baird that Athena needed a break.

Again when Baird appeared I asked that I be allowed in. Once again I was told I was a potential witness, and not allowed. Again I asked that Janna be allowed in, and I explained once again that she was not a potential witness. Again the story changed to the JP closing the hearing so it was out of his hands.

This is where I should have told him we were leaving, but we should also have refused to drop the request. I should have said I wanted duty counsel, the media, anyone. Instead, I knew I would be requesting a written transcript of the proceedings, and I would raise shit if there had been improper or unethical proceedings. There was a court recorder in the room, so the proceedings were obviously being taped.

By this point it was obvious we would not make the early afternoon doctor's appointment, so I called and plead my case to have the time moved. I have said it before, but it deserves to be said again, we are incredibly fortunate to have the doctor we do. She has been a pillar of support. Athena's appointment was changed to 4:15 p.m.

Back into the room Athena went, once again all alone. Somewhere around 1:30 p.m. the inquisition broke for lunch. Athena was near the breaking point. Her pain was extensive, her emotional health beaten near to death. Jessie wanted to go to a small restaurant nearby, famous for its poutine. I didn't care, and Athena was so emotionally upset, I doubt she even knew where we were.

The food was served around a single long table, which made talking impossible. I wondered how we appeared to the other patrons; broken, shocked, angry, or perhaps stunned. When we were finished, we moved to Coffee Culture and finally Athena spoke: This was the most humiliating experience she had ever been put through. She had not been allowed to present any of her evidence. Instead, Baird just went on and on, belittling her and calling her a liar and on the rare occasion the JP did speak, his accent was so strong she could not understand anything he said. She did not want to talk about it any further; she had been told not to discuss it with us at all, and it caused her a great deal of stress to do so.

Again I tried to have an adult allowed in with Athena; again we were all potential witnesses. Again I said Janna was not; again Baird said the court was 'in camera', and no one was allowed in.

When I tired of waiting, I went to the door and looked in the small window. I heard Baird going on and on, and could see Athena sitting on a bench, weeping. Cops regularly went in and out. What were they doing there? Was this just another creep show for their entertainment?

Athena came out a final time. She was in very bad shape. We were told there would be a small break, and then the final decision. We were all invited in for the verdict.

In we filed, Jessie, Janna, Athena and me, and to sit on a bench at the back of this very small courtroom. My first impression of the JP was that I would cast him as a hanging judge in an old west film. He was olive skinned, his hair and trimmed beard were white, his features severe and sharp.

He told us he did not believe Athena was raped.

I was absolutely shocked. We were not here to put Athena on trial; she had already been on trial, and she was found innocent. Baird asked the JP if he would explain further, and he said more words that made no sense to me. His accent made him difficult to understand, and the pounding of the blood in my head made it impossible to comprehend. I do not remember a word of his explanation only that it struck me as extremely cruel and demeaning.

This was supposed to be a fair hearing to determine if there was enough evidence to charge Conn, it was not supposed to be another witch hunt to persecute Athena.

I was literally seeing red I was so livid. If the energy of hatred could be harnessed and focused, both these men would now be dead. I told Baird I wanted a transcript. He told me there was no transcript because Conn was not going to be charged. How convenient, I said to him. No transcript and no witnesses as to what was said and done to Athena.

Baird then gave me his business card, and offered to clear up any questions I might later have.

Athena was sitting on the bench outside the courtroom, crying. "I'm done," she said. Conn will do it (rape someone) again, and there is nothing I can do to stop him. I can't go through this again. They win. They don't care about justice; they only care about preventing it from being done."

I picked up my coat and purse from the bench. Athena and Jessie walked out with Janna. I asked Baird why in god's name any woman would go to the police only to be raped repeatedly by the system that is supposed to help them.

We were already fifteen minutes late for the doctor, but another phone call confirmed we were still expected. I doubt I was really fit to drive, but I pushed the speed limit beyond the max to get to the appointment. I felt sick to my stomach, I was sick in my heart, and in my soul. On the way Athena said virtually nothing. The very few statements she made I asked Jessie to write down for me.

- When she tried to say what happened, Baird said, "You have a vivid imagination, Schuler." Athena said he only ever called her by her last name. (Just referring to Athena as *she or Schuler* is in itself degrading; implying she does not even deserve a name.)
- Athena was not allowed to present any of the evidence she brought, *and was told she could only have done so if the evidence had been seen by Baird ahead of time.* Something neither the court workers, nor the information I found on the internet ever even alluded to. The material Athena brought was left untouched and unheard. Who fucked up here, and was it intentional? Was it even true?
- Baird said to her, "The police don't believe you; why should we?" and "Why are we here? She wasn't really raped." So much for a court of law having determined her innocence.
- Athena was not allowed to explain, and was constantly told to be quiet. This was an interrogation. Baird was the interrogator, and the justice of the peace was indeed the hang man.
- Particularly upsetting to Athena was the way Dr. Rose, psychiatry in general and Athena's acquired brain injury specifically were mocked and treated with contempt.

Days later, when Athena felt strong enough to talk about it, I learned the following:

Baird had with him a written transcript of the interview from the night Athena was assaulted. He asked Athena if she had seen it. She had not, and said she had not. He then said she knew what was in it, and he told her she would accept the transcript as accurate, wouldn't she? She said no, she did not trust what was in the written transcript to be accurate. Obviously Baird could care less if Athena had seen or agreed with the transcription. He used this transcript to interrogate her, and he also used a transcript of the third interview; the one thrown out of court because of the multitude of violations and attempted inducement.

He told Athena that *I* had asked her in the third interview if she lied, and said Athena had told me she *had* lied! Where had *this* come from? This was yet another complete and blatant lie. Was this also from the notes of Delwood? Or was this Baird himself just trying to break her with lies?

I feel like I am dealing with some third-world street gang thugs, and I am again horrified that this is the alleged justice system of what is supposed to a free and democratic society.

I have no idea what the doctor said when we finally arrived. More tests were scheduled, and different drugs prescribed. On the way home from the clinic, Athena once again wished that she could die. Those were her only words the entire trip. She said nothing the rest of the night. She would not be touched, she would not talk. I learned later that she canceled her plans for the weekend because she did not want to see anyone. She finally cried herself to sleep around 3:00 a.m.

Sandy was ready to break too, only his breaking down would end in a trail of death. I told him Athena was done; she could not do anything more. His only response was: Good.

I had so many questions. Both the JP and Mike Baird were brought in from elsewhere. Why? There are two justices at the Southland court. One of them had been mislead by Officer Delwood into granting a court order to obtain Athena's text messages allegedly to investigate a sexual assault, but really to investigate Athena. I could understand there may be resentment there; but there should be no reason the other justice could not have been at the hearing.

Instead they picked a male (once again– so much for care and consideration of a rape victim and victim's rights–and brought him from elsewhere. Mike Baird works in the Regional Office of the Justice Department. He is a big gun. Why bring in the big guns? This was simply a sixteen year old girl who, in spite of everything, still *wanted to believe that justice could happen in her country*. Instead, what happened was done behind closed doors, with no adult to protect her, in complete violation of her alleged rights, like she is some terrorist or mass murderer, not a sixteen year old rape victim. No witness to what went on behind closed doors, and when I requested one, no transcript, in spite of the fact that there was a court reporter in attendance. This was a complete cover up of something; well, something including trying to cover up a sexual assault.

The bottom line is this: *all the crown needed to do was hear the evidence supporting Athena's claim of sexual assault, and if, after fair consideration, there was not enough evidence to charge Conn, then say so in a respectful manner.*

The fact that they turned what should have been an open and unbiased hearing into a witch hunt tells me that for some reason the crown felt threatened, and had a motive completely apart from seeing justice done. Who were they protecting? Conn? Delwood? Crown attorney number one who couldn't understand the laws? Or the entire broken and corrupt legal system, made worse as each level added more and more injustice in an attempt to cover the horrific and unconstitutional mess for which they were responsible?

CHAPTER 18

Kangaroo Court Continued....

I was stunned the next day when Athena announced she intended to once again pursue the private charge process to have Conn criminally charged. Through research on the internet, she learned that she can keep re-applying to the courts providing she has new evidence to present each time. There was one condition though; she wants to have Mr. Cupito go with her. Since she was not given the opportunity to present any evidence supporting a case against Connor, she thinks she has enough to go back quite a few times if necessary. She says that she will wait until we have the transcript, but she intends to keep going back until they are sick of seeing her and finally charge him.

Sandy was not happy with this. He just wants it to be over. I believe if Athena is committed to this, I have to support her. This has to be her choice. She certainly knows better than I what she will be getting into.

My anger at the indignities and injustice I witnessed has not subsided, and I want some questions answered. Baird had given me his business card, so I 'creeped' him on the internet to see if I could discover about him. I learned that he is indeed the man sent in when a big gun is needed. His cases are media worthy, high profile cases. Why on earth would he be sent in to suppress a child? What threat does Athena present, and to whom?

I also wanted to know who the justice of the peace was. It disgusted me that not just one, but two men were chosen to once again interrogate a female rape victim. This goes well beyond a lack of compassion, and

I don't believe this was an accident. I believe the players were carefully and deliberately chosen. I was also intrigued by the accent the JP sported. I hadn't heard enough to be certain, but thought it may be eastern European. I wondered where he had been educated, and what biases he might bring to his position. I needed a place to start, and as always it is best to get everything in writing. And so I sent the following, intentionally curt, email to Mr. Baird:

Thanks for offering to clear up any questions I have:

- Who was the justice of the peace, and where was he from?
- Could you explain to me again why you were sent, what your role was, and who would have played that role had you not been there.
- Why wasn't I asked to testify? When the process was started and Athena swore before the (initial) JP, she was told to bring as many witnesses as possible to testify at the hearing. She was also asked to provide any and all evidence, which seems to have changed with the new guard. I think she really felt like she was the star of the show, or perhaps, more correctly, the victim once again.
- Could you tell me who made the decision that this was a "closed" court, and what legislation mandates that a sixteen year old cannot have an adult with her.

Thank you
Marion Shuler

I received a reply from Baird the same day, thanking me for my questions, and saying he was busy for the next while but expected to 'get' me answers before the end of the next week. His choice of words made me believe someone higher up would be advising him on how to respond.

About a week later I heard back from Mr. Baird, who informed me that the name of the JP's name was Abdus Sattar. Sattar was sent as justice, he said, because "There was an obvious conflict of interest for the Southland Crown office to prosecute your daughter in a criminal case and then change sides to appear to assist your daughter as a private complainant at the pre-enquete."

This statement implies that both were brought in to ensure an unbiased hearing, which is about the last thing I believe.

Baird went on to extensively quote section 507.1 of the Criminal Code, which outlines the process by which Athena had attempted to bring about a private charge. The section talks about the importance of witnesses and evidence in such a proceeding, and was little of relevance, except to provide me with some additional disgust in paragraph forty-nine of the Code which states:" … a pre-enquete is not an adversarial proceeding."

Bull shit it isn't. The section then goes on to state that… "The Justice Department is entitled to notice of the hearing, and opportunity to attend, to cross-examine and call witnesses and to present any relevant evidence at the pre-enquete *without being deemed to intervene in the proceeding.*" Interesting that Baird controlled every aspect of every detail of the hearing, and yet according to the law, he was 'deemed' not to have intervened at all.

So Mr. Mike Baird appeared on behalf of the Justice Department, who I believe should be ashamed to have treated a child, a human being and a Canadian Citizen in the manner in which Athena was treated. In his email, Baird goes on to say that essentially he was acting under *secret government rules*:

"I performed my duties in accordance with specific policies of the Criminal Law Division of the Justice Department. Those policies are in the form of *a Confidential Legal Memorandum. Thus, I cannot share their content with you.*" So, no transcript, no witnesses and secret documents as well, which he is using to hide behind and avoid accountability for his actions. The 'secret documents' are, of course, not described; isn't that convenient. I don't know if this document is specific to Athena and her case, or if this is a blanket document that is pulled out and used whenever the questions get tough. Are secret documents that protect the actions of a public servant from public scrutiny acceptable in a democracy? I don't believe they should be. These alleged documents render Bairds' actions untouchable and unaccountable and being 'confidential' it is impossible for me to find out if they exist, let alone what is in them.

If you still aren't convinced the law is not going to help you if you are sexually assaulted, try this next statement by Baird on for size:

"There were no other witnesses to the alleged sexual assault committed upon your daughter. In my view, no other person could have assisted the Justice of the Peace with evidence relevant to the court's decision whether a case for issuing process was made out. *The fact that your daughter told others later that she was sexually assaulted* or that, for example, you say you found injuries on your daughter not found by specially trained expert sexual assault nurse examiners, would not have assisted the Justice of the Peace in this instance."

Let's look at this statement in two parts. First, Baird states that since there was no eye witness to the rape, rape cannot be proven. Athena's word counts for nothing (yet Conn's word was the only evidence in Athena's trial!) and further, if this escape clause does not apply to Athena alone, the message here is: *If you are raped, but have no witnesses to the actual event, don't expect to be believed by the legal system.* Instead of victim support, you may, like Athena, be considered the criminal for attempting to get justice, and the system itself will re-victimize you as many times as necessary until you finally get the point: they are not going to take you or your pain seriously. No wonder an estimated 88% of sexual assault victims do not report the crime to police, largely due to fear of re-victimization in the legal process. (www.statcan.ca/pub/85-002-x/2014001/article/14040-rng.htm?fpv=2693)

Secondly, according to Baird, the only witnesses that are credible are the 'trained professionals'. If, as happened in Athena's case, they failed to even check her for injuries, and this is later seen by someone else, it is completely discounted. My word, as Athena's, is worthless. If I were a cop, or a sexual assault nurse, I would be elevated to the beyond reproach status; my word would *count*. So what about the bruise on her cheek? The blood in her bra? Baird ended his paragraph by saying that he would be "in breach of the law" to discuss the "evidence" any further. And so he has, and takes, the perfect out.

Finally, he states that there is no legislation mandating that Athena could not have another person with her (in the hearing)! He again states that *potential witnesses* in the hearing room would not be prudent, and ends with: "Your daughter's friend, the counsellor and you all fell into that category of person, as we discussed outside court on the day of the hearing."

I had told Baird at least five times that Janna could not legally be a witness. I told him numerous times in several ways, and explained both why she was not, and legally could not, be a witness. He is either exceedingly dim, or he intentionally ignored my words and then pretended he never heard them. Once again, all the crown needed to do was play fair, listen to the evidence Athena was prepared to present, and give a respectful response. Instead what was done was extreme overkill at the expense of a child.

Several weeks later Athena returned to the Southland court house to pick up the papers required to initiate another hearing, but she felt extremely intimidated when the court clerk recognized her and called her by name. Athena then contacted Mr. Cupito and asked him to go with her, but he talked her out of it, saying the crown would simply do the same thing again. Once more, Cupito recommended we pursue civil suits on a number of levels once we received the transcript.

Ah, the transcript. The trial transcript that was supposed to take four to six weeks, in the end took *four and a half months*. (More on the transcript later) At one point Mr. Cupito received a phone call telling him the transcript was completed and ready for pickup at the Southland courthouse. He sent a clerk to pick it up; an hour drive there and an hour drive back, but the transcript could not be found. It resurfaced a week later, and he had it delivered to him this time. Total cost of the transcript to us: seven hundred dollars.

When I learned the name of the presiding justice, I checked him out on the internet. There was quite a bit of information. I had certainly missed the boat on his accent, however; which is Middle Eastern. I had already wondered at the possibility of bias. Many times I had thought and said that short of stoning her to death, the treatment of Athena far more resembles what goes on in some middle-eastern countries, than what I would have believed of Canada. This irony did not escape me. I go back to my statement that I feel the crown attorney and the justice of the peace were chosen with intent.

After quite some time of mulling the responses I had received, I decided to further question Mr. Baird. I wanted to know if he had been responsible for choosing a man whose English was so poor Athena could not understand him to be his co-conspirator or if that decision too had been made by someone higher up the ladder.

And so, another email to Mr. Baird, who I am certain, was thrilled to hear from me:

I have several questions in regards to the above complaint filed by Athena Schuler:

- Who made the decision not to have the complaint heard by the second JP employed in Southland?
- Why was this decision made?
- What criteria was used in choosing Justice Abdus Sattar to hear this complaint?
- Who determined the criteria, and made the choice of Justice Sattar?

Thank you.

The response from Baird took close to two weeks, and he apologized for his delay in responding. He stated that Athena's case was determined to be a conflict for the Southland office. He went on to say, "It would have been unseemly for the local Crown office to appear on a case in which your daughter was a victim. *She was being prosecuted as an accused by that office.*"

His words paralyzed me. Athena had told me Baird didn't seem to know she had already been found not guilty when he interrogated her. She told me she kept trying to tell him the trial was over, and she had been found not guilty. Obviously he is a man who hears only what he wants to hear. This statement alone should be proof of an improper hearing, whether or not his lack of understanding was intentional. There was complete misunderstanding on his part, and likely complete bias as a result. How could the 'justice' system be so completely screwed up? Did Athena not warrant a new and unbiased hearing? One that accepted she had been found not guilty in a court of law. At the very least she should be allowed to present evidence of the assault. As it stands, the entire hearing was nothing more than kangaroo court.

The rest of his email dealt with who was responsible for appointing Sattar as Justice. Bottom line: not Baird, but some other senior bureaucrat. His email prompted more questions:

> To Mike Baird:
>
> Thank you for your response. As so often happens, answers seem to lead to more questions, and greater concern. I am extremely confused by your statement that 'She (Athena) was being prosecuted as an accused by that office' (Southland). It appears you were unaware that Athena was *not* an accused, she had been found not guilty. In fact she was requesting that Connor Mann be charged because of damning admissions he made under oath *in this trial*; admissions that resulted in Athena being found not guilty. Had you allowed Athena to present this evidence, and been willing to view the trial transcript, I believe you would have found more than sufficient evidence to pursue a sexual assault charge against him. You have indicated that the reason you were not willing to hear the evidence was because you believed she was being charged at the time. This very serious misunderstanding needs to be rectified. Please let me know how this will be achieved.
>
> Marion Schuler

Amazingly, I did not get an answer back from Baird: *Ever.*

When I finally realized I did not warrant a response for what I felt was not just an outrageous and inexcusable screw-up, but a complete failure of the legal system, I sat down to write yet another formal complaint. I first contacted the Law Society for our province, but was told that Baird, as an employee of the Justice Department, was not under their jurisdiction.

The following is my letter of complaint to the Justice Department:

Please accept this as a formal complaint against Mike Baird, Counsel.

Background:

On Feb.15, 2011, my fifteen year old daughter was sexually assaulted. The Rivertown police were contacted, and subsequently charged my daughter with Public Mischief under S. 140(1)(a) of the criminal code, saying she had given consent via a text message. The case went to trial with one witness; the boy who assaulted her, and one piece of evidence: Text messages. The text messages could have been disallowed by Athena's lawyer due to the Charter rights violations in obtaining them, however they proved that contrary to what the boy claimed, he had not been granted consent to have sex via a text message. Under oath, the boy, Connor Mann changed his story numerous times, admitted he intended to have sex with my daughter one way or another, and essentially confessed. She was found not guilty.

Athena's defense lawyer suggested to us that we pursue a civil suit. He also informed Athena that she could go before a justice of the peace, and based on the admissions Mann made in court, ask that the Crown charge Mr. Mann. It was his opinion that given Mann's testimony, the Crown would have no option but to pursue a sexual assault charge. Athena then attempted the process to bring about a private prosecution.

This is where our complaint against Mike Baird begins.

A date was set for February 27, 2012, at the Southland Court House. We were told that Athena must present evidence against Mann, which she was well prepared to do, and that I would be required to be with her, as she is a minor.

When we arrived for the hearing, we were met by Mr. Baird. He had Athena's file, but claimed he was not familiar with it. He told us that he would be representing Athena, but also the Crown. He said that I would not be allowed to attend the hearing as I was a potential witness. We had brought another witness with us, and as soon as Mr. Baird heard her first name, he identified her as the friend Athena had talked to the night she was assaulted. Jessie was not allowed in the hearing either, he said, because she was a witness (yet neither of us was given the opportunity to testify at this hearing).

We also had a support worker from Hope House, where Athena has received counselling since the assault. This was NOT Athena's counsellor. Janna Mackintosh, as well as the rest of the staff of Hope House all had attended Athena's trial to provide support and send a message to the crown regarding how they felt about a rape victim being charged instead of her assailant. Janna had attended Athena's trial, and she had never been Athena's counsellor, so she was not, and could not, be a witness in any related trial. In fact she was being paid by the government to work at the court and provide support to victims.

Yet she was not allowed to support Athena in the hearing. It was obvious that Athena was being devastated by what was going on behind closed doors in the hearing, so every time Mr. Baird would leave the hearing, I asked if someone could go in to provide support for her. Each time the answer was no, although, contrary to the email attached, the reason varied. At least five separate times I asked that someone be allowed to be with Athena, and I was told no, because we were all potential witnesses. Each time this excuse was used, I explained and said that Janna could not be a witness. The story then changed to "the Justice of the Peace says this is a closed hearing." So my sixteen year old daughter was entirely alone with Mr. Baird, the justice of the peace brought in from elsewhere: Abdus Sattar, a police officer, and a court recorder.

Behind those closed doors, and with no witnesses,

Mr. Baird proceeded once again to put Athena on trial. We had been told that she would be responsible for presenting evidence, yet she was never allowed to. The entire 'hearing' was controlled by Baird. This was not a hearing to listen and objectively decide if, in fact there was sufficient evidence to charge Mann; this was a deliberate and vicious attack on a child trying to do the right thing. Athena was repeatedly bullied, insulted, and belittled; she was called a liar and told by these men that she had not been raped. In spite of the fact that *everything* the investigating officer did was thrown out of court because of Charter rights issues, attempted inducement, and lying in his notes that she had confessed when she had not, Mr. Baird said, "The police didn't believe you, so why should we?" Even after being proven not guilty, she was subjected to this brutal abuse. When I saw her, the emotional damage done to her was outrageously obvious. She had been reduced to a breakdown. Later that day she said she wished she were dead. Do you see this? My daughter *wished she were dead* because of the hours of vicious and relentless bulling by your representatives.

And all she was trying to do was prevent some other girl from being assaulted, because everything the boy has done has been condoned by the 'justice' system.

I asked Mr. Baird for a transcript, but was told there would be no transcript as the crown was not willing to prosecute Mann.

So, at this point we have an underage rape victim, and two men verbally abusing her without any adult to protect her. After being dragged through hell by the legal system, she had been trying to get her life back together, get some closure, and do the right thing. Instead she was treated worse than dirt, with no one there to protect her, and conveniently, no proof that such abuse had taken place.

I then began questioning Mr. Baird about this event by email. I have attached the emails. The last email was sent over a month ago. Apparently I do not warrant a response, although he makes the very disturbing statement that he was not aware she had been found not guilty at the time of this hearing. Had she been allowed to speak at all, this would have been obvious.

If there was not enough evidence against Mr. Mann, all the crown needed to do was let Athena present the evidence, while observing her right to have an adult present, and say so. The fact that the story kept changing and is still changing on the part of the crown, and a male JP was brought in from another area, smacks of a cover up. I can well understand the motivation to keep this atrocity quiet. The way my daughter has been treated by all levels of the legal system is appalling, and none of it should have happened starting with the police, but to have this continued by an employee of the Justice Department is inexcusable.

We are more than willing to discuss this further.

Marion Schuler and Athena Schuler

Slightly over two weeks later I received a letter in the mail, written on behalf of the Justice Department. In the letter the writer explained that a judge's order is required to obtain a transcript when there are not going to be charges laid following a pre-enqiete hearing. This means I *could* have gotten a judge's order and obtained a transcript. Yet Baird did not tell me this even when I directly asked for a transcript. Where in hell is the integrity in the legal system? Informing me that a transcript could be obtained would have shown a willingness to be transparent; not telling me says even more about his desire to remain unaccountable. It says to me he felt the need to conceal what was obviously unacceptable treatment of a child. It says to me that he knew what he was doing was completely unethical, perhaps even illegal, and as such he needed to make certain it could not come back to bite him.

He went on to state that the law sets out the rule of "in camera" ('in camera' is the easy out clause he kept using to keep us out of the hearing) and as such he cannot comment on the content of such proceedings.

Obviously the writer was adept at hiding behind the law too, something I find very unsettling. Had we known that no other adult would be allowed in to support Athena, we would have had Mr. Cupito go with her, however we were repeatedly told by the court workers that I would be required to attend. So who screwed up royally, the court workers, or Baird, or was it a deliberate misrepresentation?

The writer admits to assigning Mr. Baird to this case. He goes on to say he "understands that Ms. Schuler found the pre-enquete process to be difficult." And says Baird did not intend to "leave her feeling mistreated by his questions. He asks me to offer his apology." He says that the Crown counsel is supposed to "display sensitivity and compassion in their dealings with the public."

Sandy, tells me this is an apology; or at least as much of one as we are ever going to get. It really didn't cut it for me. The abusive treatment by Baird and Sattar was disgusting, and had someone outside of the legal profession treated a child this way, that person would be fired. Anyone thinking about going this route needs to hire a lawyer to attend with them. Once again the public is not safe from the very system that is supposed to protect them.

Athena counts this experience as one of the worst five things that have happened in her life. The other events include being sexually assaulted with a weapon; being charged with a Criminal Offence; having to see the boy who assaulted her at the trial; and finally, fearing constantly for her life.

I started to write a letter back. So much of the letter I received was meaningless garble, and so many of my questions are still unanswered. Suddenly I realized this could go on forever. I believe that for any response the Department of Justice gives, I will be able to pick apart the lies and half truths. That is the way it is with things untrue and dishonest. I don't believe there will ever be straight answers, and I will keep seeing gaping holes in the answers they do give. They will never admit that they screwed up from the day one. I believe that every time a new area of the legal system becomes involved, they try to cover up the previous atrocities by adding more lies and atrocities, and no one is willing to accept responsibility. I think if I keep asking questions, this will go on forever or, like Baird, until they just quit answering.

Nevertheless, here is my started, unfinished, and unsent letter. Fatigue has set in, and I am tired of beating my head against a wall.

Re: your letter of December, 2012.

Isn't it interesting how every response leads into more questions? Here is what I think: Every question I ask will receive a partial answer, and it will contradict a prior answer. That is what happens when each layer of the system is trying to cover up for previous mistakes, incompetency, screw-ups and generally unethical practices that went before. I believe that long before Mr. Baird walked into Southland court house, a decision had been made that there would be no charge against Connor Mann. The entire 'pre-enquete' was, as I have said to Mr. Baird previously, the epitome of a kangaroo court. This is the real reason no adult was allowed to be with Athena, the reason a woman justice was not called upon, the reason Mr. Baird failed to mention that a court order could have gotten me a transcript, the reason he pretended (and failed miserably) to convince us at the time that he knew nothing of the case history. Unfortunately, he has trouble keeping his stories straight, and while I could just keep picking away at all the lies and inconsistencies, I am done. I had hoped that somewhere in the justice system there existed honesty, integrity and professionalism, but I have to admit defeat on that one. I am horrified by all I have learned about Canada's legal system. I have gone from being a proud Canadian, to believing (sadly with more proof than I ever wanted to find) that the system is corrupt, incompetent and concerned only with self-preservation.

It is truly no wonder that an optimistic estimate (www.sexassault.ca) claims that only six out of one hundred women report a sexual assault.

The wonder to me now is why anyone does; and how we could have been so stupid as to do so.

CHAPTER 19

Learning to Live Again

We felt changes not long after our experiences at the Kangaroo Court. I remember waking up one morning not feeling overwhelmed by the dread and fear that had become so much a part of me. I felt lighter; a bit of weight had been lifted from my shoulders. When I asked Sandy he, too, felt less dread and fear of the future.

Athena started to sleep in her own room more often, always with Princess, her dog, and always with the light on. Her bedroom door had to be shut; ours had to be open. While it was not every night, it represented a definite step forward.

I believe humans have a built in mechanism that allows them to survive extreme stress: Over and over I have seen people manage to get through horrific times, only to fall apart when the event is finally over. It is as if our bodies and minds get us through what we have to in order to survive, and when that major stressor eases, our body not only demands a break, it takes one. The victim ceases to be able to function, and has absolutely no choice but to take a much needed hiatus from everyday life. I believe that is what happened with Athena.

Athena was still trying to cope with profound and ongoing depression without medication, and had quit going to counselling. A combination of not trusting authority figures, and wanting to avoid thinking or talking about her pain meant that she was not progressing: In order to be successful, counselling requires the client to be actively involved and work diligently at the process, and Athena was just not there. When I would bring up the subject, she would say that Terry was great, and if she went to counselling again it would be with her, but she just wanted to move on with her life, and not have to think about the past at all. In short, she was trying to use denial to deal with all she had been through. While I believed she needed to be in counselling, counselling falls under the category: You can lead a horse to water, but you can't make it drink. Terry assured me several times that Athena may well return to counselling: When she is ready.

Incredibly, Athena had passed all of her fall semester courses, a monumental accomplishment given the number and scope of the barriers she faced. Winter semester brought new courses: Biology, Chemistry, Math (grade 11 functions) and Photography. Shortly after the start of the semester, I attended 'meet the teacher' night, and heard encouraging and positive feedback from all her teachers. But almost the next day, calls from the school began to flood in as teachers became concerned.

Once again I found myself having to deal with biases regarding Athena having open book exams: some teachers felt it just wasn't 'fair' to other students, and I would have to explain that it is an almost insurmountable challenge for her to remember where she read the information, let alone remember details.

At first Athena believed she understood her lessons, but as the semester progressed, and her mental and physical health digressed even further, so did her ability to function in school. Her short term memory seemed even worse, and yet she was being increasingly pressured by the special education teacher to try writing exams without open book; at a time when she was literally struggling to survive. Both Athena and I felt we were constantly fighting the school to maintain the accommodations deemed necessary for her academic success.

One terrible weekend Athena tried to study for an exam. She went through all of her notes, made cue-cards, and tried to memorize from them. But the more she studied, the more confused she got. Her self-esteem was at rock bottom, she believed she was incapable of learning anything, and she was ready to quit school. Her teachers complained they could not tell if she understood what she was being taught, and essentially they believed she did not. They did not buy into the idea of giving her the benefit of any doubts. There was excessive concern on their part that she may get into university and then not be able to succeed. It was just over a year since Athena's initial head injury, and further healing was expected during the next year. We did not want to shut doors on her future. If she was not able to succeed, her grade twelve marks, and the planned re-testing would indicate this. In the meantime, we felt she should be taught and assessed in accordance with the guidelines outlined by Dr. Rose, and the Education Act. The term 'gifted' was dropped from her Individualized Education Plan, something that contributed to her plummeting self-esteem. I was told by the special education teacher that a student in their system could not be identified as both gifted and as having special needs. I expect Albert Einstein, who was considered fairly gifted but also had dyslexia would be surprised to learn this.

Not many days after the frustration of studying and trying to memorize, Athena decided she could not do the work. She felt she couldn't focus, couldn't remember, and she was in constant physical pain in spite of a feast of pain killers followed by other drugs to combat the side effects of the pain meds. She worried incessantly about what was wrong with her body. In spite of having tested negative to every sexually transmitted disease modern medicine could test for, she lived in constant fear that having been sexually assaulted had damaged her permanently. None of the tests to date had pinpointed the problem. At the school's suggestion, she dropped first math, and then chemistry.

This meant she was taking only two courses, which was a mixed blessing. On the one hand she had less school work pressure, but it added different stressors: Athena would not have enough credits to graduate in just one more year of school, and was loathe to spend another year in high school. Taking only two courses also meant she had huge amounts of free time at school.

Socially, school was really tough for Athena. She had become a target again, and she simply did not have the ability to deal with the frequent intentional rudeness. That Athena was different could not be argued. She had been through far too much to take life lightly. One factor that set her far apart was that she did not go to parties, and did not drink. In the area we live in, alcohol and parties are the social norm, even for underage teens. Choosing not to party meant she was suspect, and considered weird. But Athena had no desire to put herself in vulnerable situations. She was terrified enough just trying to get through the day.

She constantly had flashbacks and times of intense and uncontrollable fear and anxiety. All these things set her apart, and she did not explain to others what she was experiencing. While the same chronological age, she was much more mature and time wearied than other girls her age; sexual assault and the legal system had robbed her of ever feeling safe, ever fitting in, and of her teenage years.

She would leave classes suddenly, had frequent emotional breakdowns, and missed a great number of days of school. In short, she was different, and as such she was a prime target for those who derive perverse pleasure in being rude/crude/and just plain mean. Having just two classes meant she was more 'available' for verbal abuse, and I was reluctant to set her up to be a sitting duck for more bullying. She was extremely fragile, and every verbal abuse added to her growing belief that she was what she was being told she was: A loser. Athena's image of herself at this time was alarming. She believed she was stupid, gross, ugly, and a loser. And this was reinforced daily at school.

Her guidance counsellor came up with a solution, surely her brightest moment in my eyes: Athena could take a distant education class through her old school board. This would not only help get her closer to graduation, it would also give her constructive work to complete during what was otherwise free time at school. She signed up for Writer's Craft, which would give her one grade 12 University English credit.

Every day after school I would watch for her coming up the lane, secretly looking to see if she was crying, looking upset, or, on wonderful, very rare occasions, had had a relatively good day. I tried to have the kettle ready for tea or hot chocolate and sometimes popcorn if I thought the day may have been exceptionally stressful. We would sit together and talk and have tea, rebuilding our relationship. Countless days she just couldn't manage, and I often had to pick her up from school when she shattered.

She felt like she had run out of time at the school; the staff there expected her to be fine. After all, the court case was over, the rape had been some time ago. They didn't understand that healing had only just started.

I remember one day I heard her laugh. I had completely forgotten what her laugh sounded like. It was the most hopeful sound I had heard in almost two years.

☧

Athena no longer believed she would be able to achieve either college or university. All her life she had assumed she would go to university, and had always dreamed of earning at least a master's degree. These dreams became childhood fantasies. She was afraid for her future, and worried she would not be able to financially support herself. We talked about lifeguarding and teaching swimming lessons, and looked into higher qualifications through the Red Cross. At this point she worried that even this might be beyond her capabilities.

With a positive attitude, Athena started the correspondence "Writer's Craft". As soon as her brain damage information was passed on to the Distance Education Teachers, she was told she would not be required to write tests. She would, however, have extra assignments that would be marked instead. All of the course material was provided up front, as well as a list of all assignments. She would work at her own pace, but must have all the work completed by mid August. Taking this course was one of the precious few good things that happened during this entire time. Before long Athena discovered she learned best on her own, at her own pace, and with written rather than oral instruction. She loved it. She discovered that she was still capable of learning. She both enjoyed and excelled at writing and higher level thinking.

This led to her wanting to take more courses through distance education through the summer; however she had to have the consent of her 'home' school to do so. Initially, her school guidance counsellor was not willing to support her decision, and tried to convince her it was too much work; telling her she was unlikely to succeed. But Athena was adamant, and eventually he gave in.

She enrolled in College Math, Aboriginal Beliefs and Values, and Fashion Design. She had two months to complete these three courses, as well as finish up Writer's Craft.

☧

Sandy and I still lived life on pins and needles. Always afraid of where the next blow would come from, wondering if we could possible survive anything more.

I struggled constantly with feelings of intense, profound hatred. It went against my deepest beliefs to hate other human beings, I believe it is morally wrong to hate; especially with the gut wrenching intensity I felt. I knew these feelings would eat me up inside, but just the thought of police caused my stomach to clench; my lip curl in absolute distain. I felt completely victimized by the police. I trusted none of them; after all, they had clearly demonstrated how they band together to protect each other when wrongs are committed. I wore my hatred on my sleeve, and knew that with little provocation from police I could turn into a slashing, screaming madwoman. I knew I needed to get a grip on my emotions.

But that was infinitely easier said than done.

⚖

In early April Athena saw a gynecologist for the first time. Her physical problems had been somewhat narrowed down, and she was being assessed for endometriosis. As usual, I went with her, and this time she asked the question that has terrified her since the day she remembered Conn had a knife.

We assumed Conn had used the knife on her; on her tanned arm the very thin and faint scars appear to form Conn's name. One of Athena's most consuming fears was that Conn had used the knife, and cut her internally. The sexual assault centre could not perform an internal inspection as she was bleeding too heavily, something they arbitrarily passed off as her menstruation. But Athena had not felt the same since the assault, and she needed to know.

Athena's doctor had informed the specialist about the assault. The specialist referred to it simply as "non-consensual sex", which considerably diffused the emotional aspect for Athena and made it far easier to discuss her concerns.

Thankfully, he found no sign of internal scarring.

⚖

Partially as a result of the police recommendation that we get a big, intimidating dog, we had been looking to adopt. We wanted a rescue dog; we believe there are far too many unloved animals already on earth to encourage more dog breeding by buying a puppy. So Sandy started to visit the Humane Society close to where he works. He soon met and fell in love with a rescued dog.

They called him Wayne, and he had been found living on the streets in the city. He was a big dog, far too big and full of energy to live in the city, and I think the workers recognized a perfect fit when Sandy showed interest.

Wayne came home the very next day; proudly riding shotgun for well over an hour drive to his new home. Of unknown ethnic origin, Wayne looked to us to be part Great Dane; to the Humane Society, part German Sheppard. But possibly there was some Mastiff in his heritage as well. We will never know for sure, but we enjoyed speculating. His body was a very light palomino colour; all except for his head. His enormous square muzzle was dark, and his ears stood up at the base, but flopped over at the tips. He was adorable, friendly, very photogenic, and he had more energy than a lightning bolt.

We changed his name to Diesel the day he arrived, and instantly discovered that he loved to run. He took our Blue Healer, Princess, in stride, but she was terrified of what must have seemed like an enormous, uncouth brute. Although he was count-his-ribs skinny, he was not food frenzied like Princess. He was very protective of his water bowl though; perhaps water had been hard to find when he was homeless.

Diesel was a book unto himself. While we all learned to adapt to each other, he left a trail of destruction, including, but in absolutely no way limited to, a leather couch, two mattresses, the wood at both the top and bottom of the stairs, a gallon of cooking oil, an entire Easter basket including the chocolate and the hair gel, all of Timmy's old stuffed toys and a few of Athena's, a spatula–which showed up the following spring in the garden– several shirts, and my favourite sandals. He suffered from extreme anxiety, likely the result of losing his owner, and we believed this was part of what caused him to chew. He did not appear to have been abused.

There were numerous times in the first few months that the stress of having Diesel was far greater than the pleasure. This additional pressure was a huge issue at times, and several times one or another of us was ready to give up. But we take the adoption of pets very seriously. Eventually he got over his destructive tendencies, Princess got used to him, and he started to realize this was his permanent home.

Diesel was a full grown pup when he arrived, probably just over a year old. He was friendly, but also protective, and he had awesome hackles that stood up when he was worried, making him quite intimidating. His hackles ran all the way from his shoulder to the base of his tail in a strip about 15 cm wide. His incredibly strong jaws could snap an arm bone with little problem. He was loving and gentle with us, but anyone else would be a complete idiot to take a chance without a proper introduction. He was perfect.

Speaking of which, Conn was always in the background, and occasionally he would rear his ugly head. He would make new Facebook accounts, each of which allowed him a chance to make contact with Athena. We quit counting at twenty-four separate Facebook accounts. Every contact from him, no matter how small, shattered Athena's sense of security for days. She would always delete his messages instantly, as if this would stop his invasion into the safety of her world. But it never did. On Easter weekend in 2012, Athena received the following message. It was like many of the others, but she was really sick of his invasion into her home and the resulting fear and regression that it caused her. She came to me upset with this simple contact:

Connor: 'Hi'

Athena and I talked about it, and she decided this time she would answer back in hopes of finding a way to stop him from contacting her again: ever.

Athena sent back: 'You pig. After you raped me and admitted in court you planned it you have the nerve to try and contact me? What's wrong with you? You're sick. Go get help.'

Connor: 'HA HA HA it was consensual you lying little bitch learn to not lie and you wouldn't have had that problem, I think that it's hilarious that the fact you were the one that wanted it then your bf and bros did nothing about it I find that suspicious you lying cunt'

Once again, she showed me what he had written. For anyone who is not used to the short forms, bf refers to boyfriend, and bros to brothers. The entire thing seemed really weird and somehow just not right.

Together we decided to send back something that would hopefully scare him, and make him think twice about contacting her again. Athena sent the following:

Athena: 'You admitted in court you did it. The evidence is on the transcript. If you want to keep sending these messages that's fine, I'm sure you have my lawyers' name and you might as well forward them to him because all the messages you're sending me I'm sending him. By the way, I have until I'm 18 to sue you. I'm not replying to any more of your messages.'

I went and had a shower right after Athena sent this back to Conn. While I was letting the water pour over me, my mind was mulling, trying to figure out what was wrong with this message. Several things jumped out. Conn's level of literacy was extremely low, yet he used the term consensual, and very remarkably, spelled it correctly. The word 'suspicious' was not one most people would choose unless they were in the suspicion business. Even the word hilarious was an odd, higher level of language than I would expect, particularly as it too was spelled correctly. The sentence structure was also far too complex for Conn, who I would expect to say something along the lines of, you wanted to "F ... ", not 'you consented'. There were only two short forms in the message, and Athena confirmed that this was also odd. In the past he was a master of the short form, with lower-grade level grammar and spelling at absolute best. The entire thing struck me as being written by a literate person trying to convince someone they weren't.

And why on earth would Conn "find it suspicious"? Find what suspicious? Conn knew exactly what went on that day, and didn't need to rely on the reactions of other people to determine if they believed it or not. Then it hit me: This had not been written by Conn.

Athena and I came to the same conclusion at the same time. She sent one more back, saying: "Wait a second; I just realized something. This is not Conn; whoever this is can spell and doesn't use abbreviations. Whoever this is the same goes to you." She then blocked him.

So who sent this, and why? When I studied it, it seemed like an attempt to goad Athena into saying something in anger; perhaps get her to make a threat that could be used to bring a charge against her, her boyfriend or her brother. Had she responded by saying that they would like to hurt him, or planned to someday, the police would have grounds to once again lay criminal charges. Yes, I live in paranoid fear of the police, and yes they were my first choice of candidates. The only other option I could think of was the possibility of a more literate adult in Conn's family.

Even though this likely was not Conn writing, it deeply affected Athena. After thinking about it, she became very upset. Neither her boyfriend nor her brother (interesting the writer thought she had more than one brother) did "do something". Until this exact moment Athena had never wanted any violent form of revenge; quite the opposite in fact, she had consistently said that violence was not the answer. With this new contact she suddenly questioned why no one 'did anything', and seemed to be interpreting a lack of physical retaliation as no one cared enough to stand up for her. Her father and I explained that we *did* do something, even though it was far worse than doing nothing, we had done what should have been the right thing: we went to, and cooperated with, the police.

⚖

JUNE 18 2012

Athena is once again home from school, a combination of pain, and severe depression. Shortly after I left for work this afternoon, the phone at home started ringing. Each time Athena answered, the caller waited a few seconds, saying nothing, and then hung up. This went on a number of times, and with each call Athena became more and more terrified. She finally quit answering the phone, and knowing she couldn't reach me while I was teaching, she texted her dad. Sandy then called the school and left a message, which was passed on to me right away. I went home immediately.

Athena was nearly hysterical. Her greatest fear was that Conn, or Conn and some buddies would know she was home alone, and come to hurt her.

She felt extremely vulnerable. I asked her what she would do if Conn did show up. She didn't know. "That", she said, "is the whole problem".

I told her she had to phone 911. She responded, "They would know it was me, and they wouldn't come."

I told her, "They have to come; it's not a choice."

She said, "Then they would take their time, and it would be too late anyway."

I tried to get her to understand that because we live in a different county from the one she had been charged and tried in, they would come. She reminded me that the officer who came out about the phone threat had never returned my phone call in the end.

What could I say to that?

We made a list of neighbors she could call; people who lived nearby and could come quickly if there was a crisis. We discussed an emergency plan, which involved first calling 911, and then neighbors, but because it could easily be half an hour to an hour before emergency services arrived, we taught her to defend herself.

I would like to believe it would never be necessary, but the reality of stalkers is that they are unpredictably dangerous. Athena needs to feel safe; hell, has a right to not just feel safe, but to be safe, and she categorically believes the police will not help her.

Athena needs to know that she can defend herself if she has to. For anyone to get into the house and past the dogs, they would have to have a weapon, and in that case, Athena's life would be in serious jeopardy. So we taught her the skills that would allow her to save herself if her life were in imminent danger.

After all, she is absolutely correct. The police have proven they have no interest in protecting her.

CHAPTER 20

The Transcript

The trial transcript, ordered on the last day of the trial in January, arrived in late June. Instead of the four to six weeks promised, it had taken well over four months. It came in three sections, one for each day of the trial. Each of the three days separately bound.

Here is an overview of the trial; highlighting information I had not previously known.

I learned that a copy of Athena's first interview had been transcribed and was delivered to Mr. Cupito two days before the trial. This, conveniently for the crown, did not allow Cupito enough time to verify the accuracy of the document, which would have required multiple viewings of the video while reading the written version and making corrections.

The court, although requested by Cupito, had refused to transcribe Conn's interview. These difficulties did not negatively affect the trial outcome, although they certainly could have. Not giving enough time to review important documents and not transcribing Conn's interview says to me the crown was less interested in doing everything possible to ensure a fair trial than it was in winning the game.

Chompsky took the stand first. Several times she contradicted herself, with generally unimportant things, but if the table were turned, these mistakes would make you or I appear unreliable. Her first error was in saying that Athena and I traveled to the sexual assault centre with her in a marked police car.

The second, and I never have understood why this was in any way relevant, was the text Athena received while we were on our way to the sexual assault centre. When questioned by the crown, Chompsky said she noticed Athena received a text, and asked her about it. Chompsky claimed under oath that Athena did not answer her until she had repeated her question several times; and said that by the time Athena did answered her, she had already texted the person back.

Chompsky changed her story when she was cross-examined by Cupito and admitted *that it was Athena who voluntarily told her she had received a text, and it was Chompsky* who told Athena what to text back to the sender.

Cupito asked Chompsky if knowing Conn claimed he had consent caused her to change the way she interviewed Athena. She claimed no, and said she always had the victim tell the whole sexual assault story, and then left the room. When she returned to the interview room, she would then ask the victim to go through the entire event again. Cupito scored his point when he suggested she does this to help victims remember details "because (he said) they often fail to remember all the details in the initial interview." and Chompsky readily agreed.

Delwood next took the stand, and just as Chompsky had, was asked if he had added or deleted anything from his notebook. (Get this: *these cops use a spiral notebook for notes.* I was shocked by this; this is just wide open to abuse. It doesn't get any easier to remove pages, does it?)

Delwood, however, claimed he had not messed with either of the two notebooks this case apparently required. Interestingly though, the photocopies Mr. Cupito was given of Delwood's official notebooks, *did not have page numbers.* Delwood claimed his copy did. So, had someone covered *every* page number of two entire notebooks as they photocopied the rest of the page? Why would anyone do that? The lack of page numbers did sit well with Mr. Cupito, who went out of his way to comment on this bizarre omission several times.

(Note: Without page numbers, any number of pages could have been removed or even moved in sequence, allowing some serious manipulation of so-called evidence. In fact, an entire notebook could easily be rewritten. Of course, ethically no police officer would do this....)

Delwood and Conn told conflicting stories regarding the missing text message retrieval application. Delwood testified that Conn looked for the application to retrieve his text messages, but could not find it. "It had been there", Delwood said Conn claimed, "and then it was gone." Conn was then driven home because he claimed he could download the application there, which would allow him to pull up the message. But at home, Conn was unable to download messages, and so could not substantiate his claim of consent.

Delwood claimed he spoke to me the next day; the day after the assault. (In fact, neither Athena nor I spoke to him until I finally called him early the next week. He did not initiate the first contact, I did, and he did not speak to Athena until several days after that.)

When Delwood first told his version of events, he made it sound as if Athena hid the fact that she and Conn had texted. Once Cupito began questioning Delwood, his story changed, he agreed that Athena had been fully cooperative, readily gave her permission to access her texts, and when asked if any of the texts were of a sexual nature had said yes.

Given the entire criminal charge is the claim that Athena lied and said there were no texts of a sexual nature, and this was proven incorrect virtually at very beginning of the trial, one has to wonder why this trial wasn't called off after this statement.

When asked, Conn could not remember if he and Athena spoke on the phone on the night of February 14th. Less than eleven recorded sentences later, he says he thought they made arrangements to have sex during the phone call on the night of the fourteenth, the one he didn't remember having.

Conn then told a story that involved him asking and receiving consent *while* making out with Athena at his house on the day of the (ok, alleged) assault. He told an elaborate story of "I asked if I could take off her pants, and she said 'yes'. Then she asked if she could take off my pants, and I said 'yes'. This went through all the clothing parts, and concluded with him saying he asked if they could 'fuck and she said, yes'. He went on to say he asked if he could put his penis inside her, and she said ... You get the unlikely picture.

When asked by the crown attorney if the sexual position ever changed, Conn changed the sequence of events to include this, and said that Athena got on top. He claimed that after they had sex they got dressed, and he walked Athena to the door. The crown then interrupted and asked "Did you place your penis anywhere else?"

Conn replied that he asked Athena if she would give him a blow job, and she agreed.

Once again this caused the story, and the entire sequence to change again, as he said it occurred prior to intercourse. He then claimed to have obtained consent on the walk to his house, after saying only minutes before that the two of them had talked only about 'school stuff' on the brief walk. The story crashed again when Cupito asked Conn if he had taken his shirt off prior to any talk about having sex, and he admitted he had.

I lost count of the number of times Conn claimed he asked for, and received consent. At this point in the transcript Conn had sited eight separate locations where the conversation had taken place, *not one* of which was claimed in his initial interview. Conn then admitted he was surprised when Athena followed him up the stairs, thus indicating he had not obtained sexual consent at that time. If he had, he would not have been surprised by her following him up the stairs, he would have expected it.

His story completely changed when he admitted he didn't know if they had even discussed having sex when he started removing his clothes.

At one point Conn claimed that when they got inside the door of his home, he asked Athena if she wanted to have sex. Cupito's response was, "Instead of offering her a tuna sandwich, you say, do you want to have sex?"

Conn replied, "Yes."

Cupito pointed out that this statement had not been told to police when he was arrested, and had never been heard before. Conn then said the two talked about sex on the walk to his house–completely contradicting his previous statement–but not when they arrived. When questioned about this contradiction, Conn then claimed consent was given both times. Conn then returned to claiming he had consent, this time both on the way home and inside the door, but not when they were upstairs. He was unable to determine which of the times or places he had previously claimed to have gotten consent were actually true.

When asked if he was confused about what went on in the bedroom, he said "No" several times. In most cases, Cupito would clarify or restate his question to Conn, ensuring Conn would admit or agree several times. Cupito suggested that Conn took his own shirt off as soon as he entered the bedroom. Conn agreed that he had done this without Athena's knowledge, again contradicting previous statements. He did not admit to taking off his pants, but Cupito did not push this. He simply asked and let it go when Conn said no.

Conn proceeded to contradict himself regarding events following the assault: First he said they talked after sex and he decided to have lunch before going back to school, but Athena decided to return to school instead of having lunch. He said they kissed and she left. But when pressed, he admitted he had deleted his texts because it had been obvious there was a problem by how quickly Athena left following the sexual interaction.

Conn told several stories to explain why he could not retrieve his text messages, and each version contradicted the story Delwood told. Cupito pointed out that there were only two options: either Conn had deleted the application, or the police had.

Conn readily admitted that he always started any sexual texts, and the texts were just joking around. He was unable to remember any specific texts, or details of any of the texts. Cupito pointed out that Athena at times attempted to re-direct the sexual comments, responding with 'LOL' (laugh out loud) or ha ha.

When asked if he had plans on the morning of February15th to have lunch with Athena, he now said, "No". When asked if he expected to see her at all that day except possibly in the hallway, he again said "No", again contradicting his own previous statements.

Cupito then suggested to Conn that he "had already decided after all this joking around about sex that if (he) could get this woman into (his) house, (he) was going to have sex with her."

And Conn replied, "Yes."

When Cupito pushed this, saying, "And despite the fact that she didn't want to, you went ahead anyway."

Conn then said, "No." Yet he agreed when Cupito reminded him that Athena "may have" told him she did not want to have sex because she was on her period, and somehow they ended up having sex anyway.

Next, Cupito asked if there was any discussion regarding pregnancy. Conn answered, "Yes, she said she didn't want to get pregnant."

Conn then told the Court this statement was before they began intercourse, but soon amended this saying he did not know when it was said. He didn't know who brought it up or what else was said on the subject. He agreed it could have been a protest during intercourse, trying to get him to stop.

Conn admitted to locking the door when they arrived at his home, but admitted he couldn't remember if they had discussed sex before he did this or not.

Questioning ended with the following:

Cupito: You just thought, she came up to my bedroom, that is a good sign, correct?

Conn: Yes

Cupito: And you started taking your clothes off?

Conn: Yes

Cupito: And thereafter you went ahead and had sex with Athena Schuler, didn't you?

Conn: Yes

Cupito: And you never asked for or got her consent did you?

Conn: I asked her.

Cupito: You don't even know when you asked her, do you?

Conn: No, I do remember asking her though.

Cupito: And you have no idea when?

Conn: No.

That was the end of questioning.

The crown attorney then gave his closing remarks, in which he stated that under section 140 (1) (a) of the criminal code it is his submission that *"it is not an element of that subsection that the crown has to prove that the offence has not been committed."*

The crown was claiming that whether Athena had been raped or not was irrelevant. He said there was no evidence that Conn raped Athena or that Conn was standing naked and pushed her onto the bed. He said that *because there is no evidence that it happened the way Athena said it did, she therefore lied to the police, and should be convicted of lying to them.*

Mr. Crown Attorney went on to say that in Athena's first interview, she told Chompsky that Conn mostly texted to ask if he could phone her. Chompsky asked if they had discussed sex in texting. Athena said.

"Not that I remember." Chompsky then asked Athena, "Did you guys have a conversation or a text message or something about having sex on Monday?" Athena replied that she did not remember talking to him at all on Monday.

The crown said that Athena's details of "the alleged sex act" are contradicted by the evidence of Mann. (Seriously?)

He further said that "there were false statements made by this defendant (Athena) to the police that accused him (Conn) of sexual assault. Astoundingly, he then claims that *the section of the Criminal Code she was charged under doesn't say of sexual assault that was not committed.* (The crown is actually saying his interpretation of section 140 (1) (a) is not about Athena saying Conn raped her when he had not; he is saying that the rape is irrelevant to this case, what matters only is if Athena was not completely truthful in every aspect and every detail of what she told the police. In this case, about not saying there were sexual text messages on the day she was raped.)

He then pointed out the size difference between Athena and Conn, and he was done.

Cupito is an eloquent speaker. He started with: "This case began with the astonishing proposition that if a fifteen year old girl reports a sexual assault police will interview the alleged perpetrator. They will decide who they think is telling the truth and the loser of that beauty pageant will be charged with a criminal offence."

He then stated his astonishment that an offence such as public mischief could be proven by having the perpetrator say he did not do it.

He was then chastised by the judge for saying the court has "heard two even more outlandish suggestions," the first that *any* falsehood in a statement to police accusing someone of an offence could result in a criminal charge of public mischief. He said no one should dare report crime to the police without spending a great deal of time with a lawyer first to make sure the story is entirely accurate.

The second outlandish suggestion Cupito pointed out was that somehow the Crown has reversed the onus of proof, saying there was no evidence to prove it happened the way Athena said it did. "Yes, there is (proof)." Cupito said, "There is Athena Schuler's statement to the police …

So there is plenty of evidence that it happened that way, it is all written down and it is all there."

Cupito has an excellent command of English, and he proceeded to grammatically prove the meaning of section 149 (1) (a), showing it must be a statement *that falsely accuses another person of committing a crime.*

Athena, he went on to say, agreed that they had texted and talked on the phone. Many of the texts are about when was a good time to phone. That is what Athena told police, and that is correct. When asked about flirting and talking about sex, she said "not that I remember." She was then asked if he had ever expressed anything sexual to her, but Chompsky was interrupted at this point, and stopped Athena's response, Chompsky left the room, and when she returned, the question was never taken up again.

The next time she was asked about texting, by Delwood on the phone several weeks later, Athena told him there were texts and jokes about sex. Once again proving she was not trying to mislead anyone.

With regards to Conn's testimony in court, Cupito stated, "If Mr. Mann was on trial for sexual assault and put on the performance in the witness stand that he put on in this trial, the Trier of fact would be imminently justified in rejecting his evidence completely as not even raising a reasonable doubt, and certainly couldn't prove anything like I didn't do it to any standard." (Cupito was saying that had Conn been on trial for sexual assault, he would have been convicted.)

He then "touches on the high points, the six, seven big lies he told you, because his credibility is reduced to zero by that and there is no use fighting about the details."

(An interesting detail: When Cupito's was giving his closing statements, he revisited Athena going upstairs with Conn, and Conn realizing this was his 'chance' and he started to take off his clothes. Cupito commented that Conn could not say if they had even talked about having sex at this point. Judge Sheila then cut Cupito off and said, "You are talking about that day as opposed to all those text messages..."

(The judge was fixated on the text messages, and I believe this statement shows that she believes Athena deserved what she got because she had joked about sex.)

Cupito responded by reminding the court that Conn admitted he knew they were simply joking around, and nothing more.

He reiterated that, "He (Conn) had decided that if he ever got Athena Schuler alone in his house he was going to have sex with her. I asked him that question. His answer was yes ... in fact; his lies and his admissions lead almost inexorably to the conclusion that Athena Schuler was actually telling the truth about having been sexually assaulted. And for those reasons the prosecution has failed to meet its onus of proof and Ms. Schuler should be acquitted."

The judge then granted time for the prosecution (the crown attorney) to see if he could learn just what the law he had charged Athena under actually meant; to find Jurisprudence. Granting time to the crown meant we waited another six weeks for a verdict. Yet at the end of those six weeks, the crown failed to submit anything to the judge, even though he was the one who asked to be allowed to do so. Mr. Cupito made a submission showing his was the accurate interpretation.

⚖

Finally, "REASONS FOR JUDGMENT" is the title on the final document. The first two had been titled "PROCEEDINGS AT TRIAL", the screaming capitals provided by the court, not me.

Judge Sheila claimed that "Upon his arrest Conn immediately co-operated in the investigation... ", and that he testified at trial that the sex was entirely consensual, and because of the "many conflicts in their respective statements ... " Conn was released unconditionally.

She claimed that Athena's videotaped statement "undoubtedly" contained a number of falsehoods. She then gave *two* examples: One was that Athena claimed she and Conn mostly talked about when he could call her, and that they "never really texted about that much stuff." And the other, when Chompsky asked Athena about receiving a text on Monday, and Athena responded that she didn't talk to him at all on Monday. *(Example number one was actually true, according to what had come out in the court of law, the two teens had mainly texted about when Conn would phone her, and school stuff. The second, they did not text or talk or see each other on the day Chompsky asked her if they had!*

Judge Sheila then went on to read some of the texts. She then commended the police for their job in investigating this case; claiming Athena "blatantly lied about the text communication with Conn," and that the police had "ample reasonable and probable grounds to charge Athena with public mischief."

How could the judge possibly say this based only on the word of the boy Athena had accused of rape; the one who could not keep any semblance of any of his stories straight?

The judge did note that there were "a number of inconsistencies" in Conn's statement, "including when and how often Conn asked Athena if she wanted to have sex, and the order in which clothing was removed." She added that Conn admitted to knowing they were just joking around when texting.

She called Conn a "suggestible young witness". *(Thus excusing him from constantly changing all of his stories.)*

She then said she believed "Conn's trial testimony that the sexual encounter was consensual, but cross-examination did establish some inconsistencies... " and goes on to say "I do not believe her (Athena's) allegations that Conn forcibly raped her *"in the manner described"* in her statement. It is very probable that Athena Schuler intentionally made a false statement accusing Connor Mann of sexual assault."

But, in the end, she says, after all this, that she is "satisfied that the doubt (she has) is a reasonable doubt." And so Athena was found not guilty.

I would never have believed a Canadian judge would engage in such obvious, intentional victim blaming, and yet, there it is.

⚖

There were a few things I expected to find in the transcript, but did not. I had been told the Judge constantly was reprimanding Mr. Cupito, but this was not evident in the transcript. Janna McDonald, the court liaison worker from Hope House who had attended Athena's trial voiced her disgust at hearing Delwood say that Conn had come from a "good family" in the trial. I specifically looked for this, but once again this was not in the written transcript.

☪☪

During the time I was waiting for the transcript to arrive, I happened across a string of websites maintained by people who had obtained official court transcripts, and believed they had been altered. I also discovered that one can obtain a copy of the recorded audio tape of a trial. I immediately decided I would be doing this; the written word, especially transcribed from an oral, in-person event, provides extremely one-dimensional information. When people speak, voice intonation, gestures, facial and physical expressions greatly modify and even completely change the meaning of words. (This is one of the huge problems with trying to interpret the meaning of, say, text messages.) By listening to the tape, I would get a greater understanding of what was being communicated.

I decided long ago that I would be making a formal complaint to the Counsel of Judges regarding the conduct of the judge. The Counsel of Judges claims to have high expectations for those in the profession, and their website lays down those expectations. When I compare the code of ethics to what went on in court, I see major chasms. Sandy says I am wasting my time, they will be no different than anyone else in the 'justice' system, but I feel I owe it to everyone to at least give them a chance.

CHAPTER 21

~Moving on~

Summer came, and for Athena it was a summer of never unending work; the summer that had no spare time, no down time. She was a swimming instructor and lifeguard at the pool; a job she continued to love, and in one way, a job that helped to wash away some of her pain. She loved teaching children to swim. She excelled at it, and got grateful feedback from the children and the parents whose children she taught.

Virtually every minute Athena was not working at the pool she spent working on her summer courses. She took assignments to work and spent her lunch time studying. We had to force her to take breaks. She would work until she could no longer think, let alone write, and then would fall apart. But in the end, her diligence paid off: she finished Writer's Craft with eighty-three percent, Math with eighty-percent, and ninety-three percent in Aboriginal studies. She withdrew from Fashion Design, having simply run out of time.

For a child who scored in the forth percentile in her ability to focus, who was suffering from Post Traumatic Stress Disorder, was in the very early healing stages following a sexual assault and victimization by the entire legal system, her success seemed almost miraculous to us.

Athena still suffered from severe depression. Her doctor wanted her to go back on anti-depressants, but she still adamantly refused. She said she either felt no emotions when she was on the drugs, or she felt "like someone else."

Trips to the doctor and the emergency room at the hospital continued, and finally a medication was found that started to ease her physical pain.

At one point in the summer, I was talking to our closest neighbor. She was aware of what was going on in our lives, and had close ties to Rivertown. She thought I might be upset because she had shared Athena's story with a close friend: our neighbor's friend, Marcia, has a daughter in her early teens. The daughter was dating a boy that made Marcia feel very uncomfortable; there was something about the boy that just didn't seem right. The final straw came when the mother, Marcia, was sitting at her kitchen table and this boy came into her house. He walked up behind her, and started to give her a back massage. This shocked her to the point she didn't know what to think, and needed someone to concur that the behavior was indeed outrageous. My neighbor agreed with her wholeheartedly, and asked the boy's name. His name was Connor Mann. Rightfully, my neighbor felt she needed to share Athena's story.

Far from being upset, I felt this may have saved another young woman from a fate similar to Athena's.

⚖

FALL 2012

It felt like we were making some progress in the fall of 2012. I remember waking up and feeling hopeful. Throughout the day I would suddenly be struck with a feeling of profound thankfulness: I believed Athena would get through this; I believed she would survive. She was better; a relative term to be sure, but her current state of mind was no comparison to the dark places she had been. She was like the first flower on a never before seen plant. Our counsellor, Terry, had told me that Athena would never again be the same person, and that was absolutely true. We had no idea what this new flower would be like; if it would have any resemblance to the child that mentally and emotionally left us two years ago.

September brought the reality of school again. High-school would never be a good place for Athena. I expect part of the problem was dealing with the same relationship patterns that had developed when she started there as a terrified, damaged and confused girl. She had gotten stronger, but words still hurt her. She was frequently called appalling things right to her face, and she still had to deal with jokes about rape from blissfully ignorant peers.

Finally, I had enough. I called a woman's shelter that provides education on healthy dating, and asked if they would be willing to speak at this school. They were thrilled; they had been trying to convince the school to allow them to speak for a very long time. Like me, they felt it was not just important, but critical to teach students about limits, that no means no, that some relationships are toxic, and how to protect oneself from relationship violence. I explained the issues with the use of the word 'rape' and was assured this would be addressed.

I called the vice principal and once again discussed the issues Athena was dealing with. I quoted the statistics that one in four Canadian women will be assaulted, and the vast majority of these will be teenage girls. (www. sascwr.org/files/www/resources_pdfs/sexual_assault/Myths_and_Facts. pdf) I asked how these girls would be able to protect themselves if they were not even aware of the potential danger. I told the VP they need only give me a day and a time that would work for the school, and I would do all the arranging for the women's group to come and speak. She said she would get back to me.

I never heard another word from her.

Athena constantly asked the VP when she was going to do something about the issue of using the word 'rape' so inappropriately. One day in frustration the VP told her that it was just the culture of the students, and that there was nothing she could do about it.

I was not happy with this statement: The student culture included many things that were considered unacceptable, and those things were swiftly dealt with. Take the Lord's name in vain, call someone 'gay', even hike one's skirt above the 'legal' height, and discipline was immediately enforced. To me this indicated not just a profound lack of compassion on the part of the school, but a dangerous omission in their refusal to educate both girls and boys as to the reality of the world in which we live.

Ignorance is only bliss until the unthinkable happens.

☖☗

Athena had previously come to believe she wasn't capable of achieving at college or university, but following her remarkable success with correspondence courses over the summer, she re-gained some of her lost confidence. By the end summer, she had decided paramedics would be a really interesting field to go into. She changed several of her grade twelve courses with this goal in mind.

One of the courses she signed up for was law. Within days her goal changed again. She had discovered a passion; she would become a lawyer. She found the law fascinating, and remarkably easy. In some way, the written law made sense to her. Taking distance education had been the best thing that happened to her education since her head injury. She learned that she is not stupid; in fact, she is still brilliant. She now believed she could accomplish what had been impossible for her not many months ago.

Athena did well in her fall courses. She still had accommodations in place; and we still fought constantly with her home school to retain those accommodations. Dr. Rose would re-test Athena around the same time of year she had been tested two years ago. Only then would I agree to changes in her academic accommodations at school.

We started university shopping. There were factors that had to be considered. The first was to ensure that academic learning accommodations were in place, the second was to ensure an environment that would accommodate Athena's mental health needs. Athena needed to have a single room in residence, and that room had to have a secure lock. Sharing a room meant someone could enter her room at anytime, and while that was concern enough for Athena, her biggest fear was getting a roommate who would bring a boyfriend into the room, or worse, bring him in and then leave to say, go to the washroom, resulting in Athena alone in the room with a male. This possibility terrified her; a single room was vital for her success. She had one other overwhelming concern: What if something did happen to her at university? What would she do? Who would she call to help her?

Her father and I convinced her that the campus police were not 'real' police, and hence could be trusted. Was this wrong of us? I don't know. I do know that it helped to ease her fears, and allowed her to be mentally and emotionally able to attend university.

⚖

By mid fall, Athena decided for herself that she needed to be back on anti-depressants. After hearing her concerns, our doctor prescribed a different drug. Fortunately this drug worked much better for her. The difference was subtle, yet definite. In a short time Athena was turning her light off most nights, and she was sleeping.

Athena had ended the summer of 2012 with glowing recommendations from her employer. Yet she was not re-hired. What had happened? Had small town gossip caught up? Athena cried when she lost her job at the pool. It had been cathartic for her, she loved it, and she had been so very good at it. By the time she learned she had no job, it was June. She had been told at the end of the previous summer she definitely would be returning, and had trusted that would happen. By the time she learned she had no job, the summer jobs had all been filled. More stress: She would only be going to university if she had a job and saved money. We had not yet recovered from the financial damage done by the rape and criminal charge.

After a short cry, she decided she would bake for the summer, and she would sell the baking at local farmers markets. She found a summer student program that provides training and money to start a summer business. And so she worked for herself.

Not only did she learn time-management and how to run a business, she learned that small towns can be supportive and caring. The vendors at markets look after and support each other, and Athena had not had much exposure to the positive side of people. This was a wonderful new experience for her.

I spent a great deal of time with Athena that summer. We began to reconnect, and she continued to heal. She turned eighteen; an adult. She does not expect good things will happen for her, and perhaps that is why she is so grateful when they do. For the most part she relates far better to older people than people her age. She is worldly beyond her years, and it separates her from those her own age. While she has re-gained some of her sense of humor, overall she is extremely serious about life. She lost much of her outgoing nature, and does not trust people. Overall her life is better, but the scars are very deep, and a great many are not yet healed.

I loved spending the summer with her. We are as much best friends as mother and daughter; I tried to be there to support her when she needed it; and she frequently did. Conn still occasionally stalked her, and while it was mainly confined to social media, Athena lived on constant alert, and her fear was what prompted me to start going to markets with her. Always in the back of her mind was the possibility that Conn might show up. Thankfully this did not happen; emotionally I don't believe she would have been able to return to the market if he had. Unfortunately her fear awarded him huge power over her.

CHAPTER 22

Complaint to the JCRP

After much futile searching on the internet to find out what I needed to do to hear the audio recording of Athena's trial, I called the courthouse in Southland.

It took a number of days and considerable persistence to obtain the information. It appears to be almost unheard of. There were so many phone calls back and forth; the clerks began to recognize not just my name, but my voice. I found this quite disconcerting.

The process was finally determined, and the appropriate forms were forwarded to me by email. They were quite detailed, and it appeared to me that approval was not guaranteed. I decided to state my intention to file a complaint against Judge Sheila as my reason for applying, believing this may make my request harder to refuse. I said I wanted to make certain I had correct information prior to making this complaint, and hearing the trial would assist with this.

I would be required to appear in front of a judge to make my request, and I asked if this could be done at the Rivertown court. I was assured it could. The clerk confirmed that Judge Sheila would not be able to rule on the matter, as it would be a conflict of interest. She said that another judge would be brought in. I was assured everything would be taken care of, and I need only appear in court on December 14th, assigned day.

DECEMBER 13, 2012

A court clerk from Southland Courthouse, called to confirm I was definitely 'on the docket' for court tomorrow, although my request would not show up on the docket sheet. Court numbers are only assigned for active court cases, and as this was not an active case, there were no numbers. Regardless, I was assured the court was ready. I was told my case might be heard outside of the actual courtroom; perhaps in the judges' chambers.

I lost some sleep over this. I envisioned Judge Sheila and I alone, and her saying I attacked her and me ending up charged with something criminal. I decided if the hearing were in her chambers, I would not go alone. I would only enter her chamber with some impartial person; a duty council lawyer, or simply any lawyer present that I could hire for half an hour. I do not trust anyone in the Rivertown court.

DECEMBER 14, 2012

Since this was a day of lost pay anyway, I went to court early. The same court cop was there as had been at Athena's trial, and interestingly, so was Officer Firth, the school cop. I had not seen Firth since he presented Athena with the charge for public mischief, and at times I have wondered if he was absent from all the events because he had not played along with the rest of the persecution party.

As I waited my turn, I watched as a number of people went before Judge Sheila to present their plea. Of utmost interest was the fact that *not one* of them responded, when saying they understood what she was telling them, with 'yes' or 'yes your Honour', and *not once* did she correct them. Why had she corrected Athena for the exact same response the first time she met her? Was she biased before the trial even began?

Around 11:30 a.m., with the court almost empty, Judge Sheila asked if there was any other business. Her tone indicated to me she knew there was something more, but she was either playing dumb, or she actually did not know what the 'other business' was.

I stood up and said that I was making an application to obtain the recording of trial proceedings, and I had been told I would have my application heard today in this court. Thankfully I had brought copies of the application with me, as the court did not appear to have the official copy I had filed in Southland. Judge Sheila sent a court clerk to take the papers from me, a recess was called, and a flurry of activity began. I was not amused. Once again I had taken an unpaid day off work, and had done everything I could to ensure the court had done their part. Was this just to jerk me around? Or is this simply an indication of incompetence?

I had considerable time to speculate.

Finally, Judge Sheila returned, and the few of us left in the courtroom stood up to usher her in. I was asked to approach the bench.

It was a complete waste of time. Sheila said that she could not make a ruling on the application as this would be a conflict of interest.

No kidding. That was why I had been told there would be another judge present.

Sheila set a date for my application to be heard at the Southland court for January 23rd, 2013, and said that the crown may wish to be present.

My first thought was, crap, another circus performance. I didn't expect the crown would be Baird again; having made a complaint against him, he too would be in a potential conflict of interest. *I believe I felt a brief sense of achievement at that precise moment.*

JANUARY 23, 2013

We had gotten over fifteen centimeters of snow overnight, and the roads were terrible. The drive to Southland took me twice as long as normal. I rushed in fifteen minutes late; and late is something I loathe being.

As soon as the clerk behind the bullet proof enclosure saw me, she told me to go right into the courtroom, telling me they were ready for me. I was again struck by the fact that these people recognize both my name and face.

They were indeed waiting for me. This was a very different courtroom from the others I had been in: Small, but very formal with tiers from the judge down, all in light coloured wood. A woman judge I did not recognize was presiding. There were three court workers, the ubiquitous court cop, as well as a man I assume was an attorney for the crown.

I apologized for keeping them waiting, but they had been chatting from their appointed spots around the room as I came in, and seemed unconcerned. I was told to take my time, make myself comfortable, and then we would start.

It took less than five minutes. The judge read out a bit of the document, told me I would not be able to obtain a copy of the recording, however I could listen to the recording at the courthouse. I was told the recordings, contrary to what I had read and been told, were not yet digitally produced at the Rivertown court. I was told the office manager would contact me to discuss a date for me to hear the trial recording.

And that was that. We were told to raise, the judge left; then so did I.

JANUARY 28, 2013

I heard the audio recording of Athena's trial today. I took the written transcript with me so I could see if there had been any obvious omissions or mistakes. I was also listening to hear Delwood say that Conn came from a good family.

There was difficulty locating the tape, but it was eventually found. It had not been stored where it should have been, with the other tapes. Hmmm

In the recording, Judge Sheila can be heard numerous times telling Cupito to speak into the microphone, in order that everything he said would be recorded. Yet there are many sections on the tape where Judge Sheila is speaking, and the tape picks up only completely garbled speech. These breaks in audibility ranged from several seconds, to perhaps two minutes or more. Whenever there is a spot in the recording that is garbled, the written transcript indicates nothing; no break, no notation, nothing.

The written transcript held very true to the words that were audible, but one does have to wonder: Is it standard practice not to have everything the judge says on record, or had the tape been deliberately modified to downplay fringe comments made by the judge.

My suspicious nature added this to the fact that the transcript took almost three times as long as it should have to be produced, disappeared for a week before it resurfaced, and had been found today in a place where trial tapes are not usually kept.

I will never know if the tape was deliberately altered; I do know that there are many in-audible sections, and given what I have experienced in the legal system, I believe it is possible.

I did not hear Delwood say anything about Conn's family on the tape.

The woman assigned to go through the tape with me was quite new to the job. She was conscientious, and helpful. She was surprised by the tape and the trial. At the end, she asked if I would like to hear the recording of Athena's first interview. I was burnt out by this time. I appreciated her offer; I had no idea this was available to me, but I didn't feel emotionally up to hearing Athena describe being raped.

⚖️

And so, after much more research on the behavior standards expected of Judges, I made a formal complaint to the Judges Complaint Review Panel. I attested that Sheila lacked integrity and impartiality, made inappropriate and insensitive comments, belittled Athena, and showed partial treatment toward the police and Conn.

⚖️

At the beginning of May I received a response from the Judges Complaint Review Panel, advising me that a complaint file had been opened. The complaint would first be reviewed by a judge and a community member who would then submit a report to a review panel made up of two judges, a lawyer and a community member. Neither my name nor the judges' name would be made known to them. I would then "be notified of the review panel's decision in due course."

By this time Athena was taking a legal course at university. She learned that only one to two complaints made to the JCRP are heard each year. I felt somewhat hopeful that at least we had gotten an investigation.

In December of 2013, seven months after I received the letter from the JCRP, I finally phoned to inquire about the status of my complaint. Interestingly, I was not asked my name, file number, or even when I had filed my complaint. The receptionist simply informed me it could take up to a year for the process to be complete.

Just before the New Year; I received a letter of response. I was informed the committee did not find evidence that Justice Sheila had committed misconduct, and that my complaint was dismissed, and the file closed.

There was little else I learned; the committee noted that Judge Sheila was very quiet during the trial, which tells me they did not listen to the audio of the trial as I had requested, but relied instead on the transcript. They found she made no inappropriate comments, and deemed her commendation of the police was perfectly acceptable. With respect to my comments regarding violations of Athena's rights, they note that the crown attorney has the authority to decide what evidence he/she may put forward in a case. This response put the onus on the crown attorney, and entirely ignored my actual concern: that Sheila may have been bias because there were interviews that could not be used in the trial due to Charter Rights violations. They did not feel that Judge Sheila went out of her way to insult, degrade or bully Athena.

My concern that Justice Sheila appeared to pick and choose which parts of Conn's testimony she believed was not investigated. In fact, the JCRP does not have authority to investigate this area at all. The decisions of a judge are matters of judicial discretion, and the judge is not accountable to the JCRP. So, are judges accountable to anyone? If they are, this information does not appear to be obtainable, and believe me, I have tried.

For about ten minutes now I have tried to come up with something to close this chapter with. I guess I have finally accepted that the standard of ethics, professionalism and integrity I once believed existed, does not exist. I am no longer surprised by this. I am dismayed, appalled, horrified and disgusted. But not surprised.

I do think it is well past time that the entire legal system becomes accountable to the public it is supposed to protect.

CHAPTER 23

Athena: Survivor

FEBRUARY OF 2014

VICTIM'S COMPENSATION BOARD

Last summer, Athena and I entered into a contract with a personal injury lawyer. Our contract stipulates that he will be paid if and when a successful suit is settled. Only if we change our minds and decide not to sue are we required to dig into our pockets to pay, otherwise his payment comes out of the settlement.

We learned one really important detail: We believed Athena had until she was eighteen years old to initiate a civil suit. In fact, the clock begins ticking for her when she turns eighteen. She then has two years from that date to initiate a suit.

We discussed making a claim with the Victim's Compensation Board, as well as suits against Conn, his parents, and the school board for their failure to protect Athena not from the assault, but from the stalking and harassment following.

The other area we discussed was suing both the police, and Delwood. Both Athena and I were adamant that the public needs to know how sexual assault victims are treated by the police. The lawyer, Mr. McLean, said he did not have experience publicizing his cases. He believed the settlement would be lower if the media were involved, and did not feel media contact was his area of expertise. It had been his experience that the police included a "no publicity" clause in their settlements, and will pay more to keep victims from telling their stories publically. Mr. Mclean wanted me to talk to a lawyer who specialized in highly publicized cases involving human rights, and then decide if we wanted to go with him, or another lawyer. He then suggested a lawyer I should speak to.

I Googled this lawyer, and found he has an interactive website where it is possible to leave a message for him. I left a brief message.

I got a call back almost immediately: so quickly that I was caught completely off guard, and I suddenly realized how much information there was to impart to a lawyer before they could possibly have any understanding of this incredible case. As a result, I didn't get into the specifics of this case.

However, as I have consistently found, the lawyer I spoke to was very helpful and candid. I was inquiring exclusively about suing the police, and the lawyers' first question was to ask if the police had physically abused Athena. Apparently suffering physical abuse at the hands of the police is virtually the only way to bring a successful lawsuit against them. The lawyer talked about the courts, and how they generally side with the police because they trust the police over you or me. This, she said, is because of the enormous power police have.

Where is the logic in this? I believe the police should be infinitely more accountable because they have such incredible power. They should be role models for our society. We should expect; no, demand even greater adherence to the laws of our country because of their authority and the enormous potential for abuse of this power.

She explained that a suit against the police would normally cost between eighty and ninety thousand dollars. If we were successful, and she added that people rarely are; we could expect a reward of ten to fifteen thousand dollars. The process would be extremely slow, and would be constantly prolonged by the lawyer for the police, who is being paid through the never ending pot of money called tax payers' dollars. They would be very brutal to Athena, and would make her life as miserable as possible. There would be a clause attached preventing any publicity if it ever did get settled.

Once again I found myself wondering how I could have lived in Canada all my life and not realize we live in a police state.

I called Mr. McLean the next day, and asked him to proceed on our behalf.

⚖

Amy Martin was new to the law firm, and had taken over Athena's file from Mr. McLean. It was at Ms. Martin's suggestion that Athena applied to the Victim's Compensation Board (VCB). I would never have considered it. The VCB is under the Services for Victims umbrella, which is housed in the Justice Department. Unfortunately, this law firm believed the response of the VCB is an indicator of expected success in future lawsuits.

In preparation for the submission to VCB, Athena's school records were obtained, and we were sent a copy of this entire file. We really don't lack for surprises in our house: There was not even a hint that Athena had sustained an acquired brain injury in gym class in 2010 and had been taken to the hospital unconscious with a sprained jaw and broken nose. There was *not one word* in the file to represent all the emails, phone calls and meetings we had with the school over Conn stalking and harassing Athena. There was no mention of her being sexually assaulted, or of the school having reported the assault to the police. It seemed to me that this file had been scrubbed and bleached clean of any possible liability, making a lawsuit against the school board virtually impossible.

In order to learn more before the hearing, I researched the Victim's Compensation Board. It appears that every province has a variation of this as a result of the Canadian Victims Bill of Rights. It is intended to help with alleviate the hardships that come with being the victim of violent crime.

We soon discovered that our province has not considered the fact that many people live in rural settings or small communities and are at a serious disadvantage when it comes to qualifying for support through this organization.

These are a few of the costs we immediately learned would not be compensated, assuming the application was even approved:

- Because I work on call, none of my lost wages would be compensated. It did not matter that I had proof of the days I did not work, could prove that I was offered jobs on those precise days, and prove that Athena had appointments for those days because of rape trauma. It did not matter that the only way Athena could get to appointments was to be driven. This rule greatly impacts people without steady, guaranteed work: Inevitably some of the people who need it the most. Those who are in 'better' jobs have paid leave, and are not out of pocket every time they are unable to work. This ruling especially impacts women, who are statistically far more likely to work part-time jobs without benefits or a stable income. Where is the equity in this? My personal estimated loss of income as a result of this atrocity is in the thousands of dollars.
- For people in rural areas, reimbursement costs for driving is completely unrealistic. We have no public transportation. Rivertown was the closest location where we could receive counselling, and was the location of our doctor and the hospital. Return from our house to Rivertown is at least forty-eight kilometers. I looked into the cost of a cab from our home to Rivertown, and found the round trip would cost one hundred dollars; not an option. Either I drove to Rivertown, or we could not access counselling. However, in spite of having no public transportation, we were told there would be no compensation for driving to appointments in Rivertown. (This represents a few more thousand dollars.)
- Legal costs for Mr. Cupito to defend Athena could not be covered. ($33,000)
- We were informed that compensation covers only the direct victim. The emotional impact on Sandy and me does not count.
- The VCB may provide funding for counselling. Athena wanted to have a traditional Native healing ceremony, and found a healing centre in a town not too far from the university. There was no cost for the ceremony, only a symbolic donation, but transportation to and from the location was an issue. She would have to take a cab to get there. The board would not pay for this as it was under the magic distance.

Which leaves very little that may be covered if, in fact, the board determines Athena is eligible. The translation for the word "eligible" in this case is; if the board decides they believe that Athena was, indeed, raped. If they do believe this, they will then put a (small) price on her pain and suffering. If she then goes on to successfully sue Conn, she will be required to pay that money back to the VCB.

Unfortunately, the problem I see is that none of the "professional" people in the legal system, from the cops, to the Justice Department crown attorneys, have understood the law under which Athena was charged. Without exception they seem to think rape is of far lesser importance than the argument (that should have been completely settled in court) about whether or not Athena lied about texts when asked in her initial interview.

The only hope for success in this hearing is if the board members actually know the law, are smart enough to see the police have no idea what the law means, and are not of the mentality that any girls (not boys, or Conn would have been at the very least chastised for his texting contribution) who send any texts of a sexual nature deserve to be raped. Oh, and if, in fact, the decision has not already been made by the Justice Department before we even walk in the door.

If you are a victim and are pursuing a claim with your provincial form of the VCB, I recommend retaining a lawyer. Most civil lawyers will take on a client without payment up front if they believe there is a good chance of winning. The lawyer then receives payment only if a suit is successful. There are many lawyers willing to work this way, and it is a good indication of the strength of your claim. If no one is willing to take on your claim in this manner, perhaps you should re-consider. It is possible to make a claim to the VCB on your own; I would not recommend it.

FEBRUARY 5, 2014

Note: We were not given a decision at the end of this hearing. A written decision was sent later by mail and included a "ban on evidence" which means that I cannot share whatever they allege was "evidence" produced at the hearing. Given that Athena would like to completely disclose this event, and Conn's name is already protected by the anonymity required by the YCJA; this protection serves only to protect the legal system. Regardless, I will share what I can.

⚖

Well, this was an experience that solidified a number of concerns I had about the police and the legal system.

Because 2014 had brought the worst winter in many years, with constant storms and abundant road closures, we were concerned about the logistics of getting Athena to the hearing. The hearing took place an hour and a half from home, and about forty five minutes from the university Athena was attending. To pick up Athena, I had to drive past the location. We decided that Athena and I would spend the night prior to the hearing at the hotel where it was to be held. We did not want bad weather preventing us from attending. Sandy would come the day of the hearing; roads permitting. Dogs, cats, birds, frozen water and snow kept him from being able to join us ahead of time.

All week a significant storm had been predicted, and it surpassed expectations. Having watched the weather report, Sandy left early and made it on time, but we waited well over half an hour for the assigned police officer to arrive. For some unfathomable reason, the cop assigned was Chompsky, who was on the case for fourteen, maybe sixteen hours in total.

The hearing was held in a small meeting room, filled by one long table with four chairs on each side. Entry was controlled by a security guard.

Supposedly the board members who attend are not chosen by the Justice Department, and it claims to be independent of the Department. Ms. Martin did not know the process used to choose the board members for a particular hearing, and I have been unable to find out.

Chompsky eventually arrived through a back entrance, dressed in civvies', her hair down and wearing makeup. I failed to notice she was fully armed with gun, baton and handcuffs and flak jacket. But Athena and Sandy commented on this blatant show of power.

Our lawyer believed that both Sandy and I would be asked to give victim impact statements, and I understood this to be standard procedure. The board told us we would not be given the opportunity to give victim impact statements.

I discouraged Sandy from coming in, and it turned out that was the best decision. Had he seen and heard the way Chompsky spoke of Athena, he would have lost it. She might have needed her arsenal to protect herself. I was ready to get up and leave several times, but I would not leave unless Athena decided to. Had she done so, I would have been right beside her.

The board members sat on one side of the table, across from them, closest to the door, sat Athena's lawyer, then Athena, and then me. Seats were not chosen, they were assigned by the board. On the table were water and very small glasses, note paper and pens, and tissues. When Chompsky was escorted in, she was assigned the seat on my right.

The hearing was entirely controlled by the female board member. She told us that the members take turns chairing the board, and today it was her turn. There were certainly no warm fuzzies from either board member, no pleasantries were exchanged; they did not even introduce themselves. This made me wonder if the outcome of this hearing had already been pre-determined, and the chosen members just puppets on a political string.

We were only permitted to speak if invited by the board chair, or if directly asked a question. This hearing was at the same time a totally controlled inquiry, yet one that often asked Chompsky for her *opinion* when she couldn't produce facts.

Previously, when we met with Ms. Martin, she asked Athena in what manner she would prefer to swear her oath. Athena had asked her to arrange for a Sacred Eagle Feather, a legitimate and accepted form of declaration for people of First Nations in Canada. Ms. Martin had agreed to arrange for this. However, when it was time to swear in, only a bible was produced.

Chompsky was asked to speak first. I was shocked when she began to speak: Resentment was obvious in her voice, and she scoffed at anything Athena said. What the hell is it with police? The fact that someone is found not guilty should not be taken as a personal affront to the police.

Chompsky had been involved in the investigation for considerably less than twenty-four hours, and as such, knew virtually nothing. She admittedly didn't know if Athena had been charged or if her case had gone to trial. Incredibly, she had no recollection of attending the trial, in spite of having testified under oath. Interestingly, she had a copy of the trial transcript with her which really should have twigged her to the fact that there had been a trial.

How on earth could a person who could not even remember attending and *testifying* at a trial be expected to remember details of the case?

One interesting note was her reference to Delwood: She referred to him as Detective Delwood, and then corrected herself and called him Constable Delwood. Constable is a lower position than Detective. Had he been demoted? One can only hope. If I were a board member, I would question why Delwood, the investigating officer, was not at the hearing, and someone with less than a day on the case was sent instead.

When asked a question, Chompsky would half-heartedly flip through one of the stacks of paper in front of her, although I don't ever remember her locating an answer in them. She would then respond with one of two pat answers, either, "This is the first I have heard of it" or "I don't know." When she replied she did not know, the board would often ask for her opinion.

Given the integrity shown so far, I expect you can imagine Athena being tried by police opinion. Once again I wonder why in hell we pay for judges and courts and crown attorneys when the *opinion* of the police supersedes the decisions of a court of law.

Unlike a court of law, and rendering this even more of a kangaroo court, was the fact that Athena's lawyer was not allowed to ask questions that would clarify or bring out details that may be important, or were forgotten as a result of Athena's stress or anxiety. Chompsky, however, was asked after Athena spoke if what Athena had said matched what she had said the day she was assaulted. If you have read this book, you will know that it certainly would not; Chompsky was gone by the morning after the assault, and never worked the case again.

I felt like we were all wasting our time being there at all. This process is definitely not intended for people who have not been believed by the police, and, as I now know, the word of police, no matter how ill-gotten, is taken as **The Word of God**. I was so angry I could hardly sit still, but I knew if I spoke up, I would be asked to leave; I also thought it better that I not give in to my driving urge to lean over and smack Chompsky alongside the head.

I did have some hope when the second board member, asked an

intelligent question of Chompsky. This particular question cut to the chase completely, and should have changed the entire outcome by illustrating Chompsky's ignorance of the law. Unfortunately any of the intelligent questions this man asked were not included in the written decision, making me wonder why he had been invited at all. Sad, as I got the impression he may have understood Canadian law.

Once Athena was finished describing being raped, and Chompsky had sneered and scoffed at Athena's rape, she was dismissed. Athena was then asked to describe the physical and emotional effects the assault had on her.

I found it heartbreaking to hear Athena express the fear she lives with every day, and it was obvious to me that she found it very, very difficult to even talk about. She was constantly–and not politely– interrupted by the board chair.

The event was somewhat surreal as it seemed to be constantly flipping from Athena being on trial yet again, to being about compensation for being a victim. When Athena had finished talking, I was asked if I had anything to add that had not already been said. The man interrupted me, and his interruption threw off my concentration. I answered, and tried to start where I had left off. Almost immediately I was interrupted again, and I had great difficulty resuming my train of thought. I wished these people knew the value of a Talking Feather: A First Nations solution to having one's train of thought and subsequent speaking interrupted. The holder of the Talking Feather has the right to talk without interruption, and when the holder is finished, they signal this by passing the feather to the next speaker. This allows the holder to think through their answer and ensure they say all that needs to be said. The next holder of the feather may then speak without interruption until their thought is finished.

Instead, the process was completely controlled by the board chair. Not even the lawyer could speak without invitation, but this was also not a put-your-hand-up situation; having something to say did not matter. It was entirely up to the board to invite comment or ask a question. It was at the same time less formal than court or a trial, and more formal. Weird things are allowed in VCB hearings; so called 'evidence' not admissible in a court of law is acceptable here, evidence obtained illegally is just ducky too. Opinions completely unable to be substantiated were accepted if they came from Chompsky, but the only time Athena was asked an opinion she was harshly reprimanded, even though her opinion was completely valid and justifiable.

For some bizarre reason, only information sent to the board from the police could be used to make a final decision. So, if the police didn't want to support Athena's case, they need only withhold pertinent information that would benefit her. Let's say, just for the sake of example, the police decided not to provide a trial transcript, well then the VCB would not be allowed to access the transcript even if they knew of its existence.

When it was over, Athena's lawyer said that she had never experienced such tough questioning from the VCB. Sandy commented that she had never represented us before.

I realized at the end of this hearing that I do not care about the money. I just want someone in the legal system to admit that Athena was raped. But that wasn't going to happen here: Athena was once again forced to prove her innocence, which is remarkable. Obviously, once you are charged in Canada, you will never again be considered innocent, absolutely regardless of the outcome of a trial. I find this incredibly depressing, and horribly wrong.

In fact, the amount of "wrong" in this story is appalling. Athena will never be the same: none of us will be. But I believe she will survive: in spite of the arduous campaign by the legal system to drive her to self destruction, she will survive.

⚖️

Almost 5 months to the day later, on Athena's birthday in fact, she received a copy of the Hearing results from her lawyer by mail. The lawyer said that based on the results, they did not feel further lawsuits would be successful.

Once again, the police state wins, the victim loses, and the rapes continue. What woman in her right mind would report an acquaintance rape to police when the re-victimization systematically imposed by all levels of the legal system is this brutal, this demeaning, and this degrading?

Athena took the results entirely in stride. She believes the system is corrupt; and this just reinforced it once again. We went over the few pages together and pooled our comments.

First, we again speculated on the possible reasons why Delwood, who had conducted the investigation had not been sent to the hearing, but then we realized that Shepard, who had been Delwood's partner starting the day after the assault had also not been sent. She also had not attended Athena's trial. She was *also* the officer I first told about Athena's welt, and it seems pretty clear that that little fact never made it into her notebook.

Have you ever played the old game of telephone? One person at one end of a line of people whispers something into the ear of the person next to them. That person whispers what they believe they heard into the ear of the next, until it reaches the far end of the line, and the last one to be whispered to gets to say what they believe they heard, and then everyone laughs because it has changed so dramatically from the original statement. It can be very funny, but not in a legal situation.

This hearing reminded me of the telephone game, minus the fun. Since the hearing is not taped, the only records are the notes the two board members jot down while they listen to answers. As should be predictable, there were once again many inaccuracies. This was really compounded by the board's interpretation of Chompsky's responses. Whenever Chompsky responded that she 'had not heard this before' or she 'did not know this' the Board interpreted her words to mean the statement was therefore untrue. However in this case, Chompsky was being entirely honest. Most of what she was asked, she did not know, and had *not* heard it prior to that moment in time, not because this was the first time Athena had ever said such a thing, but because Chompsky's 'knowledge' ended day one. And it was true, she knew nothing of the case after February 15th, and she admitted she had not read the police file.

In fact, the only preparation Chompsky admitted was listening to the very end of the third taped interview.

One other detail I found interesting (as opposed to royally pissing me off) was that the second board member was almost completely unrepresented in the write up.

There was a new twist on victim blaming that may or may not have had to do with the welt on Athena's head. And the Police: Well, it certainly seems that once screwed by the police, always screwed by the police. Having no accountability lets them do pretty much whatever they want. I am really starting to believe that they want to keep not just the rape and persecution of Athena quiet, but also the entire rape epidemic, because there is nothing that discourages a victim from coming forward like the threat of being re-victimized. Just imagine the public outrage that would occur if there was a country where one in four girls is raped before they turn eighteen. Oh, right, there is: Canada.

⚖

Athena has now finished her second year at university. Counsellor Terry was right when she said that no one could go through what Athena has and remain the same person. Sandy and I too have been profoundly changed by the persecution of Athena.

First Athena: She and I are extremely close; we are the best of friends. I am her strongest support system. At this point she is still very often in need of emotional support. She is infinitely better than she once was, and as long as there are no additional stresses in her life, she manages.

She has some of her wonderful sense of humor and wit back, but she is far more serious about life than most people, let alone teens. She is not afraid to speak up, and she has very strong opinions; many about the law, which she studies even in her free time. For the longest time she was quite abrupt and curt, but that has softened over time, still, she does not suffer fools gladly.

She doesn't expect good things to happen for her, and that makes me very sad. She was once so full of optimism and life. She always takes notice when people are nice or go out of their way for her, and she is the most appreciative person I know. Any tidbit of politeness or respect paid to Athena is noticed, because she no longer expects it of people. And while appreciation is a wonderful quality in a person, it is sad that this is because she expects so little. The plus side, however, is that she constantly tells us how much she appreciates us and everything we do and have done for her. And she tells us every day that she loves us.

She still suffers from Post Traumatic Stress Disorder and depression. Fear is her constant companion. She trusts very few people, and certainly not police. With the exception of a handful of people, she does not believe 'anyone' cares. Athena is one of the most socially responsible, caring and genuine women I know. She is extremely responsible, trustworthy, and

- 268 -

honest, yet she is worries constantly that she may somehow come to the attention of the police, and be charged with something; or nothing. She knows she doesn't have to break the law in order to be charged, and this knowledge causes her constant and profound fear. This makes her very different than her peers: she lives in a state of constant worry, fear, and distrust.

Sandy has not dealt with the stress, or with the fact that his daughter was sexually assaulted. He, too, lives constantly with fear; every time the phone rings he is afraid something has happened to Athena. Only in the past few months has he begun to talk about the assault. This ordeal has certainly changed him. He is far more serious and far less outgoing, but he is working on re-building his life. His outlook has improved of late, and he is considerably less negative about the world. He still suffers from depression, but that, too, is not as profound as it once was.

I still worry. I know Athena is remarkably strong; she would not have survived if she were not. But I find it is impossible to stop worrying. While there are fewer fears than there were at one time, there are still many physical and emotional concerns. Now, though, we have fun when we are together, something that was lost for a very long time.

My marriage has gotten quite a bit stronger; I realized that my view of sex changed completely after the sexual assault. I no longer saw sex as 'making love'. My view became completely tainted by the violence and aggression Athena had suffered, and I could not separate it in my mind. Having realized this, I am working to deal with these emotions. I find I become very disturbed when I see any form of violence, aggression or anything that glamorizes sex or sexuality.

I am very slightly calmer about police now; the absolute hatred I felt is more a profound feeling of disgust now. But I will never trust police or anyone in the court system.

There is a new fact about myself that I find truly disturbing, and which upsets me profoundly: We have all heard of people who refuse to help others in emergencies. In the past I was appalled by this and could not understand how bystanders could walk away and forsake someone in need. In the past I would have helped in any way I possibly could.

Sadly, I no longer would. If I saw something happen, my first thought would be self-preservation. I would be terrified that if I helped, I would have to deal with police, and may for no reason at all be charged with a crime. Athena was a victim, and she was charged with a criminal offence. In Canada police regularly charge victims of crimes. Defend yourself in Canada, and you must realize you could well end up charged as a criminal. If a victim can be charged, then a bystander certainly can, and I cannot afford on any level to go through another trial.

And so, if I was a bystander to a crime or an accident, my fear of the police would be so completely overwhelming, I don't know if I would be able to force myself to take this enormous risk. This fact about myself appalls me; if you are a decent human being, I expect you, too, find this disgusting. I wish it were different: I wish I lived in a country where, as a law abiding citizen, my fear of police need not override my humanitarian and moral instincts.

I am far more critical of the world now, and especially what I see in movies, television and video games. I have far less tolerance than I once had. I also see young men differently, and I trust them far less. On a positive note though, I can now carry on a conversation without feeling like my head will blow apart with overwhelming stress. Still, it seems like a very long road back at times.

CHAPTER 24

Summary

There is a silent epidemic in North America, and it is the rape of young women by boys they know.

And we are doing worse than nothing about it: We blame the victims.

⚖

Last night, lying in bed, I had a sudden revelation. I can now tell you how the Persecution of Athena came to be:

- As a result of her acquired brain injury, Athena was in a very vulnerable state. She was befriended by a boy who excelled at taking advantage of this. He manipulated her in text messages, lured her into thinking he was a friend, then beat, and raped her.
- First the school police officer interviewed her, then Chompsky, and finally Delwood and Shepard took over. There were far too many players, no consistency, and a lot of willingness to ignore ethics.
- Athena was sent to a sexual assault centre. At the time she was suffering from shock and likely a concussion. The assault centre failed to check her head, and so, of course, did not find her head injury.
- Delwood interviewed Conn. Delwood either doesn't know Canadian sexual assault law, or chose to ignore it. Without

anything but Conn's lie that he had consent via a text message, he released Conn unconditionally, and set out to charge Athena. His modus operands to achieve this goal included any method, ethical or not. Delwood epitomizes the concept of Victim Blaming.

- Athena would not confess to something she was not guilty of. This incensed not just Delwood, but every person we had contact with in the entire legal system.
- The crown attorney for Rivertown either doesn't know the law, or once again believed Athena deserved to be raped, or both. Hence, Athena was charged and tried for a crime that literally had nothing to do with text messages, *and for which the only evidence was the alleged offender saying he had not done it.*
- Incredibly, the judge was completely pro-police. In the end it seemed she had some knowledge of the law, yet she engaged in brutal victim blaming because Athena had participated in joking around about sex.
- Athena then attempted to bring about a private charge against Conn. This action incurred the wrath of the Justice Department. The crown attorney and the justice of the peace attempted to cover up the atrocious treatment of a child with more atrocious treatment, thus preventing Athena from seeking justice,
- She then sought justice through the Victims' Compensation Board, only to find herself once again forced to prove her innocence in yet another kangaroo court.

The persecution of Athena happened for these reasons:

1) Rampant, relentless victim blaming.
2) Horrifying ignorance of Canadian Law within the legal system.
3) Each level of the legal system trying to cover up for the level below.
4) Extreme lack of integrity within the legal system.
5) Arrogant indignation that we, as a family would fight the system.

So, within the police and the legal system, it boils down to these very concerning issues:

1) The belief that Athena (and hence other women as well) 'deserve' to be raped.

2) The disturbing fact that so few alleged professionals in the legal system know Canadian law.

3) Athena pleading innocence and seeking justice were considered a personal affront by the legal system, who then acted to retaliate.

4) All levels of the legal system were willing to disregard professional integrity, ethics, Charter Rights and even laws; and incredibly, suffered no consequences as a result.

5) Being charged by police supersedes being found 'not guilty': forever.

6) The police in Canada have incredible, uncontrolled, unmonitored power that does not belong in a democratic society.

7) And finally, there is a shocking lack of compassion: *All* levels of the legal system willingly engaged in demeaning, insulting and degrading treatment of a child sexual assault victim in order to support the police, who, regardless of a complete lack of evidence, bullied her to the point she wanted to die.

⚖

There are only three ways to stop sexual assault. One is for women to protect themselves, which requires knowledge of the issue. The second is for men to stop raping. We can educate men about consent, the profound damage sexual assault causes, and the immorality of rape. But in the end, there will be many who choose immediate gratification over doing the right thing, and that is why it is imperative for police start doing their jobs with regards to rape.

If the police are unwilling to deal appropriately with sexual assaults, what choices do women and their families have? I would not want to live in a society in which vigilante justice prevails, and so far it has not. This may well be one of the reasons acquaintance rape is kept so quiet;

when it becomes known *how common rape is,* the police will be forced to explain what they are doing about it, and how it got so outrageously out of control. At this point in time the police are a major part of the problem, not the solution. Once this topic comes out of the closet, the demand for justice is going to follow, and those people who are supposed to protect us will have to step up and do their jobs. It is time to demand this happens.

The Legal System: There are two words that sum up all of the horrific treatment Athena has been subjected to by every level of the legal system starting with the police: **Victim Blaming**.

According to (www.guardchild.com/teenage-sexting-statistics/) 44% of teenagers have sent suggestive text messages in response to messages they received, and 40% of girls sent sexually suggestive text messages as a joke.

Here is my question: Do all of these girls deserve to be raped? Are they all "asking for it?" Every legal avenue we pursued from the police, the crown, the justice of the peace, the judge, the attempt to Bring about a Private Charge, and The Police Watchdog; in every single response the answer to the question would appear to be a resounding YES; if a girl sends text messages that contain sexual context, regardless of her intention, she is asking, and deserves, to be raped.

Because that is entirely what this story is about.

As I am editing this book, and going back over what we have been through, I am amazed Athena survived. Not every victim does survive, and my heart breaks for those parents. The utter loneliness, isolation and desperation overwhelms me again as I re-read what we went through, and makes me even more aware of the dichotomy of what should have been and the reality of what was. I came across the following website: (**www.sascwr.org/if-you-have-been-sexually-assaulted**) one of the subtopics is 'What to do if you have been sexually assaulted?' The article then describes the rights a victim has if they decide to report a sexual assault. According to this website, sexual assault victims have the right to be treated with respect for their personal dignity and privacy, and to be treated with compassion and courtesy.

Yet Athena was treated like absolute filth and trash, and it makes me both incredibly sad, and very angry. To be raped, and then to be treated so abominably is outrageous; and for what? Because she did not say the day she was raped that she and Conn had joked about sex in text messages. That is it. That is all there was, and all there is. Add to that, because neither the police nor the crown attorney knew or could read the law, she was charged for a criminal offence that could not be proven in any way shape or form using text messages. And not one person had either the integrity or the intelligence to end this travesty. The crime she was charged with (Section 140) (1) (a) of the criminal code demands that she had lied *about being sexually assaulted*, not about having sent text messages. Yet this 'misunderstanding' persisted through a criminal trial, Athena's attempt to bring about a private charge, and showed up again in the Victim's Compensation Board.

How can someone enforce the laws of the country if they don't even know the laws? It is obvious to me that the criteria to choose police officers are grossly inadequate. Police need to thoroughly know the law, they need to remove the chips from their shoulders, treat the public they are hired to serve respectfully, and realize that they are, in fact, paid public servants.

We pay the police, the crown attorney, and the judge very significant money to do their respective jobs. They *should* know what the hell they are doing, i.e. *they should actually understand and be able to read Canadian law, and they need to leave their bias' at home.*

And it should be a hell of a lot easier to sue them if they do not.

Which brings me to the appalling lack of accountability in the police force: When a complaint to The Police Watchdog is researched by a police sergeant of the same force, the entire concept of an independent review becomes a disturbing and pathetic joke.

When everything the police say is accepted as truth, and is not substantiated by fact and/or evidence, the Police Watchdog becomes completely self-serving for the police; and *no one* but the police would view this as a valid investigation.

It is incomprehensible to me that the police are not far *more* accountable than the rest of the countries' citizens. Legal infractions committed by police should result in the harshest punishment possible for that crime *because* of the incredible power these people have, and the astronomical potential for abuse of these powers. Instead, for some insane reason, Canada has decided to place complete trust in the integrity of officers, and demanded virtually no accountability. Yet police are constantly in the media for outrageous infractions, and the actual numbers of infractions that make it into the news are infinitely less than the ones that do not. Many infractions are overlooked, buried, or have resulted in legal settlements with conditions restricting victims of police treatment from informing the media.

We need extremely stringent repercussions, and it must be far easier for the public to hold officers accountable through law suits; but not at the public's expense. The cost of defense for a police officer successfully sued should not come out of the taxpayers' pocket. If the police truly wish to change public perception, there must be stringent expectations and harsh repercussions. We need to veer off the police-state path we are speeding down.

After four years, I have finally accepted that our Charter Rights are worthless words on paper. Until violations are enforced by punishments to violators, we don't have rights. That Athena's interviews were so full of violations they could not be used in court, yet were considered perfectly viable in *every* other legal proceeding illustrates how badly our Charter of Rights and Freedoms needs to have penalties attached that are rigorously enforced. Our rights are just a paper exercise until the violation of those rights result in serious repercussions, and they are diligently enforced.

Here is what should happen: Any police officer who violates the charter rights of Canadian citizens should first be reprimanded in writing, with a copy to his or her file. A second violation and that officer should be fired from the police force. Any officer who witness' another officer violating Charter Rights should be required to report the violation. Failure to do so should result in a written reprimand. A second violation and that officer should also be dismissed.

We have become perfect victims in Canada. Untold thousands of rape victims suffer silently in Canada, preferring that to the re-victimization by police and the legal system. Many of these women will lose their way; some will lose their lives.

It is of absolutely no wonder to me that only 8% of sexual assaults are reported to police (www.wavaw.ca/mythbusting/statistics/). This source claims that many women do not report, because they "did not feel the assault was important enough."

The victims did not believe the *police* would consider their sexual assault important enough. Why would women think this?

Well, until 2009, Statistics Canada collected data on the number of unfounded sexual assault reports by police jurisdiction. British Columbia and Ontario have continued to voluntarily collect this information, and the information is truly shocking: There are policing areas in British Columbia that claim *up to twenty-eight percent of reported sexual assaults are unfounded. Many jurisdictions are slightly lower, but are still in the twenty plus percent range. One outstanding jurisdiction in Ontario claims that more than one-in-three, or thirty-four percent of reported sexual assaults were unfounded.* (www.parl.gc.ca/Content/LOP/ResearchPublication2012-16e.htm)

In British Columbia, the rate of cases classified as unfounded is more (in some cases incredibly more) than twice the rate of any other "unfounded" reported crime, and has been for "several decades." (makingadifferencecanada. ca/pdf/LIBRARY/PDF/POLICEpolice%20classification%20of%20sexual% 20assault%20cases%20as%20unfounded.pdf

It is quite clear to me that misogynic attitudes are alive and well, and are rampant in the legal system. Statistics Canada should immediately resume the collection of unfounded sexual assaults statistics, not only for individual police forces, but for individual investigators.

If an investigating officer decides he/she does not believe an assault took place, there should be a completely independent team brought in from outside. This team should include professionals who work with sexual assault victims: counselors, psychiatrists, and medical doctors, and new, well trained police officers. There should be absolutely no further involvement by the original investigating police. As a team the professional group should evaluate the victim, and start over with the investigation.

It is generally accepted that two percent of reported crimes are unfounded (translation: the crime did not actually occur). There is no justifiable reason for sexual assault reports to be higher, and I would personally say that given the incredibly low reporting rates of sexual assault to begin with, I don't believe that that even two percent would be false. Should an investigating officer or the statistics of a police department exceed this percentage, there should be serious repercussions. An officer with a higher rate should have all his cases reviewed and have further intensive training. If this percentage does not immediately decline, he should be permanently assigned to other duties.

It is very disturbing to realize that Athena will never be considered innocent of the criminal charge regardless of being found not guilty. It does not matter that she was a juvenile when this occurred, or that she is a person with a disability. It does not matter that rights were violated, inducement was pushed, lies were told, and entire interviews could not be used in court. It does not even matter that there was absolutely no evidence to support the charge against her. The fact that the police charged her completely trumps all, and it appears it always will.

I have already pointed out how ludicrous this concept is, and how completely dependent it is on the police first being competent, and second, having integrity; both of which I found shockingly elusive. Yet, this view is rampant throughout the legal system. It renders crown attorneys and judges redundant: when a crown attorney, working for the Justice Department, actually says to someone who has been found not guilty in a court of law: "The police don't believe you, why should we," our legal system is in serious trouble.

Had Athena not had completely supportive parents willing to advocate for her, at best she would have quit school, most likely she would have become involved in serious drug or alcohol abuse, and quite possibly she would have spent her life in and out of trouble with the law; *because* of the treatment of the police and the entire legal system.

Thankfully, Athena is not about to become a criminal. She is, and has always been, far too honest, law abiding and genuine. I believe she would have killed herself instead: *because the treatment of the Canadian 'justice' system drove her so horrifyingly close to the line where her life was not worth living.*

CHAPTER 25
Conclusion

Acquaintance rape is the rape of silence. It is the least likely form of sexual assault to be reported to police, and the least likely to result in charges or convictions. Basic psychology dictates that if someone gets away with something, and receives pleasure from what they have done, that behavior will be reinforced, and will likely be repeated. It follows that once someone rapes and 'gets away' with the crime, they will likely rape again.

Which translates as this: If the persecution of Athena is any indication, our legal system is doing more to encourage rape than to discourage it.

My intent in writing this book is to bring awareness (and hopefully change) to the enormous issue of the rape of teenage girls by boys they know. Statistically, *being a teenage female in Canada means a one in four chance of being raped before your eighteenth birthday.* www.assaultcare.ca/index.php?option=content&view=article&id=49&Itemid=58 *And even more shocking, is that eleven percent of these victims will be under the age of eleven at the time they are sexually abused.*

Why are we not demanding that something be done to protect, and save, our children?

You will hear about rapes in the media, but almost exclusively these will be rapes committed by strangers, or by people in positions of powers. Plain old run of the mill acquaintance rapes are just not news worthy. Because only one to two percent of acquaintance rapes are reported to police, they simply go unnoticed. Unnoticed, that is, except for the girl whose life is destroyed. There is little value to the media in reporting acquaintance rape. Let's face it, if every rape were reported in the media, it would take the entire newspaper every day to get through them all. It is *because* acquaintance rape is so outrageously common it fails to be newsworthy.

And how, as a society, do we deal with this epidemic? We pretend it doesn't exist. We do *not* talk about it, we do not think about it, we either don't know it exists, or pretend it doesn't. This is the worst possible way to deal with what is potentially a life threatening event. Not talking about acquaintance rape means girls are all the more vulnerable: How can girls protect themselves if they don't even know there is a danger? It also means that when rape occurs, the victim is further victimized through isolation, and this silence leads to the horrific belief that they themselves are somehow to blame for being raped. It allows rapists to go unpunished, which encourages rape.

It is time we, as a society, recognize how disturbingly common, and how absolutely devastating acquaintance rape is to our young women. And we need to do something about it.

North American culture had been dubbed a 'rape culture', and when you learn the mindset of youth, this is not surprising. A study of college men concluded that *thirty-five percent* would consider raping a woman if they thought they could get away with the act. (www.uic.edu.edu/dpts/owa/sa_rapr_support.html)

Clearly, something needs to change. During the three years I have been living and writing here in hell, I have discovered how profoundly parents want to avoid talking to their children about the threat of sexual assault, particularly sexual assault committed by acquaintances and 'friends'. We make great efforts to ensure our children are protected from harm, yet this threat poses the greatest threat to our young daughters' safety and future. Had I known and talked to Athena about "date rape", would she have been spared? I don't know. I do know she would have been better prepared to protect herself.

We want to protect our children. We can't lock them up; they will be exposed to situations where assault can occur, perhaps not at your home, but at a friend's home, outings, school, dances, school trips, shopping trips, walks, sleepovers. We cannot always be with them; they themselves need to understand the danger in order to be in a position to prevent it. Yes, we all should have the right to feel and be safe anywhere, anytime, doing anything, but that is not the reality of the world we live in. The only way to make children aware of the danger is to talk frankly with them about the sexual assault of young girls by guys they know and very often trust: Guys they believe are their friends. Ignorance is only bliss until the unthinkable happens.

Parents: You now know that rape is a horrifyingly common occurrence, and it happens more often to young girls than to any other demographic group. It is not dark alleys we need to fear most. Think how you will feel if your child is one of the four who is assaulted before her eighteenth birthday; will you wish you had talked to them, made them aware that this reality is epidemic in our country?

I gave a great deal of thought to including the following information: It appears that fighting back will deter many rapists; however there is inherent risk with this. Many girls do not fight back during a sexual assault. Many are simply too shocked; they may fear that fighting back will result in their being subjected to greater violence. Statistics show that fighting back reduces the chance of being raped by half; however it increases the possibility of other bodily injury by ten percent. (From: No Safe Place: Violence Against Women www.pbs.org/kued/nosafeplace/studyg/rape.html). Obviously there is no single solution.

Were I to have the chance to live life over; to know what I know now, I would have spoken very openly to my daughter. Schools frequently teach students about body privacy and encourage children to speak out if they are touched inappropriately. While this is vital, I don't believe this is even remotely enough. Girls (and boys) need the facts. They need to know the greatest threat comes from their peers, and they need to have some idea how to respond if they find themselves in a situation they are uncomfortable or in danger in. They need to be encouraged to respond quickly to their instinct. If they feel at all uncomfortable, they need to remove themselves as quickly as possible from the situation.

Before Athena was raped it didn't occur to me to be concerned about her male friends. I never thought that she would be in danger from a 'friend'. Now I would tell my daughter that I am not worried about her being trust worthy, I am concerned that many boys do not accept that no means no, and a shocking number are willing to rape: Even some she may see as friends. It would be wonderful to trust all people, unfortunately, many are not trust worthy. If I were living life over, I would discuss potentially dangerous situations with her, and how to avoid them; I would encourage her to think of places and scenarios of potential danger. I would also discuss fighting back if she were attacked.

Athena was very passive. If I could do it over I would have enrolled her in some form of self defense training. I would encourage her to protect herself. Unfortunately for Canadians, the 'right' to defend ourselves is not much of a 'right', and defending oneself is actively frowned upon by the legal system. If your child defends herself, and in doing so injures her attacker, *she* may be charged with a criminal offence, and then, in order not to be convicted, will be required to prove in a court of law not only that she was in danger, but that she used only lesser or equal force than her assailant to protect herself. See: The Criminal Code of Canada www.efc.ca/pages/law/cc/cc.html Sections 34.(1), 34(2), 35, 36, and 37. (1) and (2))

It is really important to have a good, respectful relationship with your child. You want your child to come to you when there are problems. The first rule is this: No matter what your child tells you, you must stay calm. This goes way beyond a rape incident; this is a rule for every single day of your child's life. Overreacting will ensure your child will not share information with you. Spend time really listening. Encourage them to talk to you about anything and everything, and help them to make their own decisions through discussion. Do not pass judgment if your child volunteers information, it will only ensure you are no longer privy to what is really going on in your child's life. Discuss it, don't judge it.

Parents of boys: You have a very serious obligation to educate your son with regards to sexual assault. If you fail to teach respect for women, if you do not teach them that they must obtain consent before they have sexual relations, you are failing in your responsibilities. Teach your son that "No" means "No", and only "yes" means "yes." Do this by talking about what sexual assault is, and how the failure to obtain consent is a serious crime. Teach them that sexual assault is not only illegal, it destroys lives.

I considered providing websites with information on how to talk to your children about acquaintance rape, but found that by keying these words into a search engine you will find a vast amount of useful information:

talking to kids about date rape.

There are other societal measures that would help greatly: television, music videos, and music need to stop glamorizing forced and aggressive sexual acts. We need responsible public and media figures, especially males, to start promoting respect for women and girls.

And we need a large corporate organization to take this enormous issue out of the closet, and make it table talk. Bell Canada has done an extremely commendable job of ending the silence around mental health issues with its "Let's Talk" campaign. A public campaign promoting respect by focusing on the treatment of women and girls is urgently needed.

In Canada we spend a huge amount of time worrying about women in other countries, while our own reality is desperate. It would be a supreme social service for a sponsor to take this project under its wing. We need to start talking openly and responsibly about sexual assault. It is a huge challenge, but given the statistics, it is one that is imperative.

When I see young women who appear to be suffering: those with eating disorders, mental health issues, who are abusing themselves through cutting, drugs, or alcohol, who are completely lacking in self-esteem or who are acting out, my first thought now is to wonder if these women have been sexually assaulted. How many women lose their lives or their way because they have been raped and literally no one cares?

And it is absolutely inexcusable for those who are supposed to protect us to treat these victims as criminals.

Printed in the United States
By Bookmasters